Medieval Literacy

Medieval Literacy

A COMPENDIUM OF MEDIEVAL KNOWLEDGE
WITH THE GUIDANCE OF C. S. LEWIS

By James Grote

FONS VITAE

First published in 2011 by
Fons Vitae
49 Mockingbird Valley Drive
Louisville, KY 40207
http://www.fonsvitae.com
Email: fonsvitaeky@aol.com

© Fons Vitae

© 2011 James Grote
Louisville, KY
jimgrote@hotmail.com

Library of Congress Control Number: 2011929821
ISBN 9781891785825

Supra lunam sunt aeterna omnia.
Beyond the moon are all the eternal things.

Cicero

Naturam expellas furca, tamen usque recurret.
You can try to drive out Nature with a pitchfork,
but she will always return.

Horace

Dedication

To Elizabeth Bleecker Meigs

Acknowledgements

To Sissy Grote for helping me find my way to the Kilns; and to Carl Mitcham, bibliographic mentor and purveyor of the Scholastic adage, "Never deny, seldom affirm, always distinguish."

To express my gratitude in Aristotelian terms, this book is particularly indebted to its *causa materialis*, Rachel Grote and the generous assistance of the Trustees of the Daedalus Foundation as well as to Sara and Lauren Rice; to its *causa efficiens*, Perry Bramlett and Timothy Fout who both prodded it into existence over numerous drafts and years; to its *causa formalis*, James Lynch and Stephen Yandell who added numerous lists and insightful perspectives to the book; and finally to its *causa finalis*, Charles Breslin, who assigned C. S. Lewis' *The Discarded Image* in a Medieval Culture class I attended. This book grew out of a 30-page term paper handed in to Mr. Breslin many years ago.

In addition, I am grateful for the advice, counsel, and inspiration of Virginia Alexander, Annette Allen, Karen Britt, David Burrell, Dick and Margaret Clements, Glenda Hodges-Cook, Elias Dietz, Michael Downey, Angela Doyle, T. J. and Svetlana Durbin, Jack Ford, Edward Hackett, Philip Hanson, Junius Johnson, Rex Lagerstrom, Lucy Jones Langman, Vincent Linz, Greg and Paula Livingston, Elena Lloyd-Sidle, Anna Lynch, Thomas Maloney (particularly for his help with the chapter on Logic), Rebecca Martin, Carol Mattingly, John McGeeney, Marylee Mitcham, Anne Ogden, Gill Ring (particularly for his help with the chapters on Psychology and Philosophy), John Rounds, Julie Shinnick, William Stoddart, Abigail Tardiff, as well as colleagues and friends in the Department of Humanities at the University of Louisville.

Thanks also to Mary Jo Grote, Edward Rice, and Mary Frances Schafer for their inspiration on Dante.

Special thanks are owed to the entire editorial team at Fons Vitae, particularly to Gray Henry and to Neville Blakemore, whose wonderful manuscript and book strewn home reminds me of a Catholic Worker House of Hospitality, described by Dorothy Day as hospitality with a dash of holy chaos.

Also a special thanks to my teacher in all things Eastern, Patrick Pranke. Without his guidance, there would be no Appendix to this book.

Finally, many thanks to Mark Grote, сын Джима, for his graphic design work.

Table of Contents

Analytic Table of Contents

I. Introduction:
C.S. Lewis as Tour Guide to the Middle Ages

Tradition is the democracy of the dead.

G. K. Chesterton, *Orthodoxy*

There is nothing more wonderful than a list.

Umberto Eco, *The Name of the Rose*

"Those who cannot remember the past are doomed to repeat it." This tiresome but ominously accurate adage of George Santayana is confirmed anew every generation. Particularly in the political realm, the historically illiterate inevitably repeat the imprudent actions of the past. A similar alarm has been sounded in regards to cultural illiteracy by E. D. Hirsch, who argues that a functioning democratic nation depends for its very existence on a minimum level of cultural literacy. Obviously cultural literacy includes historical literacy as one of its components; a large part of Hirsch's famous dictionary is devoted to history. Says Hirsch, "Learning depends on communication, and effective communication depends on shared background knowledge. . . . When the schools of a nation fail adequately to transmit the literate national language and culture, the unity and effectiveness of the nation will necessarily decline."[1]

No one, not Hirsch, not even Santayana himself, was more alarmed by the consequences of historical illiteracy than C. S. Lewis. For Lewis, ignorance of the past has led to an intemperate glorification of technology that portends what he calls "the abolition of man." In theory and practice, the past is the only timeframe available to provide perspective on both the present and the future. Lewis devoted his entire education and scholarly passion to the past, particularly the medieval period. Few of his avid Christian followers are aware to what extent he considered himself a medieval specimen lost in the modern world, as if he were a creature trapped in one of his own science fiction novels. It is both ironic and unfortunate that "no role of C. S. Lewis has been more overlooked by the general public than that of a medievalist."[2]

Showing how a trip through the Dark Ages (to borrow a pejorative term) could prove enlightening was a major preoccupation of C. S. Lewis. While the Middle Ages has often been dismissed as a period of one thousand years without a bath (c.500 to c.1500), Lewis spent his adult life communicating the splendor of centuries overcast with violence, superstition, and religious totalitarianism, not to mention a distinct lack of creature comforts. For all the discomfiture and barbarism of medieval times, he admired the Medieval Model of the Universe (see descriptions of the Ptolemaic universe on pages 65-66 in chapter three on Cosmology) that was "so universally accepted" and "so satisfying to the imagination."[3] In a way that the modern world does not, this Model "provides food for

---

1. E. D. Hirsch, Jr., Joseph F. Kett, and James Trefil, *Dictionary of Cultural Literacy*, 2nd edition (Boston: Houghton Mifflin, 1993), pp. xiii-xiv.

2. Stephen Yandell, "The Allegory of Love and the Discarded Image: C. S. Lewis as Medievalist," in Bruce Edwards, ed., *C. S. Lewis: Life, Works, and Legacy*, vol. 4, Scholar, Teacher, and Public Intellectual (Westport, CT: Praeger Publishers, 2007), p. 117.

3. C. S. Lewis, *The Discarded Image: An Introduction to Medieval and Renaissance Literature* (London: Cambridge University Press, 1978), p. 203.

thought and satisfaction for our aesthetic natures."[4]

Lewis himself provides the map for this trip, a book called *The Discarded Image* based on his two most popular lecture series for undergraduate students at Oxford, the Prolegomena to Medieval Literature and the Prolegomena to Renaissance Literature.[5] "In the *Discarded Image*, C. S. Lewis' subject is the cultural literacy of the Middle Ages, which surpassed even what Hirsch describes."[6] The metaphor of touring belongs to Lewis. To understand the medievals as they understood themselves rather than through a modern lens of presumed superiority, special attention needs to be paid to how we travel back in time. For Lewis, the mode of tourism is all-important:

> There are two ways of enjoying the past, as there are two ways of enjoying a foreign country. One man carries his Englishry abroad with him and brings it home unchanged. . . . By a good hotel he means one that is like an English hotel. He complains of the bad tea where he might have had excellent coffee. He finds the "natives" quaint and enjoys their quaintness. . . . In the same way there is a man who carries his modernity with him through all his reading of past literature and preserves it intact. . . . But there is another sort of traveling and another sort of reading. You can eat the local food and drink the local wines, you can share the foreign life, you can begin to see the foreign country as it looks, not to the tourist, but to its inhabitants. . . . You can come home modified, thinking and feeling as you did not think and feel before.[7]

To return home modified is one goal of visiting the Middle Ages. Of course, one may legitimately ask of Lewis, "Why take the trip in the first place?" This Introduction to *Medieval Literacy* addresses "why" the trip is important, "how" the trip can be accomplished, and finally, once again "why" an alternative to modernity warrants serious consideration.

OLD WESTERN CULTURE AS THERAPY

Lewis' purpose resembles that of a therapist who delves into a client's past to give the client a fresh perspective on both his or her past and present. Lewis provides this peculiar kind of therapy through an immersion in Old Western Culture. When he took the job of Professor of Medieval and Renaissance English Literature at the University of Cambridge late in his life, he explained his preoccupation with Old Western Culture in his inaugural address, *De Descriptione Temporum*:

> I do not think you need fear that the study of a dead period, however prolonged and however sympathetic, need prove an indulgence in nostalgia or an enslavement to the past. In the individual life, as the psychologists have taught us, it is not the remembered but the forgotten past that enslaves us. I think the same is true of society. To study the past does indeed liberate us from the present, from the idols of our own marketplace. But I think it liberates us from the past too. I think no class of men are less enslaved to the past than historians. The unhistorical are usually, without know-

---

4. C. S. Lewis, *Studies in Medieval and Renaissance Literature* (London: Cambridge University Press, 1998), p. 49.

5. Yandell, "Medievalist," p. 128.

6. Michelle Harmon, "A Contemplation of Cultural Literacy," *Bulletin of the New York C. S. Lewis Society* 21.3 (1990), p. 1.

7. Lewis, *Studies*, pp. 2-3.

ing it, enslaved to a fairly recent past.[8]

The "recent past" Lewis particularly questioned was the popular evolutionism of the nineteenth century. Of course, his critics charge that he was not wary enough of another nineteenth century "ism" – "nineteenth century romantic medievalism."[9]

Throughout his works Lewis shows a preference for the medieval "devolutionary" scheme where spirit devolves into matter over and against the modern "evolutionary" scheme where matter evolves into spirit.[10] The former scheme confounds science, the latter simple logic. As he says regarding the latter, "If my own mind is a product of the irrational [i.e. evolution from matter] . . . how shall I trust my mind when it tells me about Evolution?"[11] Despite these logical misgivings, Lewis did accept evolution as a "biological theorem," but distrusted it as a "metaphysical statement."[12]

More to the point, he objected to evolution as a theory of social improvement, distinguishing this popular theory from scientific evolution.[13] As a scientific explanation of how organisms change, evolution shows that while some changes are for the better, the majority are wasteful or ineffective.[14] Lewis believed the popular myth of progress to be simply that – a myth. This argument is most forcefully articulated in his essay "The Funeral of a Great Myth."[15] He feared the myth of progress because it encouraged a belief in the infallibility of technology that, given the fallible state of humankind, he considered dangerous. As St. Thomas quotes the old adage: "Speed in a blind horse is no virtue" (*Summa Theologica*, I-II, q. 58, a. 4).

According to premodern thought (e.g., Aristotle, *Politics*, 1267b), since the world is finite and human desire is infinite, logic dictates that human desire must limit itself in order to conform to the natural world. Lewis believed this notion of limit distinguished the medieval from the modern mind: "For the wise men of old, the cardinal problem of human life had been how to conform the soul to reality, and the solution had been knowledge, self-discipline, and virtue. For [the modern mind] the problem is how to subdue reality to the wishes of men and the solution is technique [i.e., technology]."[16] He welcomed the arduous human adventure of conforming the soul to reality, and feared the moral and environmental consequences of a mindset bent on conforming reality to human desire. For Lewis, the study of Old Western Culture provides an antidote to this dangerous optimism. A sense of moderation can be ascertained in the famous motto of Old Western Culture, *in medio stat virtus* – virtue stands in the middle.

---

8. C. S. Lewis, *"De Descriptione Temporum,"* in *They Asked for a Paper: Papers and Addresses* (London: GeoffreyBles, 1962), p. 23.

9. Thomas L. Martin, ed. *Reading the Classics with C. S. Lewis* (Grand Rapids, MI: Baker Academic, 2000), p. 72.

10. Lewis, *Discarded*, p. 220.

11. C. S. Lewis, *Christian Reflections* (Grand Rapids: William B. Eerdmans, 1978), p. 89.

12. Mike Perry, "Evolution," in Jeffrey D. Schultz, Jeffrey and John G. West, Jr., eds., *The C. S. Lewis Readers' Encyclopedia* (Grand Rapids, MI: Zondervan, 1998), p. 158.

13. Lewis, *Reflections*, p. 58.

14. Lewis, *Reflections*, p. 58.

15. Lewis, *Reflections*, pp. 82-93.

16. C. S. Lewis, *The Abolition of Man* (New York: Touchstone, 1996), pp. 83-84.

READING OLD BOOKS AS AN EXERCISE IN DEMOCRACY

Immersion in Old Western Culture is not a Eurocentric indulgence in nostalgia, but an exercise in democracy. Free speech is a prerequisite to democracy. And if free speech entails taking everyone's view into account, why limit ourselves to the "latest" views? Free speech means letting those who have gone before us (our ancestors) speak freely.

In his autobiographical work *Surprised by Joy*, Lewis confesses to his youthful sin of "chronological snobbery." He defines such snobbery as the "uncritical acceptance of the intellectual climate common to our age and the assumption that whatever has gone out of date is on that account discredited."[17] For the chronological snob, newer is better. When arguing with a friend who believed in God, spirits, and an after-life, the young Lewis exclaimed, "Why – damn it – it's *medieval*."[18]

Unlike Lewis, one of his heroes, the metaphysical journalist G. K. Chesterton, claims to have always had sympathy for beliefs that had gone out of style. As Chesterton says, "I was brought up a Liberal, and have always believed in democracy, in the elementary liberal doctrine of self-governing humanity."[19] However, Chesterton saw an intimate connection between the idea of democracy and a respect for tradition. "Tradition is only democracy extended through time."[20] He writes:

> Tradition means giving votes to the most obscure of all classes, our ancestors. It is the democracy of the dead. Tradition refuses to submit to the small and arrogant oligarchy of those who merely happen to be walking around. All democrats object to men being disqualified by the accident of birth; tradition objects to their being disqualified by the accident of death. . . . I, at any rate, cannot separate the two ideas of democracy and tradition; it seems evident to me that they are the same idea.[21]

While this correlation of democracy and tradition may sound odd to modern students, it is important to remember that the medievals would have had an equally difficult time appreciating modern thought.

As a thought experiment, imagine a medieval hearing modern liberals champion free love (i.e. the belief that morality is a private matter) and criticize free markets (i.e. the belief that economics is a private matter), while hearing conservatives propose the exact opposite arrangement. Liberals advocate moral freedom but want to regulate what goes on in a private corporation's boardroom. Conservatives advocate economic freedom but want to regulate what goes on in a private person's bedroom. A medieval person might wonder: "Doesn't the free market that economic conservatives champion undermine the moral character that social conservatives desire?" And vice-versa, "Doesn't the regulated market that economic liberals champion limit the moral freedom that social liberals desire?"

For moderns to argue more logically, they could use an expanded time horizon, one that includes the opinions of the past. Lewis believed it undemocratic to give too much power to the present generation: "I am a democrat because I believe that no man or group

---

17. C. S. Lewis, *Surprised by Joy* (New York: Harcourt, Brace & World, 1955), p. 207.
18. Lewis, *Joy*, p. 206.
19. G. K. Chesterton, *Orthodoxy* (Wheaton, IL: Harold Shaw, 1994), p. 46.
20. Chesterton, *Orthodoxy*, p. 47.
21. Chesterton, *Orthodoxy*, pp. 47-48.

of men is good enough to be trusted with uncontrolled power over others."[22] In the *Abolition of Man* Lewis asks his reader to "picture the [human] race extended in time from the date of its emergence to that of its extinction."[23] He argues that at some point in its scientific progress, a "master generation, itself an infinitesimal minority of the species,"[24] will emerge that has unprecedented power to condition and mold future humans through genetic engineering as well as to mold human opinion about the past. Lewis is horrified by this Orwellian possibility which he describes vividly both in his philosophical work *The Abolition of Man* and in his fictional work *That Hideous Strength*.

His commitment to democracy not only makes Lewis skeptical of all power elites (which he calls "inner rings"), it also makes him skeptical of sudden social change and unbridled technology. In a word, his commitment to democracy makes him conservative: "Being a democrat, I am also opposed to all very drastic and sudden changes in society (in whatever direction) because they never in fact take place except by a particular technique. That technique involves the seizure of power by a small, highly disciplined group of people; the terror and the secret police follow, it would seem automatically."[25] Lewis is here echoing a genuine reservation that medieval scholars had about the political consequences of technological innovation.

For example, consider Thomas Aquinas' observation about the dangers of technological innovation, an observation that repeats an even earlier tradition – that of Thomas' pagan mentor, Aristotle, whom he admiringly refers to as the Philosopher: "Rules of art [i.e. technology] derive their force from reason alone: and therefore whenever something better occurs, the rule followed hitherto should be changed. But laws derive very great force from custom, as the Philosopher states: consequently they should not be quickly changed" (*Summa Theologica*, I-II, q. 97, a. 2). Thomas is not criticizing technology *per se*, only observing that while technology thrives on constant change and innovation, society thrives on routine and stability. For laws to be effective, citizens must be in the habit of obeying them.

In order for moderns to overcome both their deficiencies in logic and their sanguinity about Faustian power, Lewis proposes a gentle but radical solution – the reading of old books. By old he means written before 1800. As he recommends:

> It is a good rule, after reading a new book never to allow yourself another new one till you have read an old one in between. If that is too much for you, you should at least read one old one to every three new ones. Every age has its own outlook. It is especially good at seeing certain truths and especially liable to make certain mistakes. We all, therefore, need the books that will correct the characteristic mistakes of our own period. And that means the old books.[26]

While Lewis is not alone in questioning the validity of modern thought (see the sub-section below "Situating Lewis within the Critique of Modernity"), I am unaware of any other

---

22. C. S. Lewis, *Of Other Worlds: Essays and Stories*, edited by Walter Hooper (New York: Harcourt Brace Jovonovich, 1966), p. 81.

23. Lewis, *Abolition*, p. 68.

24. Lewis, *Abolition*, p. 69.

25. Lewis, *Other Worlds*, p. 82.

26. C. S. Lewis, *God in the Dock: Essays on Theology and Ethics* (Grand Rapids, MI: William B. Eerdmans, 1985), pp. 201-202.

author who actually claims to read medieval literature as a native. This alone makes him a unique guide to the reading of old books.

A spokesman for Old Western Culture, Lewis confesses in his inaugural address at Cambridge to being alarmed at this role, but accepts its inevitability in his life. As he concludes the address:

> I myself belong far more to that Old Western order than to yours [the modern order]. . . . Ladies and gentlemen, I read as a native texts that you must read as foreigners. . . . It is my settled conviction that in order to read Old Western literature aright you must suspend most of the responses and unlearn most of the habits you have acquired in reading modern literature. . . . And because this is the judgement of a native, I claim that, even if the defence of my conviction is weak, the fact of my conviction is a historical datum to which you should give full weight. That way, where I fail as a critic, I may yet be useful as a specimen. I would even dare to go further. Speaking not only for myself but for all other Old Western men whom you may meet, I would say, use your specimens while you can. There are not going to be many more dinosaurs.[27]

Lewis has been accused of both "playacting" and "disabling unreality" in taking this dinosaur pose.[28] But such criticism itself is open to the charge of *ad hominem* argumentation or, even worse, *petitio principii*. It may well be that, in a sincere concern for all the disappearing dinosaurs, Lewis devoted his last published work while he was alive to providing a map for students to carry with them when they toured the Middle Ages.

Old books are particularly difficult to read since the premodern worldview is so alien to modern thought. A working knowledge of medieval cosmology and psychology is indispensable for the reading of old books – a need supplied by *The Discarded Image*. A useful summary of this book can be found in Lewis' essay "Imagination and Thought in the Middle Ages" in his posthumous *Studies in Medieval and Renaissance Literature*.

It should be emphasized that Lewis had no illusions about the Medieval Model's scientific status: "[T]he medieval cosmos had of course one serious drawback. It wasn't – or a good deal of it wasn't – true. I have rather been inviting you to consider it as a work of art; perhaps, after all, the greatest work of art the Middle Ages produced."[29] His intention is not to turn the clock back. He preaches an appreciation, not an imitation, of the Middle Ages: "I hope no one will think that I am recommending a return to the Medieval Model. I am only suggesting considerations that may induce us to regard all Models in the right way, respecting each and idolizing none."[30]

OVERCOMING MODERN PREJUDICE

Contemporary historical illiteracy continues to misrepresent medieval life and thought. Two misconceptions in particular aggravated Lewis – the flat Earth misconception and the geocentric misconception. Regarding the first issue, Lewis spends a fair amount of time in *The Discarded Image* (pp. 140 ff.) dismantling the idea that medievals believed the Earth to be flat. Far from believing in a flat Earth, all educated medievals knew the

27. Lewis, *"Temporum,"* pp. 24-25.
28. James T. Como, ed., *C. S. Lewis at the Breakfast Table and Other Reminiscences* (New York: Macmillan, 1979), p. 72.
29. Lewis, *Studies*, p. 62.
30. Lewis, *Discarded*, p. 222.

Earth to be spherical (cf. St. Thomas, *Summa Theologica*, I, q. 1, a. 1) as did the ancient Greeks before them. If anything, the medievals overemphasized the importance of spheres and circles (see chapter three on Cosmology).

A few contemporary historians confirm Lewis' complaint. For example, in his book *Inventing the Flat Earth: Columbus and Modern Historians*, Jeffrey Burton Russell shows that no educated person in the fifteenth century (the age of Columbus) denied the roundness of the Earth.[31] In fact, Russell can find only two premodern scholars who believed the Earth to be flat – Lactantius (c.265-345) and Cosmas Indicopleustes (c.540). By contrast the list of scholars believing the Earth to be round would take up pages, but includes Plato (428/427-348/347 BCE), Aristotle (384-322 BCE), Aristarchus (c.310-230 BCE), Eratosthenes (276-195 BCE), Ptolemy (90-168), Augustine (354-430), Martianus (fl. fifth c.), Isidore of Seville (c.560-636), Bede (673-735), Sacrobosco (c.1195–1256), Thomas Aquinas (c.1225-1274), Roger Bacon (c.1220-1292), Dante (1265-1321), Jean Buridan (c.1300–1358), and Nicole Oresme (1320-1382). The flat Earth error was fabricated by pro-Darwinists (particularly Washington Irving) during the nineteenth century and was still being propagated as late as 1983 by the well-known historian and Librarian of Congress, Daniel Boorstin.[32]

Far from having flat Earth inclinations, the medievals may have been guilty of idolizing the circle as the perfect geometrical shape. The medievals symbolized what the perfection of God must be like through the eternal movement of this most perfect geometric figure.[33] We might note that this reverence for circularity kept the medievals from arriving at more accurate findings like the elliptical orbits of the planets discovered by Kepler.

Regarding the second misconception, the medievals were not nearly as geocentric or anthropocentric as the partisans of modernity paint them. Around 270 BCE, the Alexandrian astronomer Aristarchus of Samos asserted that the Earth revolves around the Sun. He also calculated the sizes of the Sun and Moon and their respective distances from the Earth. Aristarchus' contemporaries included other Alexandrian scholars like Euclid (geometry), Ptolemy (astronomy), and Eratosthenes (geography). What these scholars accomplished is amazing. For example, Eratosthenes calculated the circumference of the Earth within 50 miles (according to some scholars) to 195 miles (according to others) of the actual figure. Although there is evidence that Macrobius (*Commentary*, 1.19.4-7) inherited some heliocentric notions (like Venus and Mercury orbiting the Sun), ultimately Ptolemy's geocentric theory of the heavenly motions prevailed over Aristarchus' heliocentric view, and history had to wait until Copernicus for the heliocentric view to gain credence.[34]

However, while most medievals located the Earth at the center of the universe geographically, they did not believe that everything in the universe "revolved around the Earth" or around human beings in any anthropomorphic sense. The medieval Jewish scholar Maimonides notes, "Man . . . is the most perfect and the most noble thing that has been generated from matter; but if his being is compared to that of the spheres and all the more

---

31. Jeffrey Burton Russell, *Inventing the Flat Earth: Columbus and Modern Historians* (New York: Praeger, 1997), p. 14. Russell is here quoting Edward Grant, *Physical Science in the Middle Ages* (New York: Cambridge University Press, 1977), p. 61.

32. Russell, *Inventing*, p. 4.

33. Lewis, *Studies*, p. 51.

34. Thomas Cahill, *Mysteries of the Middle Ages: The Rise of Feminism, Science, and Art from the Cults of Catholic Europe* (New York: Doubleday, 2006), pp. 9-10.

to that of the separate beings, [he will appear] very, very contemptible" (Maimonides, *Guide*, III.13). Far from being philosophically geocentric, they considered the Earth and its inhabitants to be but a pale, imperfect reflection of the divine activity in the heavens. Lewis emphasizes, "To judge from the texts, medieval man thought about the insignificance of Earth more persistently, if anything, than his modern descendents."[35]

Nor were the medievals ignorant of the vastness of space. Although the medieval universe is finite, because only God is infinite, it is not small or cozy. The Earth was viewed as a point of no significant magnitude by both the ancients (Aristotle, *Metaphysics*,1072b) and by the medievals (Dante, *Paradiso*, XXVIII.41-42). The medieval astronomer Sacrobosco described the Earth in chapter one of his famous textbook *On the Sphere* (c.1220) accordingly: "the magnitude of the entire Earth is inappreciable compared to the firmament," indeed it is a "mere point."

So what exactly did this medieval universe look like? Lewis describes the architecture of the Model as follows:

> The central and (spherical) Earth is surrounded by a series of hollow and transparent globes, one above the other, and each of course larger than the one below. These are the 'spheres', 'heavens', or (sometimes) 'elements'. Fixed in each of the first seven spheres is one luminous body. Starting from Earth, the order is the Moon, Mercury, Venus, the Sun, Mars, Jupiter and Saturn. Beyond the sphere of Saturn is the Stellatum, to which belong all those stars we still call 'fixed' because their positions relative to one another are, unlike the planets, invariable. . . . They are planets as well as gods. Not that the Christian poet believed in the god because he believed in the planet; but all three things – the visible planet in the sky, the source of influence, and the god – generally acted as a unity upon his mind. I have not found evidence that theologians were at all disquieted by this state of affairs.[36]

These spheres do triple duty as the source of physical motion (spheres understood as planets), intellectual enlightenment (spheres understood as Intelligences), and existence itself (spheres understood as gods). It is interesting to note that our word influenza comes from the influences that the heavens have on human life.

As mentioned earlier, the medievals believed the universe to be enormous, but finite. In addition, they believed the heavens had a vast but distinctly vertical dimension. Lewis found these two factors enchanting. "Now these two factors taken together – enormous but finite size, and distances which, however vast, remain unambiguously vertical, and indeed vertiginous – at once present you with something which differs from the Newtonian picture rather as a great building differs from a great jungle."[37]

Lewis admires the Medieval Model for its integration of science, morality, and aesthetics. This integration follows in part from the medieval love of hierarchy. Far from seeing hierarchy in terms of power and oppression, the medievals revered hierarchy as a metaphor for growth and a signpost of a greater reality. In fact, Lewis sees medieval hierarchy as a solution to human violence. The modern disconnection of science, morality, and imagination has led not only to violence, but to atrophied imagination. To correct this fragmentation of fact and value (or of science and imagination), Lewis penned moral

---

35. Lewis, *Studies*, p. 46.
36. Lewis, *Discarded*, pp. 96, 105.
37. Lewis, *Studies*, p. 48.

fantasies/science fiction stories like the popular *Chronicles of Narnia*. In *Planet Narnia* Lewis scholar Michael Ward describes the seven Ptolemaic planets as the "controlling symbol-system" in Lewis' imaginative work, particularly in the *Chronicles of Narnia*.[38]

Ward notes that Lewis has been criticized for depicting too much violence in his children's books. However, years ago the famous (albeit somewhat infamous) psychoanalyst Bruno Bettelheim applauded Lewis' efforts in his own work, *The Uses of Enchantment: The Meaning and Importance of Fairy Tales*. Bettelheim laments contemporary efforts to whitewash evil in children's stories and documents how important it is for children to work through moral dilemmas in their imagination long before they face these polarities in reality.

Two particular gems in the Medieval Model that combined a sense of hierarchy with moral imagination were the Principle of the Triad and the Principle of Plentitude.[39] The Principle of the Triad dates back to Plato's *Timaeus* where he states, "It is impossible that two things only should be joined together without a third. There must be some bond in between both to bring them together" (31b-c). As a result, the ancients and medievals put mediating structures between everything. Between the highest part of the soul (reason) and the lowest part of the soul (animal desire) there had to be a mediating element – spiritedness or righteous indignation (see pages 78-79 in chapter four, Psychology). Between the gods (or God) and humans there had to be a mediating elements – daemons, devils, angels, spirits (see page 192 in chapter eight, Theology).

According to the Principle of Plentitude, no space in the universe is uninhabited. Wherever space occurs, the medievals speculated endlessly about whom or what inhabited that space. They end up with a very crowded universe! The Principle of Plentitude is closely linked to the Principle of the Triad. Unlike the modern Protestant God who speaks directly to the human soul, the medieval God delighted in speaking indirectly through a myriad of mediators, including natural phenomena, the heavenly spheres, and the saints. As Lewis says, "It is a continual devolution as if God, who in a sense does all things, will yet do nothing immediately which can possibly be done through the mediation of His creatures."[40]

In addition to his appreciation of medieval cosmology, Lewis also praises medieval psychology for its "objectivity." The medievals assumed everything happening inside of us must correspond to an objective reality outside of us. Their world was full of spirits and natural forces effecting what goes on inside the human mind. Conversely, according to Lewis, the modern world is governed by "subjectivity." Today, emotional conflicts tend to be explained as projections of internal mental states. Psychology has indeed become, as Nietzsche predicted in the late 1800s, the queen of the sciences.

The medievals, however, adhered to a very *object-ive* psychology (primitive by modern standards, but no less hypothetical than modern psychological theories). For the medievals, if we are mean and nasty, we may be possessed by a demon (or object) outside of us. If we are depressed and melancholy, the planet Saturn might be emitting its melancholic influence. According to the medieval worldview, it is theology (the study

---

38. Michael Ward, *Planet Narnia: The Seven Heavens in the Imagination of C. S. Lewis* (New York: Oxford University Press, 2008), p. 101.

39. Lewis, *Discarded*, pp. 43-44. On the Principle of Plentitude see also Arthur O. Lovejoy's *The Great Chain of Being: A Study of the History of an Idea* (New York: Harper and Row, 1960), p. 52.

40. Lewis, *Studies*, p. 58.

of God or the "gods") and not psychology that is the queen of the sciences. While Lewis hardly believed the planets were gods, he did lament the process of "Internalisation" that has eroded Old Western Culture.[41]

MODERNITY: GOD IN THE DOCK AND NATURE ON THE RACK

This phenomenon of Internalisation over the last few centuries led to what Lewis refers to as the "desiccation of the outer universe"[42] and E. R. Dodds calls the "progressive devaluation of the cosmos."[43] This devaluation is implied throughout Lewis' *opus*. To sketch this progressive devaluation, consider the following chart:

history	status of nature	explanation
Pre-Christian:		
The ancients (500 BCE to 500)	Nature as divine (animistic view)	Nature is "full of gods" (Thales). Nature is eternal/perfect in the heavenly realm.
Christian:		
The medievals (500-1500)	Nature as sacrament (sacramental view)	Nature is neither divine nor eternal, but a product of divine activity. Like a sacrament, creation reveals and conceals God.
Post-Christian:		
The moderns (1500-today)	Nature as raw material (materialistic view)	Nature has no spiritual status, but is merely raw material or energy to be used for "the relief of man's estate" (Francis Bacon).

The conquest of nature, while leading to astounding scientific insights and technological conveniences, has also led to a depreciation of the status of nature with disastrous environmental consequences. As other Lewis scholars have noted, Lewis' view of nature entailed a kind of "sacramental ecology, wherein man's relationship with nature would be a means by which man could – at least occasionally – experience a relationship with the sacred, with the numinous world of transcendence."[44] This sacramental view of nature is a vision Lewis shares with early Romantic poets like Wordsworth and Coleridge.

But his vision cannot be dismissed as merely Romantic, for it entails a careful historical and philosophical critique of the modern view of nature. In an essay entitled "New Learning and New Ignorance," Lewis examines what was gained and what was lost in the rise of modern natural science. He acknowledges the tremendous benefits that this science brought humanity. But he also laments the cost.

---

41. Lewis, *Discarded*, pp. 42, 215.

42. Lewis, *Discarded*, p. 42.

43. E. R. Dodds, *Pagan and Christian in an Age of Anxiety* (New York: W. W. Norton, 1970), p. 37.

44. Ed Chapman, "Toward a Sacramental Ecology: Technology, Nature and Transcendence in C. S. Lewis' Ransom Trilogy," *Mythlore* 3.4 (1976), p. 11.

> By reducing Nature to her mathematical elements [modern science] substituted a mechanical for a genial or animistic conception of the universe. The world was emptied, first of her indwelling spirits, then of her occult sympathies and antipathies, finally of her colours, smells, and tastes. . . . Man with his new powers became rich like Midas but all that he touched had gone dead and cold.[45]

The conquest of nature leads to a one-dimensional universe where humanity is granted great control at the price of nature's demotion to "raw material."

The demise of the Medieval Model puts modern humanity in the position of Midas. Control not only exacts unintended consequences, but also distorts that which is controlled. For example, everyone understands that a male predator's view of the woman he seeks to conquer is distorted. No one would disagree that his treatment of her as an object blinds him to an objective appreciation of her as a person. Lewis argues that, analogously, we have lost an objective appreciation of nature by viewing her as raw material for the satisfaction of our desires. One founder of modernity, Machiavelli, exposed this modern predatory view when he compared nature to a woman who, if she could not be cajoled, should be ravished (*The Prince*, XXV). Another founder of modernity, John Locke, referred to nature's bounty as "the almost worthless materials," without value unless transformed by human labor and ingenuity (*Second Treatise of Government*, V.43).

For Lewis, such an exploitative view of non-human nature infects our view of human nature. As nature goes through the process of de-divinization described above (from divine to sacrament to raw material), human nature goes through the same process. With human beings beginning to see themselves as "raw material for scientific manipulation," they risk surrendering their humanity to tyrants only too happy to do the manipulating.[46] Lewis explains this process in his dark fictional account of modernity *That Hideous Strength*: "All that talk about the power of Man over Nature – Man in the abstract – is only for the canaglia. You know as well as I do that Man's power over Nature means the power of some men over other men with Nature as the instrument."[47] Ironically, the disappearance of God from the universe leads to the "abolition of man."

In conquering nature, modernity reveals an aspect of nature that had heretofore remained concealed, at least in its contemporary magnitude – nature as resource or stored energy, "on call" for human consumption. The German philosopher Martin Heidegger makes this point explicitly in his famous work *The Question Concerning Technology*: "Technology is therefore no mere means. Technology is a way of revealing. . . . The revealing that rules in modern technology is a challenging, which puts to nature the unreasonable demand that it supply energy that can be extracted and stored as such."[48] The violent nature of this unreasonable demand is caught most eloquently in the dictum of Francis Bacon (an early propagandist for modernity): "We must put nature to the rack, to compel it to answer our questions."[49]

---

45. C. S. Lewis, *English Literature in the Sixteenth Century: Excluding Drama* (New York: Oxford University Press, 1975), pp. 3-4.

46. Lewis, *Abolition*, p. 80.

47. Lewis, *That Hideous Strength* (New York: Scribner Classics, 1996), p. 175.

48. Martin Heidegger, *The Question Concerning Technology and Other Essays* (New York: Harper and Row, 1977), pp. 12, 14.

49. M. D. Aeschliman, *The Restitution of Man: C. S. Lewis and the Case Against Scientism*

Lewis makes an argument remarkably similar to Heidegger's in his *Abolition of Man*. To extend Bacon's metaphor, Lewis argues that modernity puts God in the Dock (the defendant's chair) and Nature on the Rack (the instrument of medieval torture).

> We do not look at trees either as Dryads or as beautiful objects while we cut them into beams: the first man who did so may have felt the price keenly, and the bleeding trees in Virgil and Spenser may be far-off echoes of that primeval sense of impiety. The stars lost their divinity as astronomy developed, and the Dying God has no place in chemical agriculture. To many, no doubt, this process is simply the gradual discovery that the real world is different from what we expected, and the old opposition to Galileo or to "body-snatchers" is simply obscurantism. But this is not the whole story. It is not the greatest of modern scientists who feel most sure that the object, stripped of its qualitative properties and reduced to mere quantity, is wholly real.[50]

Medieval Platonic, as well as Aristotelian, science was a science of qualities as opposed to a science of quantities. This scientific worldview yielded a contemplative appreciation of nature rather than the predictive power characteristic of modern science. Aristotle himself believed the natural world to be living, animated, and divine. As he says, "All things have by nature something divine in them" (*Nicomachean Ethics*, 1153b33). Lewis contrasts this pagan view (epitomized by the character Merlin in Lewis' *That Hideous Strength*) with the "modern man to whom Nature is something dead."[51]

LEWIS' SACRAMENTALISM AND PAGAN ANIMISM

While Lewis held to a sacramental view of the universe and was captivated by the pagan animistic view of nature, he nowhere denies the facts revealed by modern science. Instead, he appeals to a view of nature broader than the quantitative model that is typified in the famous quip of the physicist Max Planck, reality is "that which can be measured."[52] Lewis was fond of pointing out that the truth of a proposition like Planck's cannot itself be measured and therefore contains a measure of circular reasoning.[53]

In addition to this logical critique of scientific reductionism, Lewis promotes a kind of epistemological democracy – "respecting each [Model] and idolizing none."[54] For Lewis the human understanding of nature is not exhausted by any singular account of nature, whether that account is animistic, sacramental, or materialistic. He simply wanted other non-scientific voices to have a vote on how nature should be treated. His belief that poetry and myth are valid forms of knowledge has taught generations of students the value of texts that might otherwise be dismissed as frivolous. For example, the ancients clearly anticipated and rejected the modern reductionist view of nature in the myth of the aforementioned King Midas. Midas was given a magical power to reduce all of nature to one specific resource – gold. But this gift proved a two-edged sword. As Ovid relates the story in his *Metamorphoses*[55] (a book referred to in the sixteenth and seventeenth

(Grand Rapids, MI: Eerdmans, 1998), p. 23.
50. Lewis, *Abolition*, pp. 78-79.
51. Lewis, *Hideous*, pp. 282-283.
52. Max Planck, *A Survey of Physical Theory* (Mineola, NY: Dover Publications, 1994), p. 53.
53. Lewis, *Reflections*, p. 89.
54. Lewis, *Discarded*, p. 222.
55. The following two lengthy quotes from Ovid are from Allen Mandelbaum's translation

centuries as the "poet's Bible"):

> As he rejoices, Midas's servants set his table – high with meats and with no lack of toasted bread. But when he reaches out to touch the gifts of Ceres, they grow hard; and if, with avid teeth, he bites a piece of meat, where they have bit that piece, his teeth meet yellow gold. . . . Amazed by his incredible mishap, a wretch among such riches, he detests what he had hoped to get; he cannot stand those treasures. There's no heap of food that can appease his hunger, and he burns with thirst – his throat is parched. And, just as he deserves, he's tortured and tormented now by gold. Lifting his hands and gleaming arms to Heaven, "Forgive me, Father Bacchus, I have sinned," he cries; "but do have mercy I implore; release me from the specious fate I sought." (XI, 120 ff.)

The ancients, as did Lewis, trembled before this "primeval sense of impiety."

Elsewhere Ovid describes another attempt by human beings to refuse to honor the sacredness of nature. As already quoted, Lewis believes that we no longer look at trees as Dryads (nymphs) or beautiful objects when we cut them down. Also in the *Metamorphoses*, Ovid tells of a man who "scorned the gods" and chose to chop down a sacred oak:

> He was about to strike the trunk aslant with his poised ax, when, trembling, Ceres' oak tree groaned aloud; its leaves and acorns paled – and its long boughs. And when that cursed stoke had hacked the trunk, out from the wounded bark, blood gushed; just as it gushed from a sacrificial bull who falls before the altar, his neck smashed. . . . Then, as he pounded, blow on blow, against the oak tree, from within the trunk, these words emerged: "I am the nymph most dear to Ceres; I live beneath this bark; now, at my death, I prophesy – and this leaves me content: your punishment indeed is imminent." (VIII, 760 ff.)

It is interesting to note that, at $2 billion and counting, the highest earning movie of all time until the year 2010, *Avatar*, revolves around a plot where evil earthlings decimate the home of the "Na'vi" on the planet Pandora (in particular a massive sacred tree) in order to mine the planet for the precious raw material scattered throughout their rich woodland.

If Lewis was a dinosaur as he describes himself, it is nowhere more apparent than his reverence for nature and horror at what he called "the murder of beauty." He complains, "The trouble is that from man's first and wholly legitimate attempt to win safety and ease from Nature it seems, step by step, to lead on quite logically to universal suburbia."[56] It is useful to note Lewis' qualification, "wholly legitimate." He did not oppose science *per se* or labor-saving devices. He feared the popularizing of scientific truths into hardened metaphysical assumptions, for example the belief that "progress is an inevitable process like decay, and that the only important thing in life is to increase the comfort of homo sapiens, at whatever cost to posterity and to the other inhabitants of the planet."[57] Lewis carefully distinguished scientific method (hypothesis, observation, and experiment) from scientism – the worship of a science that excludes the divine.

---

of the *Metamorphoses* (New York: Harcourt, Inc., 1993).

56. C. S. Lewis, *The Collected Letters of C. S. Lewis*, edited by Walter Hooper, vol. 2, Books, Broadcasts, and the War 1931-1949 (San Francisco: HarperSanFrancisco, 2004), p. 808.

57. C. S. Lewis, *The Collected Letters of C. S. Lewis*, edited by Walter Hooper, vol. 3, Narnia, Cambridge, and Joy 1950-1963 (San Francisco: HarperSanFrancisco, 2007), p. 984.

Although Lewis integrated the animistic view of nature with an understanding of nature as the creation of God, he never lost his reverence for the *anima mundi*.[58] While nature gradually came to be seen as a work of art in the Medieval Model, it was still God's work of art and hence worthy of reverence. In fact, Lewis really did not see any ultimate contradiction between the passive, pre-Christian god of Aristotle that "moves the world by being loved, not by loving"[59] and the active Christian God whose love or *agapē* for creatures extends to the remotest corner of the universe. As Ward says in *Planet Narnia*:

> Lewis was conscious that this [medieval] picture of the universe, in which God is not so much the lover as the beloved and humanity is peripheral, might be thought incompatible with the Christian picture in which God proactively seeks out the lost sheep who is the center of divine concern. However, Lewis reckoned there to be no absolute contradiction between the two pictures because the love of the spheres for God exhibits the perfect natural order of the uncorrupted translunary realm, while God's searching love for humanity represents the action of divine grace toward fallen, sublunary creatures.[60]

For Lewis, the subordination of creation to the Creator did not diminish the status of that creation worshipped by the pagans under the name of "nature." The pagans themselves struggled with the ontological status of their beloved nature, a struggle revealed in a cryptic passage from the pagan philosopher Heraclitus who observed that Nature [*physis*] loves to conceal herself.[61]

Lewis argued that "the only possible basis for Christian apologetics is a proper respect for Paganism."[62] As the above chart on page 10 indicates, Lewis divided history into three periods. He was clearly more sympathetic to the first two.

> Roughly speaking we may say that whereas all history was for our ancestors divided into two periods, the pre-Christian and the Christian, and two only, for us it falls into three – the pre-Christian, the Christian, and what may reasonably be called the post-Christian. This surely must make a momentous difference. I am not here considering either the christening or the un-christening from a theological point of view. I am considering them simply as cultural changes. When I do that, it appears to me that the second change is even more radical than the first. Christians and Pagans had much more in common with each other than either has with a post-Christian. The gap between those who worship different gods is not so wide as that between those who worship and those who do not.[63]

The pagans or "pre-Christians" had a "sympathy for nature," a "religious attitude to the family," and an "appetite for beauty." Lewis shows how much closer he is to the pre-Christian than to the post-Christian world when, in *That Hideous Strength*, he praises Mother Dimble's approach to nature by commenting, "She has not rejected it [nature],

---

58. Lewis, *English*, p. 4.

59. Lewis, *Studies*, p. 51.

60. Ward, *Planet*, p. 24.

61. Cf. Kathleen Freeman, *Ancilla to the Pre-Socratic Philosophers: A Complete Translation of the Fragments in Diels* (Cambridge, MA: Harvard University Press, 1948), p. 48.

62. Ward, *Planet*, p. 28.

63. Lewis, *"Temporum,"* pp. 13-14.

but she has baptized it."[64]

In this post-Christian world, Lewis urges the study of the Old Western Culture in order to reveal again the view of the universe as a *kosmos*. Liddell and Scott's *Greek-English Lexicon* provides an interesting array of definitions for the word, *kosmos*.

1. the world or universe
2. order
3. good behavior, decency
4. an ornament or decoration

To see the universe as natural order, moral law, and beautiful ornament is to see the world as C. S. Lewis saw it: a world of intrinsic truth, beauty, and goodness.

SITUATING LEWIS WITHIN THE CRITIQUE OF MODERNITY

Readers who find this section "Situating Lewis within the Critique of Modernity" too obscure, should feel free to skip to the next section on "How to Read *Medieval Literacy*."

It may be of interest to note that Lewis is not alone in his criticism of modernity. Within Christianity, there are two major schools of thought at odds with modernity, the Thomist School of Roman Catholicism and the Anglo-Catholic School in England. Both schools have roots in the nineteenth century Oxford Movement which itself was part of the Roman Catholic Church's elevation of St. Thomas Aquinas to a position of philosophical preeminence. A list of the more recent Thomists who have energetically resumed the old quarrel between the ancients and the moderns include:

Thomist School

- Jacques Maritain (d. 1973)
- Etienne Gilson (d. 1978)
- Josef Pieper (d. 1997)
- Henry Veatch (d. 1999)
- Alasdair McIntyre

While sympathetic to Thomas, Lewis was not a Thomist and at times was quite critical of modern neo-Thomism.

He was, however, clearly a member of the Anglo-Catholic School, albeit something of a Protestant renegade within its walls. Members of this school include:

Anglo-Catholic School

- John Henry Newman (d. 1890)
- G. K. Chesterton (d. 1936)
- C. S. Lewis (d. 1963)
- T. S. Eliot (d. 1965)
- J.R.R. Tolkien (d. 1973)

Like other members of this school, Lewis straddled the line between poet and philosopher. As he told one of his most brilliant students, the Sufi scholar Martin Lings, "You [Lings] are an intellectual, I am an imaginative man."[65] Like T. S. Eliot, Lewis was not only a

---

64. Lewis, *Hideous*, p. 311.
65. Martin Lings, "Reminiscences of C. S. Lewis in the 1930s," audiotape from an address

philosophical critic of modernity, but a literary critic as well. He had affinities with 20th century anti-modernist poets like Eliot, Yeats, and Pound who differed from Romantics like Wordsworth in the fact that they attacked modernity using modern literary forms.

A student of Lewis in the years before Lewis became famous, Martin Lings became a staunch member of the Traditionalist School or the Perennialist School.

Perennialist School

- Ananda K. Coomaraswamy (d. 1947)
- René Guénon (d. 1951)
- Titus Burckhardt (d. 1984)
- Frithjof Schuon (d. 1998)
- Martin Lings (d. 2005)
- William Stoddart

After studying with Lewis at Oxford and a stint teaching Middle English in Poland and Lithuania, Lings became a student of the French thinker René Guénon. Guénon and his followers believed that the great religions of the world all share the same essential truth, although their outward form—doctrines and practices—differ.

While most proponents of this school gravitated toward Islamic mysticism (Sufism), they did not promote Islam over other religions. Coomaraswamy, for example, was a Hindu. Guénon steadfastly maintained that "one should recognize all the great religions, but practice only one."[66] In fact the Perennialists are adamant in their defense of religious orthodoxy within various traditions.

Lings thought Lewis would be excited about the Guénon books he sent to Lewis in 1935 as both Lewis and Guénon were staunch critics of modernity (cf. Guénon's *The Crisis of the Modern World*). However, Lewis was not impressed, perhaps because Guénon insisted Roman Catholicism and Eastern Orthodoxy were the only valid forms of Christianity. North Irish to the core, Lewis was less than enthusiastic about Protestantism being dismissed as a heresy. Lings himself remarked that it did not help that the young Lings told Lewis (given Lewis' knowledge of the Middle Ages) that Lewis had no right <u>not</u> to be a Roman Catholic![67] No doubt Lewis must have seen some connections between his work and Guénon's (see page 311 of this book's Appendix), but was never reconciled to the Perennialists. He used to deride the perennial philosophy of Aldous Huxley by saying, "Christianity and Buddhism are very much alike, especially Buddhism."[68] It should be noted that Schuon later revised this critical position on Protestantism, a revision generally accepted by the Perennialist school.

Since Lewis' day, another school of thought highly critical of modernity has emerged under the tutelage of the German émigré, Leo Strauss. This school of originally Jewish scholars gradually morphed into a combative group of American academics (infamous for being a cabal of neo-cons according to liberal journalists) who proudly profess their lineage as first-generation Straussians (students of Strauss himself), second-generation

---

to the C. S. Lewis Society in Oxford, England in the early 1990s.

66. Martin Lings, "Reminiscences" audiotape.

67. Martin Lings, "Reminiscences" audiotape.

68. Cf. George Watson, "The Art of Disagreement: C. S. Lewis (1898-1963)," *The Hudson Review* 48.2 (1995), p. 230.

Straussians (students of those students), third-generation, etc. Many Straussians are agnostic, but this lack of religious orthodoxy does not weaken their view of modernity as a political disease. Strauss' major critique of modernity occurs in his book *On Tyranny*.

Straussian School

- Leo Strauss (d. 1973)
- Ernest Fortin (d. 2002)
- Harry Jaffa
- Leon Kass
- Stanley Rosen
- James Schall

Prominent Straussians include two Catholic priests, Ernest Fortin and James Schall.

In a now classic essay "The Three Waves of Modernity" Strauss himself noticed how philosophical criticisms of modernity often plunged the Western world more deeply into that same modernity being criticized.[69] The first wave identified with the work of Machiavelli created modernity through the replacement of the ancient pursuit of virtue with the novel pursuit of power and efficiency. The second wave initiated by Rousseau and continued through Hegel and Marx, criticized the first wave for ignoring the important role of history in human self-understanding. And the final wave initiated by Nietzsche ridiculed the naïve historicism of the second wave, at the same time critiquing scientific and technological culture as debased forms of culture. This cultural criticism has obvious affinities with the aesthetic criticism of Eliot, Yeats, and Pound. In its more secular versions, this cultural criticism wound up promoting "postmodern" cultural relativism.

Outside of these criticisms of modernity, one might add *social* critics like Simone Weil (d. 1943), Aldous Huxley (d. 1963), Karl Polanyi (d. 1964), Thomas Merton (d. 1968), Jacques Ellul (d. 1994), and Ivan Illich (d. 2002), many of whom were deeply religious. Ellul's book, *The Technological Society* may be the single greatest sociological critique of modern technology ever attempted. Unfortunately this sociological work is rarely read in conjunction with its theological companion, Ellul's *The Meaning of the City*.

Other prominent critics of modernity include Martin Heidegger (d. 1976) and his student, Hans Jonas (d. 1993), as well as Romano Guardini (d. 1968), Mircea Eliade (d. 1986), and the Canadian political philosopher, George Parkin Grant (d. 1988). The names of Heidegger and Eliade show fascist leanings among certain critics of modernity. It might be noted that the Protestant thinker, George Grant, has strong ties to the Anglo-Catholic School (he met his wife at Lewis' Socratic Club) and has acknowledged his intellectual debts to Simone Weil, Leo Strauss, and Jacques Ellul.

While all of the above critics have insightful criticisms of the modern world, none exceed the accessibility of Lewis' *The Abolition of Man*. For this reason, if for no other, students might turn to Lewis in their struggle to understand why modernity ought to be questioned and what might be of value in medieval thought, literature, and art.[70]

---

69. Leo Strauss, *An Introduction to Political Philosophy: Ten Essays by Leo Strauss*. Edited by Hilail Gildin (Detroit: Wayne State University Press, 1989), pp. 81-98.

70. One other reason to choose Lewis among the other critics of modernity is that, despite his enormous popularity, his work on the Middle Ages deserves to be better known. As the famous historian Norman Cantor states, "Of all the medievalists of the twentieth century, Lewis and Tol-

HOW TO READ *MEDIEVAL LITERACY*

If the lists in this book emphasize pagan more than biblical ideas, that is in keeping with Lewis' belief that the theology of the Middle Ages was primarily the theology of Aristotle, not the Bible.[71] Following medieval tradition, the chapters in *Medieval Literacy* reflect the belief that the ways of God can be read in two different books, the book of Creation or Nature and the book of Scripture.

This doctrine is clearly articulated in Alan of Lille's poem, *The Plaint of Nature:*[72]

Omni mundi creatura	The whole created world,
Quasi liber et pictura	Like a book and a picture,
Nobis est in speculum,	Serves us as a mirror,
Nostrae vitae, nostrae sortis.	Of our life, our fate.

Before the Fall of Adam, unsullied by sin, humans could read the evidence of God directly in the book of Nature. After the Fall, human reason was wounded but not destroyed. For example, in the Hebrew Scriptures, Psalm 19:1 states that "the heavens declare the glory of God." And in the Christian Scriptures, Romans 1:20 states that God can be seen in the things God has made. However, in addition to the book of Nature, God sent the book of Scripture as a supplement to wounded reason.

While the Fall of Adam made the book of Scripture necessary to human salvation, the medievals never lost the conviction that God still spoke through Nature. The founder of monasticism, St. Anthony, articulated this idea as clearly as Alan of Lille. One famous passage about St. Anthony is recorded by Thomas Merton as follows: "A certain Philosopher asked St. Anthony: Father, how can you be so happy when you are deprived of the consolation of books? Anthony replied: My book, O philosopher, is the nature of created things, and at any time I want to read the words of God, the book is before me."[73] This idea survived into early modern times. In Shakespeare's *As You Like It*, the pastoral life is revered by one who "finds tongues in trees, books in running brooks, sermons in stones, and good in everything" (II, 16-17).

In Islam, the idea of two books never went out of style. The Qur'ān encourages the study of nature because all natural wonders are signs (*ayat*) pointing to God (e.g., 2:164, 3:190-191, 24:41-42, 30:20-23, 36:33-37). Even today, Islam identifies two books, the Qur'ān and the universe itself: "According to Islam, the Qur'ān in its inner reality is uncreated, this archetypal Qur'ān being at once the origin of the Noble Book or the composed Qur'ān (*al-Qur'ān al-tadwini*) and the universe or the 'cosmic Qur'ān' (*al-Qur'ān al-takwini*)."[74]

The basic outline of *Medieval Literacy* follows this doctrine of the two books. In Part

---

kien have gained incomparably the greatest audience, although 99.9 percent of their readers have never looked at their scholarly work" (*Inventing the Middle Ages* [New York: William Morrow and Company, 1991]), p. 207.

71. Lewis, *Studies*, p. 50.

72. Willemien Otten, "Nature and Scripture: Demise of a Medieval Analogy," *Harvard Theological Review* 88.2 (1995), p. 283.

73. Thomas Merton, *The Wisdom of the Desert* (New York: New Directions, 1960), p. 62.

74. Seyyed Hossein Nasr, *The Need for a Sacred Science* (Albany, NY: SUNY Press, 1993), p. 101.

One of *Medieval Literacy* on Nature, the most primitive attempts of ancient humanity to understand the natural world are presented in the chapter on Mythology. A more sophisticated treatment of the world or "macro-cosmos" is presented in the chapter on Cosmology. The treatment of the soul or "micro-cosmos" is presented in the chapter on Psychology. Since medieval tradition held that logic is a tool for philosophy and that philosophy is the "handmaiden of theology," the chapters on Logic, Philosophy, and Theology are presented in Part Two of *Medieval Literacy* under the rubric of Knowledge. The medieval method of education is explained in the Interlude. The Epilogue shows how the development of art and literature in the twelfth century paved the way for the modern world.

While this book may not cause the reader to run out and join the nearest monastery, at the very least it provides a useful reference to the reading of the old books. At the very best it provides the crucial perspective on modernity encouraged by C. S. Lewis. Similar to books like E. D. Hirsch, Jr.'s *Dictionary of Cultural Literacy*, Stephen Prothero's *Religious Literacy*, Joseph Telushkin's *Jewish Literacy*, and even Lynn Arthur Steen's *Mathematics and Democracy: The Case for Quantitative Literacy*, this work serves as an exercise in literacy, specifically medieval literacy. Like a Map Quest road map, *Medieval Literacy* provides a minimum of narrative detail. This annotated compilation of lists reflects the bookish medieval mind at work, relentlessly compiling an inventory of the universe.

The making of lists appears to be native to human civilization. Humans are apparently list-making as well as tool-making animals. Centuries before David Letterman's "Top Ten" lists, Homer went into great detail listing the famous catalog of Greek ships and countries in the invasion of Troy (*Iliad,* 2.584 ff.). The Hebrew Scriptures often go on for pages describing genealogies of who "begat" whom.

The Buddhists may have outdone the West in their fabrication of lists. In medieval times, the Buddha's enormous number of lists (a sample found in the Appendix to this book), were gathered into manuals and memorized by monks in their barest forms. These manuals resemble the *Summae* of the Western medieval world, collected lists of pro and con arguments. The enormous number of lexical lists from ancient Mesopotamia has even spawned a particular branch of knowledge – *Listenwissenschaft,* or the science of lists.[75]

Medieval thought favored the condensed form of scholastic manuals. In this regard, *Medieval Literacy* provides an introduction to things medieval within a format that is definitely medieval. *Medieval Literacy* shares the distinct advantage of a roadmap by showing the reader how to move around inside the medieval world. In his preface to *The Discarded Image*, Lewis makes the general recommendation that we "consult a map before we set out" to understand the Middle Ages.[76] *Medieval Literacy* expands on Lewis' work. In fact Lewis scholar Perry Bramlett refers to *Medieval Literacy* as *The Discarded Image* on steroids! If you are studying medieval art, literature, philosophy, theology, or history (or just like lists); this book should prove an agreeable traveling companion.

The interconnections between these lists reveal a highly developed and conscious "world view," a structure first articulated in ancient works like Plato's *Republic*, then blending with Christianity in late antiquity by Augustine in the *City of God*, and finally reaching its pinnacle in Thomas Aquinas' *Summa Theologica* and Dante's *Divine Comedy*. To put the Medieval Model in historical perspective, it might help to recap a few other

---

75. Jack Goody, *The Domestication of the Savage Mind* (New York: Cambridge University Press, 1977), pp. 80, 94.

76. Lewis, *Discarded*, p. vii.

important dates (note that St. Augustine is often seen as a transitional figure between the ancient and medieval worlds).

Graeco-Roman Antiquity	500 BCE–500
Plato (student of Socrates)	428/7-348/7 BCE
Aristotle (student of Plato)	384-322 BCE
St. Augustine (Platonist)	354-430
Middle Ages	500–1500
Boethius	c.480-c.525
St. Thomas Aquinas (Aristotelian)	c.1225-1274
Dante (greatest medieval poet)	1265-1321

While the Medieval Model outlived Dante, it never surpassed his grand synthesis of paganism and Christianity or of poetry and philosophy. According to Lewis, Dante's *Divine Comedy* is the "supreme achievement" of the Middle Ages, followed closely by the *Summa Theologica* and the cathedrals dotting the European landscape.[77]

In conjunction with this supreme achievement, I have outlined the entire *Summa Theologica* and *Divine Comedy* in the Theology chapter. Only in one other instance in *Medieval Literacy* was a specific book outlined. In the Mythology chapter I have outlined the entire *Metamorphoses* of Ovid because of its prominent place within the medieval mind. While Virgil was the greatest Latin poet, Ovid was the most popular. His influence on the medievals in general and Dante in particular is incalculable. W. R. Johnson said, "No other poem from antiquity has so influenced the literature and art of Western Europe as has the *Metamorphoses*."[78] The *Metamorphoses* is the best classical source for over 250 Greek myths.

Furthermore, it is helpful to note that the Middle Ages is often subdivided into the Early Middle Ages (500-1000), the High Middle Ages (1000-1300) and the Later or Low Middle Ages (1300-1500). One other helpful note regards my placing Islam within the West along with Judaism and Christianity. This was done for two reasons. First, Islam refers to all three monotheistic religions as the People of the Book in the Qur'ān (3:110, 187). Second, Islam helped create the medieval West through its translations of the works of Plato and Aristotle. Islamic scholars provided Western Europe with its own history and are thus pivotal figures in the history of the West. Just as Judaism prepared the way for Christianity, Islam prepared the way for the reintegration of classical philosophy into Western Christendom.

A comparison of this book's lists reveals the ways in which a synthesis between Judeo-Christian revelation and Greek reason (mediated through Arab translation) was attempted by the medieval mind. Following each list are bibliographic references to the relevant primary sources (A) that are listed in chronological order by the author's lifetime and secondary sources (B) that are listed in alphabetical order by the author's name. The lists themselves sometimes follow a chronological order (earlier historical lists precede later historical lists), sometimes a thematic order (based on the material), or even a quantitative

---

77. Lewis, *Studies*, p. 44.

78. Allen Mandelbaum, afterword to Ovid's *Metamorphoses* (New York: Harcourt, Inc., 1993), p. 551.

order (lists of threes, then fours, then fives, etc.). Please note that for ease of reference a small number of lists and charts are repeated in different chapters. Also note that in the bibliography dates for books are for later editions (not original copyright dates) in order to give the reader a clue as to the availability of the book.

I hope that these lists will act as a catalyst for more in-depth lectures by professors and/or further reading by students. I have found the lists helpful in preparing both lectures and exams for students. Umberto Eco states in his medieval murder mystery *The Name of the Rose*, "There is nothing more wonderful than a list."[79] That said, let the lists begin!

POSTSCRIPT

After reviewing this manuscript before publication, three lacunas have come to my attention. First, although major scholarly opinion holds that Plato's influence during the Middle Ages was meager, a case could be made that Christian Platonism has been given short shrift compared to Christian Aristotelianism within *Medieval Literacy*. This difference of opinion has been noted explicity in appropriate places in the text.

Second, despite occassional exceptions, lists from the Later or Low Middle Ages as well as certain Northern European and Italian sources have not been mentioned despite their importance to C. S. Lewis and their reference in *The Discarded Image*. These gaps include mention of Ango-Saxon and Norse Epics as well as Boccaccio and Chaucer. For example, in the chapter on Art and Literature, almost all literary references are to the Old French tradition. In the current edition of *Medieval Literacy* lists have stopped around the time of Dante and the end of the High Middle Ages.

Finally, aside from references to Maimonides and the Hebrew Scriptures, medieval Judaism and the entire tradition of rabbinic literature has been inadequately treated. This would include discussion of the written Torah and the oral Torah (the Mishnah) as well as the Talmud, Midrash, and medieval Bible commentaries like those of Rashi. For an excellent introduction to rabbinic literature, the reader might consult Barry W. Holtz's *Back to the Sources: Reading the Classic Jewish Texts*. Hopefully a second edition of *Medieval Literacy* will be able to fill in all of these gaps.

---

79. Umberto Eco, *The Name of the Rose* (New York: Harcourt Brace Jovanovich, 1980), p. 73.

PART ONE: NATURE

II. Mythology

"Don't you understand," said Socrates, "that we begin by telling children fables [myths], and the fable is, taken as a whole, false, but there is truth in it also?"

Plato, *Republic*, 377a

Modern slander against medieval beliefs includes much more than the myth of the flat Earth. Another modern prejudice holds that the ancients and medievals believed the stories of Zeus, Aphrodite, and the myriad gods and goddesses to be literally true. The above text from Plato shows that twenty-five centuries ago, educated people knew such myths to be false in the literal sense, but useful and even beneficial in the education of children (see the discussion of children and mythology on page nine in chapter one, the Introduction to this book). Following this Platonic tradition, Dante, the greatest storyteller of medieval times, acknowledges the truth of myths to be allegorical, not literal. "The allegorical is a truth hidden beneath a beautiful fiction" (*Convivio*, II.i). Despite the bizarre surface of myths (e.g., Prometheus being chained to a rock and having birds of prey eat his liver for eternity), these tales hold a kernel of truth (e.g., Prometheus being a symbol of human pride or *hybris*).

Originally, the Greek word *mythos* simply meant "word" or "speech" – any word or any speech. With time *mythos* came to refer to a poetic or legendary tale as opposed to a historical account. Believing the universe to be eternal rather than created, ancient pagans expressed little interest in historical accuracy. They had no sense of "making history" and did not attach much significance to the uniqueness of historical events.[80] Since history would inevitably repeat itself (given the eternity of the world), what mattered to them were the timeless lessons to be drawn from events – the morals, the stories (*mythoi*), and the archetypes. The Hebrew belief in the uniqueness of the Exodus event and the Christian belief in the uniqueness of the death and resurrection of Christ gradually transformed this pagan view of history, but only slowly and over many centuries. The medievals retained an avid devotion to mythology.

C. S. Lewis found enormous significance in pagan myths. Mythology holds a central place in his account of his conversion to Christianity *Surprised by Joy*. His first three religious experiences as a youth, or "stabs" of Joy as he called them, were all mythic: (1) holding his brother's miniature garden in his hand and feeling the bliss of Eden, (2) being overwhelmed by the Idea of Autumn after reading a children's story, and (3) reading a passage from Norse mythology. These pagan ecstasies prefigured his conversion and he laments that as a young man, "No one ever attempted to show in what sense Christianity fulfilled Paganism or Paganism prefigured Christianity."[81]

He was particularly taken by Norse mythology and Wagner's music. He confesses that his first true understanding of "worship" came from the Norse gods, not the Christian God.

---

80. Cf. the summary of archaic thought in Mircea Eliade, *The Myth of the Eternal Return* (Princeton, NJ: Princeton University Press, 1991).

81. Lewis, *Joy*, p. 62.

> We are taught in the Prayer Book [Anglican Book of Prayer] to "give thanks to God for His great glory," as if we owed Him more thanks for being what He necessarily is than for any particular benefit He confers upon us; and so indeed we do, and to know God is to know this. But I had been far from any such experience. I came far nearer to feeling this about the Norse gods whom I disbelieved in than I had ever done about the true God while I believed.[82]

His appreciation of myth remained unchanged throughout his life; if anything increasing as he aged. He wrote the *Chronicles of Narnia* to give children an appreciation of myth. And he declared on one occasion that no one should be allowed to die without having read Plato's *Symposium*, a work that examines various myths about the goddess of love. Lewis' definition of Joy is Platonic. He refers to Joy as an "unsatisfied desire which is itself more desirable than any other satisfaction."[83] This definition has close affinities with the courtly love tradition discussed in chapter nine on Art and Literature.

This metaphor he uses to describe these religious experiences or "stabs" of Joy betrays a medieval worldview. Love (divine or human) is a passion to be endured; it is a painful bliss. Andreas Capellanus defines the medieval courtly love of knights and their ladies in similar fashion. "Love is a certain inborn suffering derived from the sight of and excessive meditation upon the beauty of the opposite sex" (*Courtly Love*, I.1). In the medieval worldview, we are possessed by love as by a superhuman power beyond our control.

> By saying that love, or victory, is god, or to be more accurate, a god, was meant first and foremost that it is more than human, not subject to death, everlasting. It is not for nothing that the Greeks ordinarily referred to their gods as οἱ ἀθάνατοι, the deathless ones. Any power, any force we see at work in the world, which is not born with us and will continue after we are gone, could thus be called a god, and most of them were.[84]

The myths of love form one piece of the mosaic of stories about these forces beyond human control.

Perhaps the hallmark of the medieval worldview (as first popularized in Book II of Boethius' *The Consolation of Philosophy* and later in Chapter VII of Dante's *Inferno*) is the story of the goddess, Fortuna. "[Boethius'] *De Consolatione Philsophiae* was, in Lewis' opinion, among the most influential books ever written in Latin; he thought that to acquire a taste for it was almost to become naturalized in the Middle Ages."[85] At the heart of this naturalization lies the myth of fortune that challenges the modern myth of progress. Lewis was hostile to progress because he did not find it a comforting myth, but a cruel one. He proposes the myth of fortune as a defense against the progressive view, "common to vulgar Pagans and to vulgar Christians alike, which 'comforts cruel men' by interpreting variations of human prosperity as divine rewards and punishments."[86] He regarded all notions of progress as forms of social Darwinism – perversions of the Christian doctrine of providence.

Lewis found the myth of fortune closer to the Christian truth where God "makes

---

82. Lewis, *Joy*, p. 77.
83. Lewis, *Joy*, p. 17-18.
84. G. M. A. Grube, *Plato's Thought* (Boston: Beacon Press, 1966), p. 150.
85. Ward, *Planet*, p. 111.
86. Lewis, *Discarded*, p. 82.

his Sun rise on the evil and on the good, and sends rain on the righteous and on the un-righteous" (Matthew 5:45). In the myth of fortune human beings find themselves on an inexorably turning wheel. Dante identified Fortuna as the "terrestrial Intelligence" that steers the Earth, not through an orbit, but "in the mode proper to a stationary globe."[87] At the 12:00 position (the top of the wheel) sits a king confident, powerful and strong, who says, "I rule." At the 3:00 position is the figure of a king who has lost his crown and says, "I have ruled." At the 6:00 position a king is dressed in rags and has lost everything on the wheel of fortune. He says, "I have no kingdom." At the 9:00 position sits the figure of a cunning young prince clawing his way to the top who says, "I will rule."

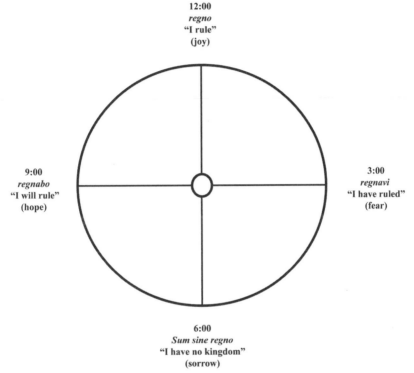

12:00
regno
"I rule"
(joy)

9:00
regnabo
"I will rule"
(hope)

3:00
regnavi
"I have ruled"
(fear)

6:00
Sum sine regno
"I have no kingdom"
(sorrow)

Fortune teaches the valuable lesson that no human being or group of human beings can claim mastery of the universe. Even the technological "conquest of nature" (the conquest of chance or fortune) may turn out to be a temporary 12:00 victory giving way to any number of 6:00 calamities like global warming, environmental disaster, and nuclear accident.

Middle class Westerners outwardly may live life at 12:00 on the wheel, but the major-ity of humanity does not. Historians estimate there were roughly 400 million people on Earth before the advent of modern science and technology.[88] Let's assume that 95% of these people lived at or below a harsh subsistence level. By the year 2000, world popula-tion exceeded 6 billion people and by 2012 over 7 billion. However, today, although a greater percentage of humanity lives above a harsh subsistence level, in absolute numbers a far greater number of people live at or below the level of a medieval serf. According

---

87. Lewis, *Discarded*, p. 139.

88. Ronald Wright, *An Illustrated Short History of Progress* (Toronto: House of Anansi, 2006), p. 152.

to the World Bank, 1.4 billion people now live on less than $1.25 a day. And 3 billion live on less than $2.50 a day. So there are six times as many people living at or below a harsh subsistence level today than there were in the Middle Ages. Is this progress? It is if your perspective on life is from the 12:00 view, but not necessarily if your perspective is from the 6:00 position.

Regarding the barbarity of medieval times (and no one can deny the barbarity of slavery/serfdom, torture, the Inquisition, and the Crusades), it is only fair to note that, in sheer numbers, medieval atrocities pale before the technological barbarism of modernity. Medieval tactics were indeed gruesome, but their effect was limited compared to contemporary warfare. Modern libertarian economists (devoted to the ideal of limited government) have spent decades calculating the slaughter imposed by modern governments on their opponents and their own citizens. In the 20th century alone, estimates of people killed through war, genocide, and liquidation run from a low of 80 million to a high of 300 million people. Ronald Wright calculates "at least 100 million people" died in 20th century wars.[89] Even given the lower estimates, during the 20th century far more people were slaughtered than in all previous centuries combined. From a strictly utilitarian calculus (i.e., the greatest good for the greatest number), the moral superiority of modernity is debatable. Furthermore, however barbaric the medievals may have been, they did not have the power to destroy the world.

According to the myth of fortune no one stays on top forever. This medieval myth may well provide a more accurate understanding about the human condition than the myth of progress. Of course, neither story is scientific in any rigorous sense. However, since it is impossible to live without stories and myths, an educated person might be defined as one with a wide exposure to all of humankind's stories, not just the modern ones. One need not accept all of Lewis' neo-Romantic notions to entertain the possibility that Western culture buried some of its gems along with its crimes in the past. At the very least, in order to face the adage of Santayana ("those who cannot remember the past are doomed to repeat it") head on, there is no harm in digging them up and seeing if they still shine.

Remember, following each list are bibliographic references to the relevant primary sources (A) that are listed in chronological order by the author's lifetime and secondary sources (B) that are listed in alphabetical order by the author's name.

---

89. Wright, *Progress*, p. 42.

CHRONOLOGY OF THE GODS

Primordial Gods (natural forces)

1. Chaos

2. Eros (Love)

3. Gaia (Earth)

4. Uranus (Sky)

5. Pontus (Sea)

    A. Hesiod, *Theogony*, 115-135
       Plato, *Timaeus*, 40e
    B. Vernant, Jean-Pierre, *The Universe, the Gods and Men;*
       Ancient Greek Myths, pp. 3-6

CHRONOLOGY OF THE GODS (CONTINUED)

First Generation of Individualized Gods (12 Titans)

6 sons	who married:	6 daughters
1. Cronus (leader of the Titans)		Rhea
2. Iapetus		Themis
3. Oceanus		Tethys
4. Hyperion		Theia
5. Crius		Mnemosyne
6. Coeus		Phoebe

    A. Hesiod, *Theogony*, 133-137
       Plato, *Timaeus*, 40e
    B. Hamilton, Edith, *Mythology*, pp. 21-22

Second Generation of Individualized Gods (Olympian gods)

1. Zeus (leader of the Olympians)
2. Poisedon
3. Hades
4. Hestia
5. Demeter
6. Hera

    A. Hesiod, *Theogony*, 453-457
       Plato, *Timaeus*, 41a
    B. Vernant, Jean-Pierre, *The Universe, the Gods and Men; Ancient Greek Myths*, p. 17

CHRONOLOGY OF THE GODS (CONTINUED)

Genealogy of the Gods

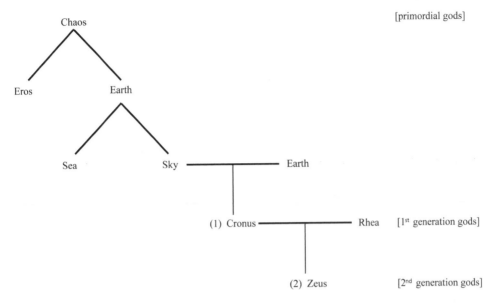

1. Cronus is the youngest of the Titans born to Uranus (Sky) and Gaia (Earth). Sky continually lies on Earth and impregnates her but refuses to separate from her. To liberate his fellow siblings, Cronus castrates Uranus who recoils from Gaia, thereby creating space between the heavens and the Earth.

2. Zeus is the youngest of the Olympians born to Cronus and Rhea. Cronus eats all children born to Rhea. Zeus feeds an emetic to Cronus so that Cronus vomits forth Zeus' siblings, thereby freeing the Olympians. The Olympians and Titans fight for dominance among the gods with the Olympians ultimately winning.

    A. Hesiod, *Theogony*, 116 ff.
    B. Vernant, Jean-Pierre, *The Universe, the Gods and Men;*
        Ancient Greek Myths, pp. 3-19

LISTS OF MYTHOLOGICAL FIGURES

The Three Graces (daughters of Zeus & Eurynome; reside on Mt. Olympus)

goddess	patron
1. Aglaia	splendor
2. Euphrosyne	mirth
3. Thalia	good cheer

A. Hesiod, *Theogony*, 905-910
B. Hamilton, Edith, *Mythology*, p. 39

The Three Furies (born of Gaia's & Uranus' blood; they punish evildoers in Hades)

1. Tisiphone

2. Megaera

3. Alecto

A. Hesiod, *Theogony*, 185
Virgil, *Aeneid*, VI.550 ff. and VII.325 ff.
Dante, *Inferno*, IX.45-48.
B. Hamilton, Edith, *Mythology*, p. 44

Lᴵꜱᴛꜱ ᴏꜰ Mʏᴛʜᴏʟᴏɢɪᴄᴀʟ Fɪɢᴜʀᴇꜱ (ᴄᴏɴᴛɪɴᴜᴇᴅ)

The Three Fates

1. Clotho = goddess who spins the thread of life

2. Lachesis = goddess who weaves the thread (assigns the lot) of life

3. Atropos = goddess who cuts the thread of life

A. Hesiod, *Theogony*, 218 and 905
   Plato, *Republic*, 617c
B. Hamilton, Edith, *Mythology*, p. 49

The Four (Five) Rivers of Hades (some authorities do not include Lethe)

1. Acheron = river of woe

2. Cocytus = river of lamentation

3. Styx = river of unbreakable oaths

4. Phlegethon = river of fire

(5.) Lethe = river of forgetfulness

A. Plato, *Phaedo*, 112e-114b
   Virgil, *Aeneid*, VI.295 ff.
   Macrobius, *Commentary on the Dream of Scipio*, I.x.10-11
   Dante, *Inferno*, XIV.116-130
B. Hamilton, Edith, *Mythology*, p. 43

LISTS OF MYTHOLOGICAL FIGURES (CONTINUED)

The Four Winds (Aeolus = King of the Winds)

1. Boreas, the north wind

2. Zephyr, the west wind

3. Notus, the south wind

4. Eurus, the east wind

   A. Virgil, *Aeneid*, I.69 ff.
   B. Hamilton, Edith, *Mythology*, p. 48

The Five Ages of Humanity

age	description	Plato's regime
1. Golden Age	eternal springtime, fruitful Earth, no labor, no law, no fixed dwellings, no old age	aristocracy
2. Silver Age	four seasons, need for protection from the elements, houses, agriculture, afterlife of spirits, honor still exists	timocracy
3. Bronze Age	war, violence, weapons	oligarchy
4. Heroic Age	love of gain, mining the Earth's resources, heroes are descendents of the gods, war	democracy
5. Iron Age	deceit, envy, private property, Justice leaves Earth for Mt. Olympus	tyranny

   A. Hesiod, *Works and Days*, 110 ff.
   Plato, *Republic*, 546e ff.
   Ovid, *Metamorphoses*, I.89 ff.
   B. Lings, Martin, *Ancient Beliefs and Modern Superstitions*, p. 2

Lists of Mythological Figures (continued)

The Seven Days of the Week

day	god/planet	planet
1. Sunday	Sun day	Sun
2. Monday	Moon day	Moon
3. Tuesday	Tiw's day (Norse god Tiw)	Mars
4. Wednesday	Wotan's day (Norse god Wotan)	Mercury
5. Thursday	Thor's day (Norse god Thor)	Jupiter
6. Friday	Frigg's day (Norse goddess Frigg)	Venus
7. Saturday	Saturn's day	Saturn

    A. Isidore of Seville, *Etymologies*, V.xxx
      (Isidore does not mention the Norse gods)
    B. Calter, Paul, *Squaring the Circle*, p. 448

The Nine Muses (daughters of Zeus & Mnemosyne [Memory]; reside on Mt. Olympus)

muse	patron	sphere
1. Calliope	epic poetry	Mercury
2. Clio	history	Moon
3. Euterpe	lyric poetry	Jupiter
4. Thalia	comedy, bucolic poetry	Earth
5. Melpomene	tragedy	Sun
6. Terpsichore	dancing	Venus
7. Erato	erotic poetry	Mars
8. Polyhymnia	sacred song	Saturn
9. Urania	astronomy	Stars

    A. Hesiod, *Theogony*, 77-19
    B. Hamilton, Edith, *Mythology*, pp. 39-40

Lists of Mythological Figures (continued)

Types of Nymphs

nymphs	types	famous nymphs
1. Dryads	forest nymphs	
2. Hamadryads	wood nymphs, guardians of trees	
3. Heliades	guardians of poplar trees	Aegiale Aegle Aetheria
4. Hespirides	guardians of Hera's tree of golden apples	
5. Oreads	mountain nymphs	
6. Naiads	guardians of rivers & springs (freshwater nymphs)	Daphne Lethe River
7. Nereids	sea nymphs (specifically the Mediterranean Sea)	Thetis (mother of Achilles) Galatea
8. Oceanids	ocean nymphs	Clymene Eurynome Pleione
9. Mermaids	special water nymphs	
10. Pleiades	seven stars/sisters (daughters of Atlas & Pleione)	Electra Maia

NOTE: Nymphs are female nature deities, protectors and personifications of natural forces. Portrayed as beautiful young girls, they are often the prey of lustful Olympians as well as satyrs (their male counterparts in the world of nature divinities). The nymphs mentioned here are just a few of innumerable types. Often nymphs are identified with one specific locality.

> A. Hesiod, *Theogony*
> Ovid, *Metamorphoses*
> Isidore of Seville, *Etymologies*, VIII.xi.96-97
> B. Lewis, C. S., *The Discarded Image*, pp. 122-138

LISTS OF MYTHOLOGICAL FIGURES (CONTINUED)

The Twelve Months of the Year (Julian calendar)

month	god/emperor/other
1. *Januarius*	From Janus, Roman god of the doorway
2. *Februarius*	Latin for "month of purification rituals"
3. *Martius*	From Mars, Roman god of war
4. *Aprilis*	Latin for "month of Venus"
5. *Maius*	From Maia, Roman goddess of fertility
6. *Junius*	From Juno, queen of the Roman gods
7. *Julius*	From Julius Caesar, who was born in this month
8. *Augustus*	From Augustus Caesar, who named this month after himself
9. *September*	*septem* = seven (seventh month in the calendar of Romulus)
10. *October*	*octo* = eight (eighth month in the calendar of Romulus)
11. *November*	*novem* = nine (ninth month in the calendar of Romulus)
12. *December*	*decem* = ten (tenth month in the calendar of Romulus)

A. Isidore of Seville, *Etymologies*, V.xxxiii
B. "Calendars," *Dictionary of the Middle Ages*, vol. 3

LISTS OF MYTHOLOGICAL FIGURES (CONTINUED)

The Olympian Deities (some authorities omit Hades and others Demeter)

	Greek	Roman	relation	ruler
1.	Zeus	Jupiter/Jove		king of the gods
2.	Poseidon	Neptune	brother of Zeus	ruler of sea
3.	Hades	Pluto	brother of Zeus	ruler of underworld
4.	Hesita	Vesta	sister of Zeus	hearth and home
5.	Demeter	Ceres	sister of Zeus	agriculture (cf. "cereal")
6.	Hera	Juno	sister/wife of Zeus*	queen of the gods
7.	Ares	Mars	Zeus/Hera's son	war (cf. "martial" law)
8.	Athena	Minerva	born of Zeus' head**	wisdom
9.	Aphrodite	Venus	born of foam from sea	love/beauty (cf. "venereal")
10.	Apollo	Apollo	Zeus & Leto's son, Aretmis's twin	music, the arts, the Sun
11.	Artemis	Diana	Zeus & Leto's daughter, Apollo's twin	moon and hunting
12.	Hermes	Mercury	Zeus & Maia's son	messenger of the gods
13.	Hephaestus	Vulcan	Hera's son (not by Zeus)	fire & forge (cf. "volcano")

*Zeus' second wife
** Born after Zeus swallowed his first wife, the pregnant Metis (meaning cunning)

A. Hesiod, *Theogony*, 886 ff.
   Isidore of Seville, *Etymologies*, VIII.xi
B. Hamilton, Edith, *Mythology*, pp. 21-37

Triangular Relationships in the *Iliad*

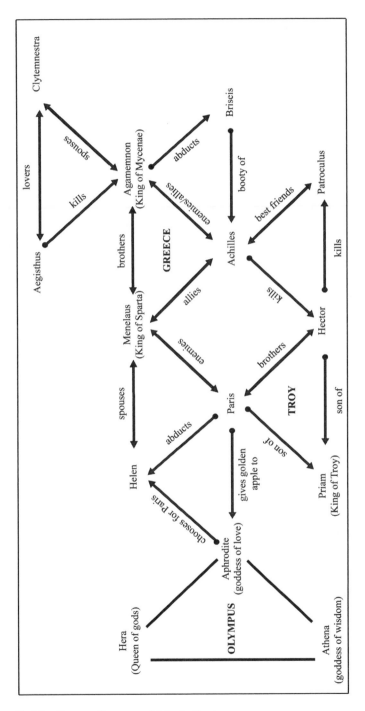

Source: Compiled by James Grote and Mark Grote

The Underworld in Homer's *Odyssey*

1. Ulysses descends into the underworld to meet the blind prophet Teiresias and to ask him how long he must wander before reaching his homeland. Ulysses digs a trench a cubit square and fills it with blood from his animal sacrifices to the dead. Ghosts must drink of the blood to converse with Ulysses.

2. Ulysses meets his comrade in arms from Troy Elpenor who has not yet been laid beneath the Earth and who begs Ulysses for burial so his soul will not wander.

3. Ulysses encounters his dead mother Anticlea but does not let her drink of the blood.

4. Ulysses meets the prophet Teiresias who tells Ulysses of his future hardships, his final triumphal homecoming, and his death at the hands of the sea and Neptune.

5. Ulysses allows his mother to taste of the sacrificial blood and learns from her about his family. He is deeply saddened that he cannot embrace her ghost.

6. Ulysses meets and converses with the ghosts of the wives and daughters of famous men including Tryo, Antiope, Alcema, Jocasta, Chloris, Leda, Iphimedeia, Phaedra, Procris, Ariadne, Maera, Clymene, and Eriphyle.

7. Ulysses is addressed by the god Arete and by King Alcinous.

8. Ulysses is accosted by King Agamemnon who weeps and relates how he was murdered by his wife and her lover after he returned home from Troy.

9. Ulysses meets Achilles and hails him as the greatest of princes, even though Achilles is dead. Achilles utters the famous words that he would rather be a servant in a poor man's house above ground than a king of kings among the dead. Ulysses also sees Achilles' friend Patroclus as well as Antilochus.

10. Ulysses tries to engage Ajax in conversation, but Ajax is still bitter about the armor of Achilles that Ulysses won.

11. Ulysses sees other gods and heroes including Minos, Tityus, Tantalus, and Sisyphus (who is eternally rolling a large stone up a hill).

12. Ulysses' final conversation is with Hercules who seems to prefer his life underground to his life above ground.

    A. Homer, *Odyssey*, Book XI
    B. "Inferno," *Dante Encyclopedia*

Sources of Mythology (continued)

The Underworld in Virgil's *Aeneid*

1. Aeneas descends into the underworld in order to see his father Anchises. Once underground he encounters the boatman Charon at the banks of the river Acheron. Charon objects to ferrying a living soul across the river Acheron, the river that pours into the river Cocytus, and then into the river Styx.

2. Before crossing Acheron, Aeneas also meets the souls of unburied men, particularly two sailors, Leucaspis and Orontes, returning like himself from Troy and lost at sea. They cry out, "Throw earth on me."

3. Aeneas also meets the three-headed watchdog of the dead, the Great Cerberus.

4. Aeneas is permitted into the boat by Charon after displaying "the golden bough" he has brought with him from the world above (cf. James Frazer's *The Golden Bough*).

5. Aeneas sees the souls of infants who have died.

6. Aeneas sees the souls of the falsely accused.

7. Aeneas sees the souls of suicides.

8. Aeneas sees the Fields of Mourning and the souls "whom pitiless love consumed." He sees the soul of his Phoenician lover Dido who has committed suicide.

9. Aeneas sees the souls of numerous famous warriors who died in battle.

10. The road forks before the mighty walls of Dis. Aeneas fixes the golden bough on the walls of Dis in order to continue his journey.

11. The road to the left leads to Tartarus, the heart of Hell. Here Aeneas sees the ancient gods, the Titans, who threatened the power of the Olympian gods. Here also are humans guilty of treason and incest.

12. The road to the right leads to Elysium. Here Aeneas encounters his father, Anchises, as well as famous Romans like Romulus, Julius Caesar, and Augustus Caesar.

NOTE: Compare Aeneas' journey with that of Dante in the *Inferno* outlined in chapter eight, Theology.

    A. Virgil, *Aeneid*, Book VI
    B. "Inferno," *Dante Encyclopedia*

SOURCES OF MYTHOLOGY (CONTINUED)

Outline of Ovid's *Metamorphoses* (chiastic structure)

Part One: The Divine Comedy (Books 1-2):

Gods Acting Like Humans (Gods Loving Humans)

A Myths of Creation and the Fall of Man
    B Myths of the Flood and Re-creation
        C Divine Love (Apollo and Daphne)
           D Divine Love (Jupiter and Io)
              E Epic Story of Phaethon's Tragic Chariot Ride
           D' Divine Love (Jupiter and Callisto)
        C' Divine Love (Apollo and Coronis)
    B' Divine Love (Hermes and Herse)
A' Divine Love (Jupiter and Europa)

Part Two: The Avenging Gods (Book 3 – Book 6, line 400):

Humans Suffering at the Hands of Gods (Gods Punishing Humans)

A Divine Vengeance Episodes (Actaeon, Semele, Narcissus & Echo, Pentheus)
    B Love Tales of the Minyades
        C Epic Stories of Perseus, Andromeda and Phineus
    B' Love Tales of the Muses
A' Divine Vengeance Episodes (Arachne, Niobe, Lycian Peasants, Marsyas)

SOURCES OF MYTHOLOGY (CONTINUED)

Outline of Ovid's *Metamorphoses* (chiastic structure)

Part Three: The Human Pathos of Love (Book 6, line 401 – Book 11):

Humans Suffering at the Hands of Humans

A First Pathos of Love (Philomela, Procne, Tereus)
  B   Second Pathos of Love (Scylla)
    C   Epic Stories (Meleager-Althaea)
      D   Theodicies (Philemon-Baucis, Erysichthon)
    C' Epic Stores (Hercules-Deianira-Apotheosis)
  B' Third Pathos of Love (Byblis)
A' Fourth/Fifth Pathos of Love (Myrrha, Ceyx-Alcyone)

Part Four: Rome and the Deified Ruler (Books 12-15):

Humans Becoming Gods

A Troy (Lapiths and Centaurs)
  B   Judgment of Arms
    C   Troy (Hecuba)
      D   Stories of Aeneas
    C' Rome (Native Gods, e.g., Romulus)
  B' Philosophy of Pythagoras
A' Rome (Foreign Gods, e.g. Hippolytus; and Deification of Caesar)

  A. Ovid, *Metamorphoses*
  B. Otis, Brooks, *Ovid as an Epic Poet*, chapter three

43

Sources of Mythology (continued)

Outline of Ovid's *Metamorphoses* (book by book)

Part One: The Divine Comedy: Gods Acting Like Humans (Books 1-2)

Ovid's work begins with the myth of creation including the origin of the four elements, the five geographic zones, the four winds, and the four ages of man as well as myth of the flood and Jove's destruction of sinful humanity.

Book One includes Apollo's attempted rape of Daphne (transformed into a tree) and Jove's (hidden in heavy fog) rape of Io.

Book Two includes Jove's (disguised as Diana) rape of Callisto (transformed into a bear by an outraged Juno), Apollo's attempted rape of Coronis (transformed into a bird to escape), the House of Envy, and Jove's (disguised as a bull) abduction of Europa.

Part Two: Avenging Gods: Humans Suffering at the Hands of Gods (Books 3-6)

Book Three includes Actaeon being turned into a stag by Diana for accidentally seeing her virgin goddesses bathing, Semele being reduced to ash for witnessing Jove's unveiled glory, the nymph Echo being reduced to an echoing voice by Juno for hiding Jove's philandering, Narcissus dying of frustrated love for himself and being turned into a flower, and Pentheus being murdered by his mother Agave after being transformed into a bull.

Book Four includes myths by Minya's daughters, the Pierides (avoiding the Bacchic rites) who are transformed into bats by Bacchus for ignoring his rituals. Book Four also includes Neptune's rape of Medusa and the transformation of her beautiful hair into snakes by Minerva.

Book Five includes myths by the Muses themselves including Perseus' use of the Gorgon's face to turn his enemies into stone and Pluto's rape of Ceres' daughter Proserpina who is condemned to live six months a year in the underworld. The human sisters are turned into birds in Book Five for daring to compete with the Muses.

Book Six includes myths of human women competing with gods. Arachne claims to be a better weaver than Minerva and is turned into a spider to weave for eternity. Niobe brags about having more children than the goddess Latona, whereupon Apollo kills Niobe's seven sons, seven daughters, and husband with his deadly arrows.

Part Three: Pathos of Love: Humans Suffering at the Hands of Humans (Books 6-11)

Book Six also tells of King Tereus' rape of his sister-in-law Philomela and the cutting out of her tongue to hide his crime. In revenge her sisters cut up the King's son and serve him his son for dinner. The sisters and King are transformed into birds at the end of the myth.

Book Seven includes the story of Jason and the Golden Fleece as well as the story of Jason's unfaithfulness to Medea and Medea's murder of her own children and of Jason's new wife. Book Seven introduces the war between King Minos of Crete and King Theseus of Athens, including the story of a terrible plague sent by Juno.

Book Eight includes the story of Daedalus' son Icarus who flies too near the Sun

SOURCES OF MYTHOLOGY (CONTINUED)

Outline of Ovid's *Metamorphoses* (book by book)

with his engineered wax wings and dies (later to be turned into a bird by Minerva). It also includes the story of the hospitality of the pious old couple, Philemon and Baucis, towards gods disguised as travelers. Also told is the myth of Eriysichton's ecological impiety in trying to fell the sacred oak grove of Ceres.

Book Nine includes myths of tragic and unnatural loves like Byblis's love for her brother, Caunus (Byblis is turned into a fountain of water) and Iphis's (disguised as a boy) love of the blonde Ianthe. Iphis is transformed into a real boy just before the wedding ceremony.

Book Ten includes myths told by Orpheus including the Pygmalion story where Pygmalion falls in love with his own statue of a girl; of Myrrha's incestual love for her father Cinyras; and of Venus' love for the beautiful boy Adonis whose blood is transformed into a flower that is light, delicate, and fragile.

Book Eleven includes the myth of the collective murder of Orpheus by the crazed women followers of Bacchus (who are transformed into an oak tree as punishment), the myth of King Midas and his golden touch, and tales of King Ceyx and his trusted wife, Alcyone.

Part Four: History of Rome: Humans Becoming Gods (Books 12-15)

Book Twelve begins the history of Rome with an account of the Trojan War that includes the sacrifice of Iphigenia by Agamemnon and the funeral of Achilles. Other myths include a visit to the House of Rumor and a bizarre wedding where the Lapith family of Thessaly engages in a bloody fight with centaurs that are guests at the banquet.

Book Thirteen continues the story of the Trojan War with Ajax and Ulysses' argument over which one of them deserves to inherit the armor of Achilles (Ulysses wins the debate and Ajax commits suicide). The Fall of Troy and enslavement of the Trojan women is described as well as the voyage of Aeneas after the war.

Book Fourteen continues the aftermath of the Trojan War including tales from the voyages of Ulysses and of Aeneas, culminating in the myth of Romulus, the first King of Rome.

Book Fifteen moves from a dry summary of early Roman kings to a surprising philosophical treatise on Pythagorean number theory and reincarnation to the death of Julius Caesar from the perspective of the gods (Caesar's soul becomes a star) and Augustus' deification of Caesar. Ovid ends on a note of self-glorification: "My name and fame are sure. I shall have life."

A. Ovid, *Metamorphoses*
B. Otis, Brooks, *Ovid as an Epic Poet*

Types of Change in Ovid's *Metamorphoses*

types	examples
1. gods	Jove disguises himself as the goddess Diana in order to approach the nymph Callisto before he ravishes her. (Book Two)
2. humans	Juno takes on the form of a wrinkled old woman in order to trick Semele who has been impregnated by Jove. Juno advises Semele to convince Jove to show his undisguised divinity the next time he and Semele embrace. Semele does so and is reduced to ash by Jove's heavenly glory. (Book Three)
3. animals	The master weaver Arachne is taught by the goddess Minerva how to weave and then angers the goddess by bragging about her superior weaving ability. In retribution, Minerva transforms Arachne into a spider so that she and her progeny will weave webs forever. (Book Six)
4. plants	The handsome Adonis, human lover of the goddess Venus, is accidentally gored to death by a wild boar. As he lies dying Venus changes Adonis into a special type of wind-flower to commemorate his transient beauty which parallels the beauty of flowers. (Book Ten)
5. stones	Perseus' uncle Phineas is jealous of Perseus' bride Andromeda. At the wedding party Phineas and his followers attack Perseus and his guests. In order to stop the brawl, Perseus shows the Gorgon's head to over two hundred brawling guests and turns them all to stone. (Book Five)
6. water	The river nymph Cyane witnesses Pluto's rape of Proserpine. She attempts to thwart Pluto's abduction of Proserpine to the underworld but is unsuccessful. She is outraged and cries endless tears until she herself dissolves into a pool of water. (Book Five)
7. birds	Scylla is turned into a bird to save her from her father King Nisus' murderous rage due to her treason in Nisus' fight with Minos of Crete. (Book Eight)

A. Ovid, *Metamorphoses*
B. Otis, Brooks, *Ovid as an Epic Poet*

Sᴏᴜʀᴄᴇs ᴏғ Mʏᴛʜᴏʟᴏɢʏ (ᴄᴏɴᴛɪɴᴜᴇᴅ)

The Wheel of Fortune

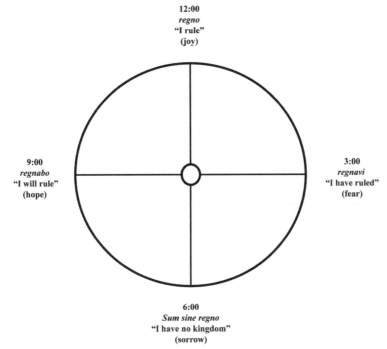

12:00
regno
"I rule"
(joy)

9:00
regnabo
"I will rule"
(hope)

3:00
regnavi
"I have ruled"
(fear)

6:00
Sum sine regno
"I have no kingdom"
(sorrow)

12:00 Figure of a king confident, powerful and strong, who says, "I rule."

3:00 Figure of a king who has lost his crown and says, "I have ruled." He has tumbled down the wheel of fortune and is desperate and frightened.

6:00 Figure of a king dressed in rags who has lost all on the wheel of fortune and says, "I have no kingdom."

9:00 Figure of a cunning young prince clawing his way to the top who says, "I will rule."

The Wheel of Fortune (Continued)

"Fortuna: I am that Fortuna who has made and unmade kings and emperors. It is of no avail to worship me. Let him beware who sits at the top of the wheel. Let each hold fast to his treasure."

Joy

"Regno: I reign at the top of the wheel, as Fortune has destined me. But if the wheel turns, I may be derived of power. Be moderate, you who are in power, lest you fall to Earth. Behold the honor I am paid because I sit at the top of the wheel."

Fear

"Regnavi: I reigned for a while, then Fortune put me down and deprived me of everything good. Her friendship avails not. No friend remains when a man falls. Be not confident when you are rising; Fortune makes you fall with deadly blows. Hearken to my case, how I gained and lost this honor."

Sorrow

"Sum Sine Regno: I am, as you see, without reign, down low in wretchedness. Fortune has disclaimed me. If I should mount on this wheel, every man would be friendly to me. Let each take warning who considers me."

Hope

"Regnabo: I shall reign as Fortune pleases and the wheel turns to the fourth place. I shall be above and rule the entire world. How great is my pleasure then! Virtue moves me to speak such words, because I plan to do justice and punish those who have maliciously robbed the men of good estate. What joy I shall have to be able to punish them!"

NOTE: Quotes are from Howard Patch's *The Goddess Fortuna in Medieval Literature* for this description of the wheel of fortune. Also, see the list "Four Main Passions of the Soul" on page 80 in chapter four on Psychology for another view of the four emotions on the wheel of fortune.

NOTE: The wheel of fortune was also described in more cosmological terms as a wheel whose heart is at the center rather than the circumference of the world (a complete inversion of the Ptolemaic system). "As in a wheel the nearer we get to the center the less motion we find, so every finite being, in proportion as he comes nearer to participating in the Divine (unmoving) Nature, becomes less subject to Destiny, which is merely a moving image of eternal Providence . . . . All luck, seen from the center, is good and medicinal. The sort we call 'bad' exercises good men and curbs bad ones – if they will take it so. Thus, if only you are near the hub, if you participate in Providence more and suffer Destiny less, 'it lies in your own hands to make your fortune what you please.'"

C. S. Lewis, *The Discarded Image*, p. 87

    A. Boethius, *The Consolation of Philosophy*, II Pros. i and IV Pros. vi-vii
       Dante, *Inferno,* VII.67-96
    B. Lewis, C. S., *The Discarded Image*, pp. 81-87
       Patch, Howard, *The Goddess Fortuna in Medieval Literature*, pp. 165-166

SOURCES OF MYTHOLOGY (CONTINUED)

Illustration of the Wheel of Fortune

Source: Among numerous other sources, see early editions of *Le Roman de la Rose.*

III. Cosmology

> Hardly any battery of facts could have persuaded a Greek that the universe had an attribute so repugnant to him as infinity; hardly any such battery could persuade a modern that it is hierarchical.
>
> C. S. Lewis, *The Discarded Image*, p. 222

The study of the cosmos or universe can be understood in two different senses. The first analyzes the motions of the heavenly bodies (astronomy). The second inquires into the purpose of those motions, including the effects of the heavenly bodies on human consciousness (astrology). The medievals did not distinguish between astronomy and astrology. For them cosmology and psychology (see chapter four) were intimately connected. Following an idea first suggested by Plato (*Philebus 29*), they thought the universe to be a macrocosm or extension of the human person and the human person to be a microcosm or miniature reflection of the universe.

Medieval thought remained fiercely (some might say perversely) devoted to the only dialogue of Plato's to be translated from Greek into Latin in the Early Middle Ages, the cosmological *Timaeus*. This work remained a foundation for medieval thought to such an extent that Plato scholar Paul Shorey once quipped, "The shortest cut to the study of the philosophy of the Middle Ages is to commit the *Timaeus* to memory."[90] As the *Timaeus* is notoriously obscure, the reader is advised to approach medieval cosmology through the more accessible *Commentary on the Dream of Scipio* by Macrobius. Macrobius' work could easily have been titled the "Commentary on the *Timaeus* of Plato." In the *Timaeus* the reader will find every aspect of cosmology – the four contraries, the four elements, the four humors, and the celestial spheres. Since the human being is the universe in miniature, it is not surprising that the celestial motions affect human life and that a jovial person is born under the sign of Jupiter while a saturnine personality is born under the sign of Saturn.

A universe devoid of meaning and purpose was inconceivable to the medieval mind. The medievals pictured the world as a rational, structured, and beautiful ornament, or to use the term coined by Pythagoras – a *kosmos*. The very word implies purpose and design. To discover the meaning of the universe is synonymous with finding one's self at home in the universe. Self-knowledge (psychology) leads to knowledge of the Whole (cosmology).

The notion of hierarchy was built into this medieval search for meaning and purpose. To describe their world in terms of general systems theory, they saw the world as a nested as opposed to a non-nested hierarchy. Nested hierarchies involve levels that consist of lower levels, for example, an army with its many ranks. Non-nested hierarchies may have but do not necessitate such lower levels, for example, the food chain. The ancients and medievals believed "the cosmos was constructed as a set of nested spheres, with each

---

90. Frederick B. Artz, *The Mind of the Middle Ages: An Historical Survey*, third edition, revised (Chicago: University of Chicago Press, 1984), p. 456.

sphere moving the one interior to it, so that activities on Earth were controlled, to some extent, by the movements of the heavenly sphere."[91] While this assumption of rational order led to some irrational speculation, the beauty of the Medieval Model has never ceased to fascinate modern thought. Finding purpose in the universe may appear a difficult task, but it seems that humans are hard wired for that search.

Although many medieval institutions were oppressive, the medieval mind never viewed the notion of hierarchy *per se* as a tool of oppression. On the contrary, the medievals viewed hierarchy in terms of beauty rather than (like Michel Foucault) in terms of power. The purpose of hierarchy is nowhere better articulated than in Pseudo-Dionysius' text on the nine choirs of angels.

> The goal of hierarchy, then, is to enable beings to be as like as possible to God and to be at one with him. A hierarchy has God as its leader of all understanding and action. It is forever looking directly at the comeliness of God. A hierarchy bears in itself the mark of God . . . . It ensures that when its members have received this full and divine splendor they can then pass on this light generously and in accordance with God's will to beings further down the scale. (*Celestial Hierarchies*, III.2)

This affirmation of the world as a hierarchical cosmos rather than a meaningless chaos is reflected by the popularity in medieval times of the biblical passage regarding Jacob's dream at Bethel. "And he dreamed that there was a ladder set up on the Earth, the top of it reaching to Heaven; and the angels of God were ascending and descending on it" (Genesis 28:12). Nothing could be more medieval than this metaphor of a ladder. According to medieval cosmology, the Earth is nestled in the center of the universe within a series of spheres that do triple duty as the source of physical motion (spheres understood as planets), intellectual enlightenment (spheres understood as Intelligences), and existence itself (spheres understood as gods). To quote C. S. Lewis' description of this Medieval Model once again:

> The central and (spherical) Earth is surrounded by a series of hollow and transparent globes, one above the other, and each of course larger than the one below. These are the 'spheres', 'heavens', or (sometimes) 'elements'. Fixed in each of the first seven spheres is one luminous body. Starting from Earth, the order is the Moon, Mercury, Venus, the Sun, Mars, Jupiter and Saturn. . . . They are planets as well as gods. Not that the Christian poet believed in the god because he believed in the planet; but all three things – the visible planet in the sky, the source of influence, and the god – generally acted as a unity upon his mind.[92]

Church teaching took this cozy view and put a theological spin on it. Since the Fall of Adam, the center of the universe (the Earth) had been polluted by sin and became a center of physical and spiritual gravity, a kind of sinkhole for evil. Dante's picturesque view of the medieval cosmos puts Hell at the center of the Earth and Satan at the center of Hell where his three heads continuously devour the bodies of the three greatest earthly traitors – Brutus, Cassius, and Judas.

Although Dante Christianized this cosmology that the medieval Church inherited from the ancient Greeks, he did not fundamentally change the pagan/Aristotelian physics

---

91. Richard Rubenstein, *Aristotle's Children* (New York: Harcourt, Inc., 2003), pp. 182-183.
92. Lewis, *Discarded*, pp. 96, 105.

that gave birth to it. Aristotle too blended physics and ethics (in his *Physics* and *On the Heavens*) to provide an explanation both for physical motion and for all the e-motions that plague the human race. In typical hierarchical fashion, he divided the world into two main regions – the sublunary world below the moon's orbit (comprised of the four elements of earth, water, air, and fire) and the superlunary world beyond the moon's orbit (comprised of a fifth celestial element called aether). The four sublunary elements move up and down from the center of the Earth while the superlunary element moves in circles around the Earth, the center of the universe. In Aristotle's thought, circular motion symbolized the unchanging divine perfection of God because a circle has no beginning and no end.

The sublunary world had a natural hierarchy as did the superlunary world. In the sublunary world the four elements formed concentric shells around the sphere of the Earth, creating a hierarchy of elements – earth, water, air, and fire. Like everything else in the "fallen" sublunary world, nothing was arranged perfectly so that areas of land sometimes protruded above the water. The essence of fire was considered to be invisible and found its natural place above the air but below the orbit of the moon. In general the heaviest element earth naturally moved downward (e.g. a falling stone) and the lightest element, fire, naturally moved upward.

To recap, as Plato taught in the *Timaeus*, the entire universe is round, "the most perfect and uniform of all shapes" (33b). Within this gigantic sphere, everything below the moon's orbit (the terrestrial realm) is subject to change, generation, and decay. Creatures dwelling here fall prey to the six imperfect rectilinear motions (up and down, forwards and backwards, right and left), imperfect because they are always changing their path or direction. Above the moon's orbit, the heavens maintain their perfect circular motion, nothing is subject to change and decay, and celestial creatures dwell in a state of perfect bliss. Keep in mind that the authority for this worldview ultimately lies with Plato and Aristotle, not with the medieval Church. The Church, in a sense, merely baptized Plato and Aristotle.

As mentioned in chapter one of this book, Aristarchus of Samos who has been nicknamed the ancient Copernicus, dared to challenge Aristotle and maintained (about 270 BCE) that the Earth revolves around the Sun. But Aristarchus' view did not prove persuasive and the geocentric view (based on the authority of Aristotle, not the Church), remained virtually unchallenged until Copernicus published *On the Revolution of the Celestial Spheres* in 1543.

However, one astronomer, a Greek-Egyptian named Claudius Ptolemy (c.100–175), did successfully modify some of Aristotle's system, albeit without changing the essential structure. Ptolemy's famous *Almagest* codified astronomical findings up to his time in such elegant fashion that the medieval system came to be known as the Ptolemaic universe. Ptolemy knew that Aristotle's perfect circles could not account for the observed movements of celestial bodies. He added epicycles and other constructions to more accurately chart the path of the heavenly bodies. These modifications altered the mechanics of perfect circular motion in the heavens, but never did away with that ideal. Medieval universities adapted to this compromise situation and tended to teach Ptolemy's calculations in the mathematical part of their curriculum and Aristotle's speculations in the philosophical and theological parts of their curriculum.

The reader should keep in mind the first two lists on page 54 in this chapter carefully. There the complete medieval cosmology is presented as follows:

1. The One
2. The Divine Mind
3. The World-Soul
4. Matter
    a. Celestial Bodies (see page 65, "Celestial Spheres of the Ptolemaic Universe")
    b. Terrestrial Bodies (see page 56, "The Four (Five) Elements")

The universe is the result of a series of emanations or devolutions from the completely transcendent God (who is "beyond being") to the Mind of God which remains like God when it fixes its attention on God, but when it looks away creates from itself the World-Soul. The World-Soul remains incorporeal as long as it contemplates God, but degenerates into the creation of bodies when it looks away from God. The World-Soul first creates celestial or aetherial bodies (who imitate God in their circular, eternal motion); but this creative process degenerates into the creation of terrestrial (i.e., earthly) bodies composed of the four elements of earth, air, fire and water.

Human souls (discussed in chapter four, Psychology) enter into matter by falling from their heavenly home in the sphere of the stars through two portals in the heavens (where the Milky Way and Zodiac intersect); and then falling through the celestial spheres where they pick-up the characteristics of the spheres, for example, reason from Saturn and bold spirit from Mars (see the list on Astrological Influences on page 67 in this chapter); and finally enter into earthly bodies. While earthly bodies were considered to be tombs of the soul, through the practice of virtue (see chapter four, Psychology), human souls could return to their true home in the heavens. The difficult question of how immateriality (souls) could devolve into matter (bodies) was often described in mathematical terms. According to Plato's *Timaeus*, the One or the number one devolved into the even (number two) and the odd (number three). The material world resulted from the interaction of odd and even numbers (which were themselves immaterial). See the list on Plato's Lambda on page 165 in chapter seven, Philosophy, for more information on the emergence of matter (cubed figures) from immaterial forms (points, lines, and planes).

Remember, following each list are bibliographic references to the relevant primary sources (A) that are listed in chronological order by the author's lifetime and secondary sources (B) that are listed in alphabetical order by the author's name.

The Neo-Platonic Triad

	Greek	Latin	description
1. The One/Good	*agathon*	*Deus*	Nothing can be predicated of the One "beyond being" (*hyperousia*).
2. The Divine Mind	*nous*	*mens*	Emanation of the One, the highest form of being.
3. The World-Soul	*psychē*	*anima*	Emanation of Mind, containing all particular souls including human souls.

NOTE: Both St. Paul and Plotinus spoke of a human triad of body (*sōma*), soul (*psychē*), and spirit (*pneuma*).

 A. Plato, *Republic*, 509b
  I Thessalonians 5:23
  Plotinus, *The Enneads*, V.i.7-8
  Macrobius, *Commentary on the Dream of Scipio*, I.vi.20 and I.xiv.6ff.
 B. Knowles, David, *The Evolution of Medieval Thought*, pp. 22-26

The Neo-Platonic Universe

1. The One

2. The Divine Mind

3. The World-Soul

4. Matter

 a. Celestial Bodies

 b. Terrestrial Bodies

NOTE: Regarding Celestial Bodies see "Celestial Spheres of the Ptolemaic Universe" on page 65 of this chapter. Regarding Terrestrial Bodies see "Four (Five) Elements" on page 56 of this chapter.

 A. Macrobius, *Commentary on the Dream of Scipio*, I.xiv.6ff.
 B. Knowles, David, *The Evolution of Medieval Thought*, pp. 22-26

THE TERRESTRIAL WORLD

The Four Contraries

1. hot   (= summer)

2. cold   (= winter)

3. wet   (= autumn)

4. dry   (= spring)

    A. Aristotle, *Physics*, 188b
       Aristotle, *On Generation and Corruption*, 329b ff.
       Manilius, Marcus, *Astronomica*, I.145
       Macrobius, *Commentary on the Dream of Scipio*, I.vi.26-28, 59-60
    B. Lewis, C. S., *The Discarded Image*, pp. 94-95, 169-170

THE TERRESTRIAL WORLD (CONTINUED)

Four (Five) Elements (sublunary spheres)

element	symbol	contraries	natural location
1. earth		cold & dry	center of universe
2. water		cold & wet	above earth
3. air		hot & wet	above water
4. fire		hot & dry	elemental fire is pure fire, invisible and transparent, found just below the orbit of the moon
(5.) aether			above the orbit of the moon

NOTE: Combination of elemental symbols = the Seal of Solomon:

A. Plato, *Timaeus*, 32b-c
   Aristotle, *On the Heavens*, 270b
   Avicenna, *The Canon of Medicine*
   Martianus Capella, *The Marriage of Philology and Mercury*, VIII (814)
   Isidore of Seville, *Etymologies*, XIII.3
B. Burkhardt, Titus, *Alchemy: Science of the Cosmos, Science of the Soul*, pp. 74-75, 92-96
   Lewis, C. S., *The Discarded Image*, p. 95

THE TERRESTRIAL WORLD (CONTINUED)

Representation of Sublunary Elements

SOURCE: http://internetshakespeare.uvic.ca/Library/SLT/ideas/sublunary.html

The Terrestrial World (continued)

Four Bodily Humors

humor	contrary	element	temperament
1. sanguine	hot & wet	air	courageous, hopeful, amorous
2. choleric	hot & dry	fire	angry, irritable, passionate
3. melancholic	cold & dry	earth	gloomy, brooding
4. phlegmatic	cold & wet	water	indolent, apathetic

humor	predominant humor and time of day
1. sanguine	12:00 a.m. through 6:00 a.m.
2. choleric	6:00 a.m. through 12:00 p.m.
3. melancholic	12:00 p.m. through 6:00 p.m.
4. phlegmatic	6:00 p.m. through 12:00 a.m.

A. Isidore of Seville, *Etymologies*, IV.v
   Avicenna, *The Canon of Medicine*
B. Lewis, C. S*., The Discarded Image*, pp. 169-174

THE TERRESTRIAL WORLD (CONTINUED)

Diagram of the Four Contraries, Elements, Humors, and Seasons

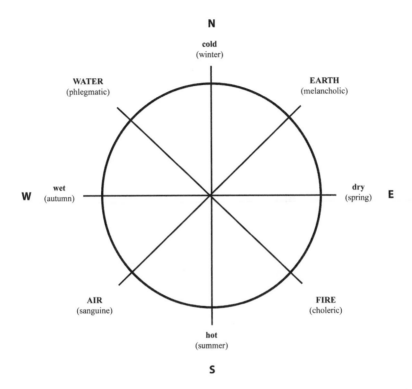

SOURCE: Titus Burckhardt, *The Essential Titus Burckhardt: Reflections on Sacred Art, Faiths, and Civilizations*, p. 122

THE TERRESTRIAL WORLD (CONTINUED)

Four Grades of Terrestrial Reality

1. mere existence (e.g. stones)

2. existence with growth (e.g. plants)

3. existence with growth and sensation (e.g. animals)

4. existence with growth, sensation and reason (e.g. humans)

    A. Gregory the Great, *Moralia*, VI.16
       Dante, *Convivio*, III.iii
    B. Lewis, C. S*., The Discarded Image*, p. 93
       Lewis, C. S., *Studies in Medieval and Renaissance Literature*, p. 50 ff.

The Arc or Four Ages of Human Existence

phase	ages	dominant contraries	temperament
1. adolescence (ascent)	up to 25	hot & wet (air)	sanguine
2. maturity	26-45 yrs	hot & dry (fire)	choleric
3. old age (descent)	46-70 yrs	cold & dry (earth)	melancholic
4. senility	over 70	dry & wet (water)	phlegmatic

NOTE: The peak of life's arc according to Dante is age 35.

    A. Dante, *Convivio*, IV.xxiii
    B. "Convivio," *Dante Encyclopedia*
       Southern, R. W., *Medieval Humanism*, p. 165

THE TERRESTRIAL WORLD (CONTINUED)

Five Geographical Zones

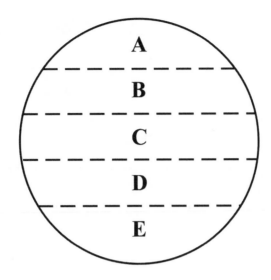

Frigid Zone = A & E (includes north and south poles)
Temperate Zone = B & D (inhabitable)
Torrid Zone = C (includes equator)

NOTE: The globe is a giant ocean. There is an elongated island in B that comprises the known world (Europe, Africa, and Asia) and its borders run over into A and C. C, for the most part is a boiling ocean. Another elongated island, of which we can know nothing, exists in D (the Antipodes) and its borders run over into C and E. Apparently at the poles there is only water. A and E are too cold for anything living to survive, and C is too hot.

A. Ovid, *Metamorphoses*, I.48
   Macrobius, *Commentary on the Dream of Scipio*, II.v-ix
   Martianus Capella, *The Marriage of Philology and Mercury*, VI (602-608)
   Isidore of Seville, *Etymologies*, III.xliv and XIII.vi
   Sacrobosco, *On the Sphere*, chapter II
B. Lewis, C. S., *The Discarded Image*, p. 28

THE TERRESTRIAL WORLD (CONTINUED)

Illustration of the Five Zones

SOURCE: Marcrobius' *Commentary on the Dream of Scipio*, Brescia issue of 1483

THE TERRESTRIAL WORLD (CONTINUED)

T-O Map or Medieval World Map

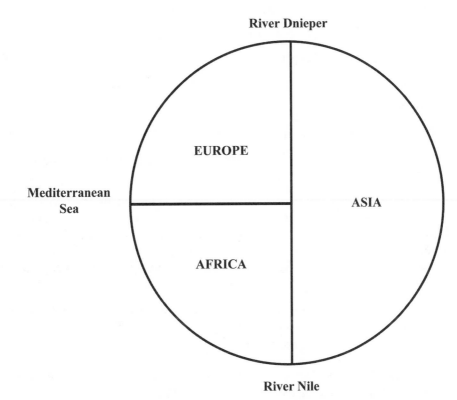

NOTE: The "O" as a whole represents the northern temperate zone described above (the inhabited world). Sometimes the "O" is seen as an encircling Ocean or the god Oceanus. The sideways "T" represents the three main bodies of water dividing the known world into Asia, Europe, and Africa. The river Dnieper is to the north, the river Nile to the south, and the Mediterranean Sea to the west. Says Isidore of Seville, "The Ocean flowing around [the inhabited world] is contained in a circular limit, and it is divided into three parts, one part being called Asia, the second Europe, and the third Africa."

> A. Martianus Capella, *The Marriage of Philology and Mercury*, VI (622-626)
>   Isidore of Seville, *Etymologies*, XIV.ii
> B. Southern, R. W., *The Making of the Middle Ages*, p. 69

THE TERRESTRIAL WORLD (CONTINUED)

The Seven Climes (following Sacrobosco)

1. Clime of Meroe (ancient city on the upper Nile)

2. Clime of Syene (ancient city on the Nile; today Aswan)

3. Clime of Alexandria (Egypt)

4. Clime of Rhodes (Greek island southwest of Turkey in eastern Aegean Sea)

5. Clime of Rome

6. Clime of Boristhenes (ancient city at mouth of the Dnieper river on the Black Sea)

7. Clime of Ripheon (the Ural Mountains in Russia were know as the Riphean Mountains in antiquity)

NOTE: The seven climes represent lines of latitude in the inhabitable, northern temperate zone (zone B on page 61). In the middle of each clime is an invisible line or latitude that passes through the above cities. As the climes move north, the length of each line from east to west decreases as the earthen sphere narrows. The climes are not always consistently named, nor even consistently numbered. Martianus for example mentions eight different climes. Here we follow Sacrobosco both in name and number.

    A. Martianus Capella, *The Marriage of Philology and Mercury*, VIII (876)
       Cassiodorus, *An Introduction to Divine and Human Readings*, II.vii.3
       Isidore of Seville, *Etymologies*, III.xlii
       Sacrobosco, *On the Sphere*, chapter III
    B. Thorndike, Lynn, *The Sphere of Sacrobosco and Its Commentators*, pp. 236
       ff. (commentary by Robertus Anglicus)

THE CELESTIAL WORLD

Celestial Spheres of the Ptolemaic Universe

sphere   glyph   human influence

Earth = center of the universe

1. Moon   ☽   bodily movement and generation

2. Mercury   ☿   reason (analytic thought)

3. Venus   ♀   amorous passion

4. Sun   ☉   heart (sensory soul)

5. Mars   ♂   courage

6. Jupiter   ♃   will (decision making)

7. Saturn   ♄   intellect in general

8. The Fixed Stars = the *Stellatum* (where the constellations of the Zodiac reside)

9. *Primum Mobile* (or the Crystalline) = Aristotle's "Unmoved Mover"

Empyrean = The Dwelling Place of God, the highest heaven (outside the last sphere)

A. Plato, *Timaeus*, 36d ff.
   Ptolemy, *Almagest*
   Dante, *Convivio*, II.iii
B. Burckhardt, Titus, *Alchemy: Science of the Cosmos, Science of the Soul*, pp. 79-91
   Lewis, C. S., *The Discarded Image*, p. 96

The Celestial World (continued)

Representation of the Ptolemaic Universe

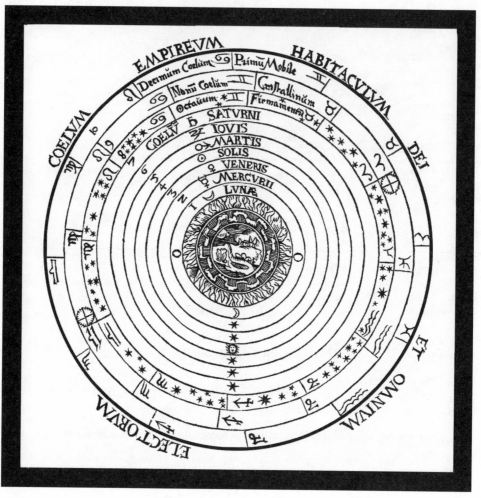

SOURCE: Peter Apian's *Cosmographia*, Antwerp, 1524

THE CELESTIAL WORLD (CONTINUED)

Astrological Influences

planet	human function (following Macrobius)
1. Moon	bodily growth (*phytikon*)
2. Mercury	ability to speak and interpret (*hermēneutikon*)
3. Venus (Lesser Fortune)	passion (*epithymetikon*)
4. Sun	sense perception (*aisthētikon*), imagination (*phantastikon*)
5. Mars (Lesser Misfortune)	bold spirit (*thymikon*)
6. Jupiter (Greater Fortune)	power to act (*praktikon*)
7. Saturn (Greater Misfortune)	reason (*logistikon*), understanding (*theōrētikon*)

planet	emotion	metal
1. Moon	mad (insane)	silver
2. Mercury	eager	quicksilver
3. Venus (Lesser Fortune)	amorous	copper
4. Sun	generous	gold
5. Mars (Lesser Misfortune)	warlike	iron
6. Jupiter (Greater Fortune)	jovial	tin
7. Saturn (Greater Misfortune)	melancholic	lead

NOTE: Each sphere produces different temperaments and metals.

A. Ptolemy, *Tetrabiblos*
Macrobius, *Commentary on the Dream of Scipio*, I.xii.14
B. Burckhardt, Titus, *Alchemy*, pp. 76-91
Lewis, C. S., *The Discarded Image*, pp. 105 ff.

THE CELESTIAL WORLD (CONTINUED)

Illustration of the Music of the Celestial Spheres

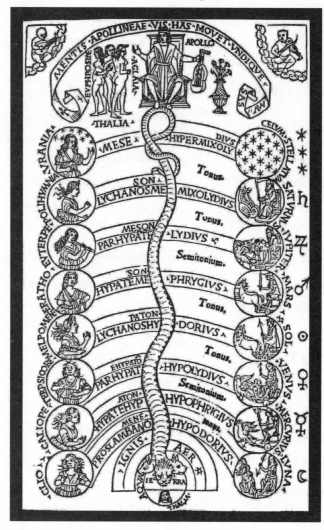

NOTE: The Muses or patrons of the arts (see the list on page 35 of this book) on the left side of the picture are linked to their corresponding celestial spheres of influence (see the list on page 65 of this book) on the right side. To the direct right and left of the central figure – the three-headed monster – are the fifteen tones of the Greek musical scale according to Pythagoras (see Cassiodorus, *An Introduction to Divine and Human Readings*, II.v.8). Pythagoras believed the celestial spheres emitted heavenly music, hence the close connection between music and astronomy. The three Graces (see the list on page 32 of this book) are standing to the right of Apollo (and to the reader's left). Apollo, the god of music and the arts is enthroned at the top of the picture.

SOURCE: Franchinus Gaffurius, *Practica Musicae* (Florence, 1496)

THE CELESTIAL WORLD (CONTINUED)

Signs of the Zodiac (zodiac meaning "circle of animal figures")

sign	glyph	animal	element	energy/dates
1. Aries	♈	ram	fire	pioneering energy (March 21 – April 19)
2. Taurus	♉	bull	earth	deliberation and determination (April 20 – May 20)
3. Gemini	♊	twins	air	abstract curiosity (May 21 – June 21)
4. Cancer	♋	crab	water	healing and nurturing (June 22 – July 22)
5. Leo	♌	lion	fire	confident self-expression (July 23 – August 22)
6. Virgo	♍	maiden	earth	refinement and discrimination (August 23 – September 22)
7. Libra	♎	balance	air	balance and harmony (September 23 – October 23)
8. Scorpio	♏	scorpion	water	intense emotional power (October 24 – November 21)
9. Sagittarius	♐	archer	fire	quest for truth (November 22 – December 21)
10. Capricorn	♑	goat	earth	self-discipline and austerity (December 22 – January 19)
11. Aquarius	♒	water-bearer	air	freedom and eccentricity (January 20 – February 18)
12. Pisces	♓	fish	water	mystical dreaminess (February 19 – March 20)

A. Manilius, Marcus, *Astronomica*, I.255 ff. and IV.122 ff.
   Isidore of Seville, *Etymologies*, III.lxxi.23-32
   Sacrobosco, *On the Sphere*, chapter II
B. Burckhardt, Titus, *Alchemy*, p. 88
   Park, David, *The Grand Contraption: The World as Myth, Number, and Chance*, p. 157

THE CELESTIAL WORLD (CONTINUED)

Zodiacal Man

celestial constellation	body part
1. Aries	head
2. Taurus	neck and throat
3. Gemini	lungs, arms, and shoulders
4. Cancer	chest and breasts
5. Leo	heart and upper back
6. Virgo	stomach and intestines
7. Libra	kidneys and lumbar region
8. Scorpio	genitals
9. Sagittarius	hips and thighs
10. Capricorn	knees and bones
11. Aquarius	calves, shins, and ankles
12. Pisces	feet

NOTE: Each part of the body is ruled by one of the signs.

A. Manilius, Marcus, *Astronomica*, II.453-465
B. Park, David. *The Grand Contraption*, p. 157

THE CELESTIAL WORLD (CONTINUED)

Illustration of Zodiacal Man

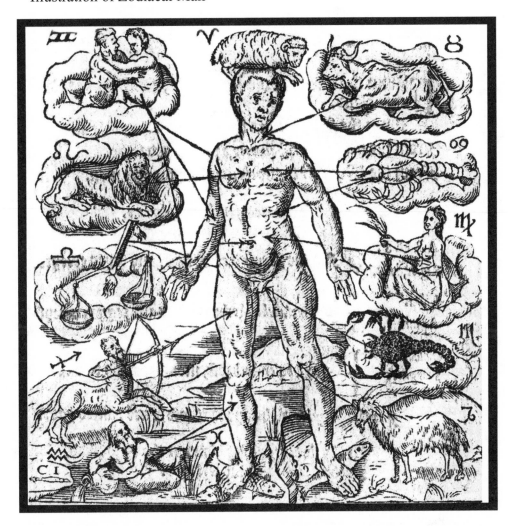

SOURCE: Zodiacal man, showing how parts of the body are governed by zodiacal signs. From Digges 1556; courtesy of J. M. Pasachoff and the Chapin Library of Williams College.

THE CELESTIAL WORLD (CONTINUED)

The Ten Celestial Circles (incorporeal lines dividing the universe)

1. Horizon (observer's "latitude")	Celestial circle with no fixed location; a "horizontal" circle with respect to the observer's perspective looking out into space
2. Meridian (observer's "longitude")	Celestial circle with no fixed location; perpendicular to horizon; a "vertical" or overhead circle with respect to the observer's perspective
3. Equinoctial (celestial equator)	Perpendicular to the axis of the world and equidistant between the north and south poles; passes through east & west points of the horizon
4. Ecliptic (Zodiac)	Sun's annual path through the Zodiac; inclined at an angle of 23 degrees to equator; changes orientation with respect to the horizon
5. Equinoctial Colure	Passes through the equinoxes and celestial poles; changes orientation with respect to the horizon
6. Solstitial Colure	Passes through the solstices and celestial poles; changes orientation with respect to the horizon
7. Tropic of Cancer (summer tropic)	Parallel to the equator (23.5 degrees N) and tangent to the ecliptic at the summer solstice
8. Tropic of Capricorn (winter tropic)	Parallel to the equator (23.5 degrees S) and tangent to the ecliptic at the winter solstice
9. Celestial Arctic Circle	Parallel to the equator (66.5 degrees N); everything north of this circle is the Arctic proper
10. Celestial Antarctic Circle	Parallel to the equator (66.5 degrees S); everything south of this circle is the Antarctic proper

A. Plato, *Timaeus*, 36c-e
   Macrobius, *Commentary on the Dream of Scipio*, I.xv.8-19
   Martianus Capella, *The Marriage of Philology and Mercury*, VIII (818-837)
   Sacrobosco, *On the Sphere*, chapter II
B. Heilbron, J. L., *The Sun in the Church: Cathedrals as Solar Observatories*, p. 63

THE CELESTIAL WORLD (CONTINUED)

Diagram of the Celestial Circles

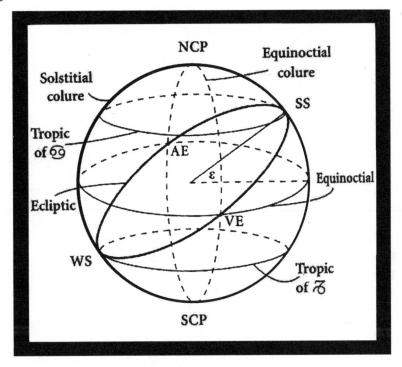

NOTE: Diagram does not include horizon & meridian.

NCP = north celestial pole
SCP = south celestial pole
WS = winter solstice
SS   = summer solstice
AE = autumnal equinox
VE = vernal equinox
"e" = angle between equinoctial and ecliptic

SOURCE: Reprinted by permission of the publisher from *The Sun in the Church: Cathedrals as Solar Observatories* by J. L. Heilbron, p. 58, Cambridge, MA: Harvard University Press (c) 1999 by the President and Fellows of Harvard College.

IV. Psychology (Ethics)

Two things cannot rightly be put together without a third.
Plato, *Timaeus*, 31b

As this book illustrates, the medievals loved the number three and loved to borrow whatever they could from the ancient Greeks. Since originality was neither a medieval virtue nor concern, it is not surprising that when it comes to psychology (literally the science of the soul) the medieval soul would have three parts borrowed from the theories of Plato and Aristotle. In Plato and Aristotle's time, "soul" was both a scientific concept and a religious concept. According to Greek scientific views, soul or *psychē* was the principle of self-motion or the animating principle of the body.

Today the word "person" approximates but is not equivalent to what the Greeks meant when they talked about the "soul." For example, in the modern debate over abortion the question is asked whether the fetus is a person, not whether the fetus has a soul. Unfortunately the modern concept of person has a moral and political, but not a scientific status. The ancients and medievals were more integrated in their approach to morality as the soul was both a scientific and a moral concept. To appreciate this integrated approach, compare the biological and psychological notions of the tripartite soul in the lists towards the beginning of this chapter.

The notion of soul held a central place in premodern psychology, ethics, and politics. These different disciplines were all part of a seamless garment, so to speak. The ancient Greeks (and the medievals after them) were particularly intrigued by what causes human bodies to move. What unique force animates human action? The heart of psychology (and ethics and politics) lay in the specific human motions referred to as e-motions. For Aristotle in particular, psychology entailed the study of what is now referred to as emotional intelligence. But, in order to understand Aristotle's psychology, we must first turn to the psychology of his teacher, Plato.

When Plato examines the human soul in the *Republic* (439d ff.), he notices two diverse elements – a calm rational element and an agitated irrational element. Upon further observation he finds that the irrational part of the soul comprises two distinct parts itself – the spirited or competitive part and the desiring or appetitive part. Plato's tripartite soul includes a rational part, love of knowledge and wisdom; a spirited part, love of combat and honor; and an appetitive part, love of wealth and pleasure. The spirited or competitive part is often called the angry part of the soul for it avenges infractions against reason and dignity.

Plato teaches that each part of the soul has a bodily center – the head for reason, the heart or chest for spiritedness, and the belly for appetite. Furthermore, each part has a corresponding cardinal virtue and civic class in the ideal city. Wisdom, the virtue of the rational part, is embodied in the philosophers who rule the ideal city. Courage, the virtue of the spirited part, is embodied in the military guardians who protect the ideal city. Temperance, the virtue of the appetitive part, is embodied by the workers who serve the economy of the ideal city. Justice, the fourth cardinal virtue, balances all the various civic classes and insures that each group "minds it own business" (441e). The soul is in perfect harmony when reason rules appetite by means of spirit, the policeman of the soul.

The medievals assumed this tripartite division when they talked about the three orders of medieval society: the *oratores* or clergy (analogous to the philosopher rulers) who pray, the *bellatores* or knights (analogous to the guardians) who protect the Church and the people, and the *laboratores* or serfs (analogous to the artisans and workers) who produce the wealth of the feudal society. Note that the Church often had to cajole the nobility to protect rather than to pillage the people through a variety of methods like the Peace of God and Truce of God movements initiated by Church Councils around the year 1000 as well as through chivalric codes and courtesy books.[93]

C. S. Lewis laments the contemporary disregard of this natural hierarchy within the soul, particularly the neglect of the middle mediating principle, the spirited part. To Lewis modernity has become a world of disembodied intellects serving animal appetites – a world, as he calls it, of "men without chests." In debunking all emotions as subjective sentiments, modern thought replaced noble objective *virtues* (like courage) with personal subjective *values*, none of which can claim an objective precedence over the others. Lewis argues: "We make men without chests and expect of them virtue and enterprise. We laugh at honor and are shocked to find traitors in our midst. We castrate and bid the geldings be fruitful."[94] It should be noted that, while Lewis was an avid proponent of this natural hierarchy or natural law within each human soul (a law he called the *Tao*), he remained opposed to political hierarchies like the one suggested by Plato in the *Republic*.

Since Lewis wrote, more recent developments in brain research (e.g., the theory of "three brains") seem to confirm the ancient intuition of a tripartite soul (see Daniel Goleman, *Emotional Intelligence*).[95] The primitive brain or brain stem surrounds the top of the spinal cord and regulates basic life functions. Also known as the reptilian brain, humans share this sensory-motor brain with innumerable species including reptiles. Over millions of years the old mammalian brain or limbic system grew up and around this stem, adding a more complex sensory system and an intricate emotional system. Unlike reptiles that eat their young, mammals have feelings and are capable of sympathizing with other creatures' feelings. Finally, the third brain or neo-cortex evolved, adding language and thought onto these neural systems. Hence the three-brain theory of a sensory brain, an emotional brain, and a rational brain that is analogous to Plato's soul.

Aristotle's psychology, more biological than Plato's, identifies three faculties in the soul – vegetative, sensitive, and rational. These faculties roughly approximate the Platonic tripartite soul. Aristotle's psychology mirrors his other scientific studies. Just as his physics studies the motions of inanimate bodies (rocks) and his metaphysics studies the motions of the lower celestial bodies (planets = gods), so his psychology and ethics study the motions (or e-motions) of bodies with rational souls, i.e., humans.

The mixing of psychology and ethics may sound odd today, but for Aristotle, ethics was a natural offshoot of psychology. Ethics studied the perfection (or best functioning) of the human *psyche*. Similarly, politics was a natural offshoot of ethics in that it studied the perfection of the *polis* that both Plato and Aristotle believed to be "the soul writ large."

---

93. Philip Daileader, *The High Middle Ages*, CD-ROM, Lecture Three (Chantilly, VA: The Teaching Company, 2001).

94. Lewis, *Abolition*, p. 37.

95. Daniel Goleman, *Emotional Intelligence* (New York: Bantam Books, 1995), p. 10.

Daniel Goleman also makes this connection today between politics and psychology in his popular book, *Emotional Intelligence*. Goleman says, "The first laws and proclamations of ethics – the Code of Hammurabi, the Ten Commandments of the Hebrews, the Edicts of Emperor Ashoka – can be read as attempts to harness, subdue, and domesticate emotional life."[96]

As well as lamenting the emotional illiteracy and general lack of manners in modern life, Goleman claims at the beginning of his book that we have yet to understand "Aristotle's Challenge." What is this challenge? Nothing more than the challenge of controlling emotions in order to become a good person. What Aristotle adds to Plato's psychology is an explanation for why it is so hard to become good as well as a method for achieving that goodness. For Aristotle the secret to goodness lies in finding the rational mean or virtue between vicious, irrational, emotional extremes – the golden mean. Virtue is not a matter of having good intentions (far from it), but a matter of acquiring the right moral skills (just like a carpenter acquires the right technical skills).

Emotional skill or intelligence is the avoidance of excess and defect in particular emotions or dispositions. For example, courage is the rational mean or virtue between the irrational extremes or vices of recklessness (the excess) and cowardice (the defect). Self-respect is the rational mean or virtue between the irrational extremes or vices of vanity (the excess) and humility (the defect). Finding the golden mean in our emotions and dispositions is a lifelong task, as Aristotle says in the *Nicomachean Ethics* (1109a):

> It is no easy task to be good. For in everything it is no easy task to find the middle, e.g. to find the middle of a circle is not for every one but for him who knows; so, too, anyone can get angry – that is easy – or give or spend money; but to do this to the right person, to the right extent, at the right time, with the right motive, and in the right way, *that* is not for every one, nor is it easy; wherefore goodness is both rare and laudable and noble.

Aristotle's ethics focuses on eleven particular emotions that can be found on page 82 in the list "Virtues as the Golden Mean."

You may have noticed that Aristotle lists humility as a vice rather than as a virtue. This classification should alert us to the fact that however much the medievals tried to reconcile classical culture with biblical faith, and however beautiful the synthesis they achieved, a perennial tension exists between the philosophical approach to the world (epitomized by the city of Athens) and the religious approach to the world (epitomized by the city of Jerusalem). One need only compare the detached god of Aristotle (see the introduction to the Philosophy chapter) who exists blissfully beyond all sordid human affairs and the active God of the Bible who creates the world (the Creation), works to liberate the world from its fallen state of sin (the Exodus), and suffers with the world (the Crucifixion) in that redemptive process.

Before the dominance of Judeo-Christian morality, the highest morality was considered beyond the grasp of the common man. The classical philosophers distinguished common or vulgar virtue from the most complete virtue, that is, philosophic virtue. Vulgar virtue was even compared to the manners of a well-trained dog by some philosophers. As Macrobius says, "Hence those who maintain that virtues are found only in men who philosophize openly affirm that none are blessed except philosophers" (*Commentary,* I.viii.3). The

---

96. Goleman, *Emotional*, p. 5.

masses or *hoi polloi* did not have the necessary equipment (intelligence, ancestry, wealth) for the highest virtue. The masses were no more expected to be moral than cattle and were treated accordingly. However, in the Judeo-Christian tradition full morality was expected of everyone. According to St. Paul, "All have sinned and fall short of the glory of God" (Romans 3:23). Likewise all are expected to be moral. But Judeo-Christian morality takes place on a different playing field from the morality of the pagans.

For the classical philosophers, virtue is a function of knowledge and vice a function of ignorance. Socrates believed this so fervently that he claimed, "If you know the good, you will do the good." He considered it impossible for a person to knowingly choose bad over good. People educated properly will naturally choose what is good.

C. S. Lewis emphasizes this same point in reference to Aristotle: "The really temperate man abstains [from sin] because he likes abstaining. The ease and pleasure with which good acts are done, the absence of moral effort is for him [Aristotle] the symptom of virtue."[97] In other words, someone who is tempted to vice is not truly virtuous. This ethical worldview is a far cry from St. Paul's description of sin in the Epistle to the Romans: "I do not understand my own actions. For I do not do what I want, but I do the very thing I hate. . . . It is no longer I that do it, but sin that dwells within me" (Romans 7:17).

In the Judeo-Christian tradition, while sin is acknowledged to be something that clouds the intellect, it is also an act of the will – infidelity to God. The battle between good and evil does not take place only in the intellect, but in the heart, in the spirited part of the soul as well. This struggle is a fierce battle, not an intellectual exercise (cf. Prudentius's *Pyschomachia* or *Battle of the Soul*). Within this new framework, the medieval obsession with lists of sins may be seen in a more positive light as a teaching tool to protect the souls of the common people. In order to simplify morality for the masses while still providing a psychological basis for morality (based on the classical tripartite theory of the soul), St. Paul's radical notion of "sin" in the Epistle to the Romans gradually evolved into the medieval doctrine of "sins" that has left such a deep impression of the Western psyche. Far from being only a negative obsession, these lists of sins may well reflect the medieval tendency toward the democratization of morality.

Remember, following each list are bibliographic references to the relevant primary sources (A) that are listed in chronological order by the author's lifetime and secondary sources (B) that are listed in alphabetical order by the author's name.

---

97. C. S. Lewis, *The Allegory of Love: A Study in Medieval Tradition* (New York: Oxford University Press, 1985), p. 59.

OUTLINE OF THE SOUL

Pythagoras and Aristotle's Doctrine of the Three Lives

type of life	type of person attending Greek festivals
1. life of contemplation (*bios theōrētikos*)	spectators
2. life of action/politics (*bios politikos*)	competitors
3. life of pleasure (*bios hēdonēs*)	vendors

    A. Plato, *Republic*, 581c
        Aristotle, *Nicomachean Ethics*, 1095b17
        Diogenes Laertius, *Lives of the Eminent Philosophers*, VIII.8
    B. Jones, W. T., *The Classical Mind,* 2nd edition, p. 34.

The Tripartite Soul in Plato

faculty	virtue	bodily seat	civic class
1. reason (*logos*)	wisdom	head	philosophers/rulers
2. spiritedness (*thymos*)	courage	chest	military/guardians
3. appetite (*epithymia*)	temperance	belly	workers/producers

faculty	political regimes
1. reason	aristocracy (love of wisdom)
2. spiritedness	timocracy (love of honor)
3. appetite	oligarchy (love of money) democracy (love of freedom) tyranny (love of license)

    A. Plato, *Republic*, 441e-442a and 546e ff.
       Plato, *Timaeus*, 69c ff.
       Macrobius, *Commentary on the Dream of Scipio*, I.vi.42
       Averroes, *Averroes on Plato's Republic*, 51.10
       Thomas Aquinas, *Summa Theologica*, I-II, q. 22, a. 2 and q. 23, a. 1
    B. Lewis, C. S., *The Abolition of Man*, pp. 35-36
       Lewis, C. S., *The Discarded Image*, pp. 57-58

OUTLINE OF THE SOUL (CONTINUED)

The Tripartite Soul in Thomas (psychological approach)

faculty	Thomistic nomenclature	three orders of feudal society
1. reason	apprehensive appetite	clergy who pray (*oratores*)
2. spiritedness	irascible appetite	knights who fight (*bellatores*)
3. appetite	concupiscible appetite	serfs who work (*laboratores)*

NOTE: If one substitutes the rule of philosophers with the rule of priests, there is a strong similarity between the classes of society in Plato's *Republic* and the three orders of feudal society ordained by nature. Theoretically at least, rulers of the medieval Church, like the rulers in Plato's ideal city, rule by intellectual insight (intellectualism), not by force or will (voluntarism).

NOTE: "The house of God, which is thought to be one, is therefore triple. Now [some] pray, others fight, and others work. These three are together and they suffer no split; the workings of two thus stand on the office of one, [and] alternately they offer support to everyone. This triple connection is therefore single."

Adalbero of Laon (quoted in Cook and Herzman below)

 A. Adalbero of Laon, *Carmen ad Robertum Regem* [Song to King Robert] in
   Jacques-Paul Migne, ed., *Patrologia Latina* (PL), vol. 141, col. 782
   Thomas Aquinas, *Summa Theologica*, I-II, q. 22, a. 2 and q. 23, a. 1
 B. Cook, William R. and Ronald B. Herzman, *The Medieval World View:*
   An Introduction, 2nd edition, p. 174
   Duby, Georges, *The Three Orders: Medieval Society Imagined*

The Tripartite Soul in Aristotle and Thomas (biological approach)

faculty	powers (powers of lower souls included in powers of higher souls)
1. rational soul	intellect (includes active and passive intellect) will (rational appetite)
2. sensitive soul	appetite (sensitive appetite) locomotion sensation (includes five exterior and five interior senses)
3. vegetative soul	nutrition (includes growth and reproduction)

 A. Aristotle, *On the Soul*, 413a-415a
   Thomas Aquinas, *Summa Theologica*, I, q. 78, a. 1
   Dante, *Convivio*, III.ii
   Dante, *Purgatorio*, XXV.52-75
 B. Copleston, Frederick C., *A History of Philosophy*, vol. I, part IV, chapter 30
   "Faculties of the Soul," *New Catholic Encyclopedia*, 2nd edition, vol. 5

OUTLINE OF THE SOUL (CONTINUED)

Sensation in the Sensitive Soul

<u>exterior</u>   <u>interior</u>

1. sight   1. memory (memory of particular sense experiences)

2. hearing   2. estimation (animal instinct, e.g. distinguishing friend from foe)

3. smell   3. imagination (retaining sense perceptions)

4. taste   4. phantasy (higher imagination, separating and uniting images)

5. touch   5. common sense (distinction/collation of sense experiences)

    A. Thomas Aquinas, *Summa Theologica*, I, q. 78, a. 3-4
    B. Lewis, C. S., *The Discarded Image*, pp. 161-165

Four Main Passions of the Soul

1. desire/hope (see 9:00 on the Wheel of Fortune)

2. joy (see 12:00 on the Wheel of Fortune)

3. fear (see 3:00 on the Wheel of Fortune)

4. sorrow (see 6:00 on the Wheel of Fortune)

    A. Virgil, *Aeneid*, VI.733
       Augustine, *City of God*, XIV.5
       Macrobius, *Commentary on the Dream of Scipio*, I.viii.11
       Thomas Aquinas, *Summa Theologica*, I-II, q. 25, a. 4
    B. "Appetite," *New Catholic Encyclopedia*, 2nd edition, vol. 1

OUTLINE OF THE SOUL (CONTINUED)

Five Passions of the Irascible Appetite (Thomas)

1. hope = seeking a good object that is difficult to obtain

2. courage = energetic attack on an evil thing that is difficult to overcome

3. despair = giving up of a good object because of difficulties

4. fear = avoidance of an evil thing that is difficult to escape

5. anger = movement toward an evil thing (that is difficult to overcome) for the sake of destroying it

    A. Thomas Aquinas, *Summa Theologica*, I-II, q. 25, a. 3
    B. "Appetite," *New Catholic Encyclopedia*, 2nd edition, vol. 1

Six Passions of the Concupiscible Appetite (Thomas)

1. love = tendency toward a good thing

2. desire = tendency toward a good thing not yet possessed

3. joy = possession of a good thing

4. hate = turning away from an evil thing

5. aversion = repugnance to an evil thing presenting itself

6. sorrow = suffering affliction from an evil thing

    A. Thomas Aquinas, *Summa Theologica*, I-II, q. 25, a. 2-3
    B. "Appetite," *New Catholic Encyclopedia*, 2nd edition, vol. 1

VIRTUES AND VICES

Virtues as the Golden Mean between Extreme Emotions

	excess emotion	virtuous mean	deficient emotion
1.	Rashness	Courage	Cowardice
2.	Self-indulgence	Temperance	Insensibility
3.	Extravagance	Liberality (Generosity)	Stinginess
4.	Vulgarity	Munificence	Niggardliness
5.	Vanity	Magnanimity (Self-Respect)	Humility
6.	Ambitiousness	Love of Honor	Unambitiousness
7.	Anger	Gentleness	Apathy
8.	Flattery	Affability (Friendliness)	Grouchiness
9.	Boastfulness	Truthfulness	Self-deprecation
10.	Buffoonery	Wittiness	Boorishness
11.	Envy	Justice	Malice
(12.)	Shamelessness	Modesty	Bashfulness

A. Aristotle, *Nicomachean Ethics*, 1107a-1108b
  Dante, *Convivio*, IV.xvii (Dante does not include Modesty in his list)
B. Ross, W. D., *Aristotle*, p. 210

Five Intellectual Virtues in the Rational Soul (Aristotle)

speculative intellect

1. intuitive reason (*nous*) = intuitive grasp of first principles or ultimate premises
2. science (*epistēmē*) = certain knowledge that is communicable by teaching
3. wisdom (*sophia*) = union of intuition and science; theoretical wisdom

practical intellect

4. art/applied science (*technē*) = right reason about something to be made
                                    (carpentry, sculpture)
5. prudence (*phronēsis*) = right reason about something to be done
                              (politics, ethics); practical wisdom

A. Aristotle, *Nicomachean Ethics*, 1138b-1145a
  Thomas Aquinas, *Summa Theologica*, I-II, q. 57, a. 2-4
B. Joseph, Miriam, *The Trivium*, p. 11
  Ross, W. D., *Aristotle*, pp. 221-227

VIRTUES AND VICES (CONTINUED)

Human Responsibility in Aristotle

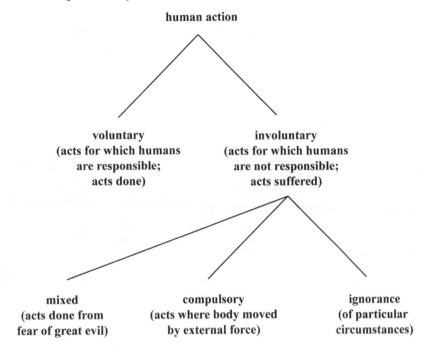

human action

voluntary
(acts for which humans
are responsible;
acts done)

involuntary
(acts for which humans
are not responsible;
acts suffered)

mixed
(acts done from
fear of great evil)

compulsory
(acts where body moved
by external force)

ignorance
(of particular
circumstances)

A. Aristotle, *Nicomachean Ethics*, 1109b ff.
B. Jones, W. T., *The Classical Mind*, 2nd edition, p. 279

Four Cardinal Virtues (following Thomas)

1. prudence (wisdom) = right reason about moral actions

2. courage = reason overcoming fear of danger or toil

3. justice = right relation to other individuals and to the common good

4. temperance = reason curbing the passions of the flesh

    A. Plato, *Republic*, 427e ff.
    Macrobius, *Commentary on the Dream of Scipio*, I.viii.3-10
    Thomas Aquinas, *Summa Theologica*, I-II, q. 61, a. 2
    Dante, *Purgatorio*, XXIX.130-132
    B. Lewis, C. S., *Mere Christianity*, pp. 74-78
    Pieper, Josef, *The Four Cardinal Virtues*

Personifications of the Four Cardinal Virtues

1. Prudence (compass in right hand reflects measured action; mirror in left hand reflects all thoughts back in time representing the wisdom of the ages).

2. Temperance (clock in left hand reflects changing seasons and managing ones passions).

3. Courage (represented in armour and helmet as a warrior, killing a dragon).

4. Justice (book in left hand reflects law/fairness; sword in right hand reflects punishment).

Prudence   Temperance   Courage   Justice

SOURCE: Tomb of Francis II, Duke of Brittany, Cathedral of Nantes (France). Permission granted under the terms of the GNU Free Documentation License.

Three Theological Virtues (following Thomas)

1. faith = assent of the mind and will to the revealed word of God

2. hope = confidence in the goodness of God leading to eternal happiness

3. charity = friendship with God

   A. I Corinthians 13:13.
      Thomas Aquinas, *Summa Theologica*, I-II, q. 62, a. 3
      Dante, *Purgatorio*, XIX.121-129
   B. Lewis, C. S., *Mere Christianity*, pp. 115-132

VIRTUES AND VICES (CONTINUED)

Seven Gifts of the Holy Spirit (which Isaiah saw in the Messiah)

gift	corresponding virtue	planetary sphere
1. understanding	faith	Moon
2. knowledge	hope	Mercury
3. wisdom	charity	Venus
4. counsel	prudence	Sun
5. fear of the Lord	temperance	Saturn
6. piety	justice	Jupiter
7. courage	courage	Mars

    A. Isaiah 11:2
       Thomas Aquinas, *Summa Theologica*, I-II, q. 68, a. 1
       Dante, *Convivio*, IV.xxi
    B. "Holy Spirit, Gifts of," *New Catholic Encyclopedia*, 2nd edition, vol. 7

Three Pagan Moral Defects (Aristotle)

1. vice = emotional extremes

2. incontinence = moral weakness

3. violence = brutality, bestiality, brutishness

    A. Aristotle, *Nicomachean Ethics*, 1145a15-16
       Dante, *Inferno*, XI.79-84
    B. Ross, W. D., *Aristotle*, pp. 227-231
       "Virtues and Vices," *Dante Encyclopedia*

VIRTUES AND VICES (CONTINUED)

Three Deadly Sins/Temptations (Augustine)

sin	I John 2:16	Genesis 3	growth of sin in the soul
1. concupiscence or gluttony	lust of the flesh	fruit of tree	serpent's *suggestion* of sin
2. curiosity or avarice	lust of the eyes	knowledge of good/evil	Eve's *delectation* or delight in sin
3. pride or vainglory	pride of life	desire to be like gods	Adam's rational *consent* to sin

    A. I John 2:16
       Augustine, *Confessions*, X.30 and XIII.21
    B. Howard, Donald, *The Three Temptations*, pp. 56-65

Three Categories of Sin (Thomas)

1. sin against God (e.g. heresy, blasphemy)

2. sin against one's self (e.g. gluttony, lust)

3. sin against one's neighbor (e.g. theft, murder)

    A. Thomas Aquinas, *Summa Theologica*, I-II, q. 72, a. 4
       Dante, *Inferno*, XI.30-33
    B. "Virtues and Vices," *Dante Encyclopedia*

Three Internal Causes of Sin (Thomas)

1. ignorance (sin on the part of reason)

2. malice (sin on the part of will)

3. passion (sin on the part of appetite)

    A. Thomas Aquinas, *Summa Theologica*, I-II, q. 76 & q. 77 & q. 78
    B. "Sin, (Theology of)," *New Catholic Encyclopedia*, 2nd edition, vol. 13

VIRTUES AND VICES (CONTINUED)

Seven Deadly Sins

<u>sin</u> (following Dante's order of gravity)	<u>cure</u> (Prudentius)

1. pride (*superbia*) = inordinate desire to excel   humility
   For the beginning of pride is sin.
   > Ecclesiasticus 10:13

2. envy (*invidia*) = resentment of another's fortune   charity
   Through the devil's envy death entered the world.
   > Wisdom 2:24

3. anger (*ira*) = inordinate desire for vengeance   patience

4. sloth (*acedia*) = avoidance of physical/spiritual work   diligence

5. avarice (*avaritia*) = inordinate desire for material wealth frugality
   The desire of money is the root of all evil.
   > 1 Tim 6:10

6. gluttony (*gula*) = inordinate desire for food & drink   sobriety

7. lust (*luxuria*) = inordinate desire for sex   chastity

NOTE: In the Western tradition, the seven deadly sins have also been paired with (as a corruption of) the seven planets or luminaries — pride (Sun), envy (Mercury), anger (Mars), sloth (Moon), avarice (Saturn), gluttony (Jupiter), and lust (Venus). For reference, see Lings below.

    A. Prudentius, *Psychomachia*
       St. Gregory the Great, *Moralia*, XXXI.17 ff.
       Thomas Aquinas, *Summa Theologica*, I-II, q. 84, a. 4
       Dante, *Purgatorio*
    B. Bloomfield, Morton, *The Seven Deadly Sins*
       Lings, Martin, *Symbol & Archetype,* p. 88
       "Seven Deadly Sins," *Dictionary of the Middle Ages*, vol. 11

NATURAL AND DIVINE LAW

Types of Law in Thomas Aquinas

1. eternal law (Divine Providence)

2. natural law (universal moral standards discovered through the light of reason)

3. positive law (necessary due to generality of natural law that does not provide for all the specific situations that human beings face)

   a. human positive law (specific laws further deduced from natural law)

   b. divine positive law (necessary on account of uncertainty of human judgment)

      i. Old Law = the Decalogue in the Old Testament

      ii. New Law = the law of the Gospel in the New Testament

   A. Thomas Aquinas, *Summa Theologica*, I-II, q. 91, a.1 ff.
   B. "Law," *The New Dictionary of Theology*

Three Main Precepts of Natural Law (fundamental human inclinations)

1. inclination to self-preservation (common with all substances)

2. inclination to propagate species and educate offspring (common with animals)

3. inclinations of nature according to reason (proper only to human beings)

   a. to know the truth about God

   b. to live in society

   A. Thomas Aquinas, *Summa Theologica*, I-II, q. 94, a. 2
   B. Copleston, Frederick C., *Aquinas*, p. 223

NATURAL AND DIVINE LAW (CONTINUED)

Divine Law (the Decalogue)

Catholic List	Protestant List
1. You shall have no false gods before me	You shall have no false gods before me
2. You shall not take God's name in vain	You shall not make for yourself an idol
3. Keep holy the sabbath day	You shall not take God's name in vain
4. Honor your father and your mother	Keep holy the sabbath day
5. You shall not murder	Honor your father and your mother
6. You shall not commit adultery	You shall not murder
7. You shall not steal	You shall not commit adultery
8. You shall not bear false witness	You shall not steal
9. You shall not covet your neighbor's wife	You shall not bear false witness
10. You shall not covet your neighbor's goods	You shall not covet your neighbor's wife or goods

NOTE: The Protestant list splits the first commandment from the Catholic list into two and combines the ninth and tenth commandments from the Catholic list into one.

NOTE: For comparison with other faiths, see the the Five Pillars of Islam on page 202; Hinduism's "Ten Commandmants" (the five do's and don'ts of Patanjali) on page 339; and Buddhism's Eightfold Path on page 350.

> A. Exodus 20:1-17
> Deuteronomy 5:7-21
> Thomas Aquinas, *Summa Theologica*, I-II, q. 100, a. 5
> B. "Ten Commandments," *New Dictionary of Theology*

NATURAL AND DIVINE LAW (CONTINUED)

Three Kinds of Justice*

1. Commutative justice (reciprocal obligations between individuals)

   Requires the honest adherence to contracts established by private parties (e.g. labor law, contract law, and perhaps international law).

2. Distributive justice (obligations of the state to the individual)

   Requires the fair distribution of pubic benefits and burdens among the members of a given political community (e.g. tax law).

3. Contributive justice (obligations of the individual to the state)

   Requires that each individual contributes his or her proper share toward the common good (e.g. criminal law, tax law).

*NOTE: Later traditions divide the Aristotelian/Thomistic dual division of commutative and distributive justice into the tripartite division of commutative, distributive, and contributive justice.

> A. Aristotle, *Nicomachean Ethics*, 1130b ff.
>   Thomas Aquinas, *Summa Theologica*, II-II, q. 61, a. 1-3
> B. "Justice," *New Dictionary of Theology*

Prerequisites for a Just War (Thomas)

1. Just authority (only a legitimate sovereign, not private individuals, can wage war)

2. Just cause (force can be used only to correct a grave public evil)

3. Just intention (the intention of the belligerents must be the protection of human rights, not material gain)

NOTE: Later just war traditions added other criteria for a just war, most notably:

- Last resort (force can be used only after all viable alternatives have been exhausted)
- Probability of success (deaths and injury incurred in a hopeless cause are not morally justifiable)
- Proportionality (the good to be achieved by the use of force must outweigh the destruction expected from the use of force)
- Discrimination (the weapons used must discriminate between combatants and civilians; civilians are never permissible targets of war)

> A. Thomas Aquinas, *Summa Theologica*, II-II, q. 40, a. 1
> B. "War," *New Dictionary of Theology*

INTERLUDE

V. Seven Liberal Arts

Wisdom has built her house; she has hewn her seven pillars.

Proverbs 9:1

The ink of the scholar is holier than the blood of the martyr.

Mohammad

If one list holds a preeminent place in the map of the medieval mind, it would have to be the seven liberal arts. Roughly twenty-five centuries before college ACT and SAT scores were divided into verbal and mathematical abilities, the liberal arts tradition divided the "basics" of human knowledge into the trivium of verbal skills (grammar, rhetoric, and logic) and the quadrivium of mathematical skills (arithmetic, geometry, astronomy, and music). By the time Plato wrote *The Republic* he could refer to these arts as an accepted tradition (*Republic*, 522c ff.).

However, in Plato's time the major pedagogical distinction was not between the trivium and quadrivium, but between *mousikē* and *gymnastikē*. In the *Republic* (376d), he refers to *mousikē* as the arts that train the soul and to *gymnastikē* as the arts that train the body. Gymnastics not only referred to athletics, but especially the training of the body for war. As a martial art, gymnastics reflected the "noble warrior culture" of the ancient Greek aristocracy that is the focus of Homer's *Iliad*. Over time, the warlike deeds of the *Iliad* took a back seat to the poetic speeches of the *Iliad*. As Greek culture became a more intellectual or "scribe culture," gymnastics lost its primacy (but not its place) and *mousikē* gradually became synonymous with education.[98]

The word *mousikē* reflects the liberal arts curriculum before the distinction of trivium and quadrivium became prominent. Verbal and mathematical disciplines were originally integrated into one artistic expression. As Will Durant notes:

> The word *mousikē* among the Greeks meant originally any devotion to any Muse. Plato's Academy was called a *Museion* or Museum – i.e., a place dedicated to the Muses and the many cultural pursuits which they patronized; the Museum at Alexandria was a university of literary and scientific activity, not a collection of museum pieces. . . . In Arcadia all freemen studied music to the age of thirty; everyone knew some instrument; and to be unable to sing was accounted a disgrace. Lyric poetry was so named because, in Greece, it was composed to be sung to the accompaniment of the lyre, the harp, or the flute. The poet usually wrote the music as well as the words, and sang his own songs; to be a lyric poet in ancient Greece was far more difficult than to compose, as poets do today, verses for silent and solitary reading. Before the sixth century there was hardly any Greek literature divorced from music. Education and letters, as well as religion and war, were bound up with music: martial airs played an important part in military training, and nearly all instruction of the memory was

---

98. For the distinction of warrior culture and scribe culture see H. I. Marrou, *A History of Education in Antiquity* (New York: Sheed and Ward, 1956), p. xiv.

through verse."[99]

Since literature was always sung and songs were part of military training, there was a natural affinity between body training and soul training in ancient Greece. This integration of literature, music, and physical exercise continued to a lesser extent in the Middle Ages through the monk's chanting of the Psalms in the Divine Office – an exercise physically strenuous enough to be referred to as the work (*labora*) of God.

As education became more intellectual and less physical, the distinction between soul training (music) and body training (gymnastics) gave way to the distinction between verbal training (trivium) and mathematical training (quadrivium). The three language arts of grammar, rhetoric, and logic reflected the operations of the human mind and the four mathematical arts reflected the operations of inert matter (pure quantity). In modern society where the study of matter is given primacy and the very existence of mind independent of matter is suspect, the three language arts of the trivium take on the current connotation of being trivial.

There is another sense in which the liberal arts conjure the notion of something trivial and that is in the transmission of this liberal arts tradition during the Early Middle Ages. Although the liberal arts were originally viewed as a means to an end, as preparatory studies for the "three philosophies" of physics, ethics, and theology; during the Early Middle Ages they became ends in themselves. The Early Middle Ages barely had the capacity to master the preparatory studies, and then only in a highly abbreviated form that created a distinct literary genre (a forerunner of our modern encyclopedia) and earned these transmitters the title of "Latin encyclopedists."

The earliest Latin classification of the liberal arts was in a work that is now lost, the *Disciplinarum Libri* of Terrence Varro (116-27 BCE). Centuries later, St. Augustine (354-430) started to write an encyclopedia of the seven liberal arts, *Disciplinarum Libri*, but did not finish the task. And Boethius (c.480-c.525), "the last of the Romans and the first of the Scholastics" (Lorenzo Valla), provided textbooks or summaries of the liberal arts, which unfortunately have not survived.

While Boethius, as well as Chalcidius and Macrobius were considered Late Latin encyclopedists, the three encyclopedists whose chief works consciously followed a liberal arts outline were Martianus Capella (fl. fifth c.), Cassiodorus (c.490-c.583), and Isidore of Seville (c.560-636). Martianus wrote an elaborate allegory, *The Marriage of Philology and Mercury*, symbolizing the marriage of learning (Philology = quadrivium) and eloquence (Mercury = trivium). The first two books of this allegory narrate the wedding and the next seven books present brief digests of the liberal arts in the guise of speeches by the seven bridesmaids who personify these arts. Despite his love of things medieval, Lewis cannot resist a jab at Martianus: "I have heard the scholar defined as one who has the propensity to collect useless information, and in this sense Martianus is the very type of the scholar."[100]

After a career devoted to politics, Cassiodorus, a high-ranking minister to the Ostrogothic emperor, Theodoric, retired to a monastery to compose *An Introduction to Divine and Human Readings*. The first book on divine readings discusses the Bible and

---

99. Will Durant, *The Story of Civilization*, vol. 2, The Life of Greece (New York: Simon and Schuster, 1939), p. 226.

100. Lewis, *Allegory*, p. 79.

establishes precise rules for copying and preserving manuscripts. It is Cassiodorus who helped transform monasteries into theological schools and scriptoriums. The second book on human readings surveys everything then known about the seven liberal arts, a sketchy endeavor at this point in history.

Archbishop Isidore of Seville rounds out this trivium of encyclopedists with his lengthy work, the *Etymologies*. Couched as a study of words, Isidore collects every piece of information and misinformation available in the Early Middle Ages, including a hefty dose of medieval bestiaries or animal studies (where unicorns and lions are catalogued with equal seriousness) borrowed from Pliny the Elder. However, the first three books of the *Etymologies* are devoted to the seven liberal arts. Book one is devoted to grammar, book two to rhetoric and logic, and book three to the four mathematical arts.

Dante allegorized this liberal arts tradition by matching each art with its patron heavenly sphere. His discussion of the arts in the philosophical treatise *Convivio* (II, xiii-xiv) exemplifies the exalted status of these seven arts. The heaven of the Moon resembles grammar. Like the shadows and variations in the luminosity of the Moon, grammar falls in and out of academic fashion according to the vagaries of human history.

The heaven of Mercury resembles dialectic or logic because (a) Mercury is the smallest of the seven medieval planets, and (b) the path of Mercury is more veiled by the Sun's rays than any other planet. Likewise, dialectics is the most compact body of knowledge (being wholly contained in Aristotle's *Organon*), and its method of argumentation is veiled from all but the most diligent minds.

Rhetoric is like the planet Venus (a) because of the brightness of Venus and (b) because of its change in appearance, once in the morning and once in the evening sky. Likewise, rhetoric is the sweetest and most appealing of the sciences and it changes its appearance when the rhetorician speaks before his audience as distinct from its appearance when he writes to his audience.

The heaven of the Sun can be compared to arithmetic because (a) all the other heavenly bodies are enlightened by the light of the Sun and (b) the human eye cannot directly behold the Sun. Similarly all other sciences are illuminated by arithmetic because they can all be considered under some numerical aspect. Furthermore, "the eye of the intellect cannot look upon [arithmetic] because number insofar as it is considered in itself is infinite, and this we cannot comprehend."

The heaven of Mars can be compared to music because (a) as the middlemost of the nine heavenly bodies (including the fixed stars and the *Primum Mobile*) Mars forms a series of ratios with these bodies and because (b) it is hot and fiery in appearance. Similarly music is composed of harmonies and ratios and has the power to melt the vapors of the heart by its beautiful melodies.

The heaven of Jupiter can be compared to geometry because (a) Jupiter is a temperate planet between the cold Saturn and the hot Mars and (b) Jupiter appears the whitest or silvery of all the planets. Similarly geometry moves between two antithetical things (the point and the circle) and is the science that is most white or free from error.

Finally the heaven of Saturn can be compared to astronomy because it is the slowest and highest of the planets. Similarly astronomy takes a great deal of time to master and is the highest in nobility and subject matter of the seven sciences.

One thing to keep in mind when reading the lists describing the seven liberal arts is the unusual way the medievals approached music and astronomy. Both arts were viewed as branches of mathematics. Music uncovered the numeric ratios inherent in harmony, and astronomy revealed the geometry of the stars. Music and astronomy were linked in the medieval notion of the "harmony of the spheres," the belief that the celestial bodies emitted a heavenly music that could only be heard by humans well advanced along the spiritual path.

The immaterial nature of mathematics (any triangle we draw can only approximate a perfect, real triangle) held a mystical significance for the medieval mind, a significance inherited from both Pythagoras and Plato. Since mathematics measures material entities but is itself immaterial, it functioned as a bridge between the material and spiritual realms. For more information on mathematics, see chapter seven on Philosophy.

It might be noted that until Latin translations of the Greek classics began pouring into Europe in the twelfth century, Europe had a paucity of Greek works for understanding the liberal arts tradition. During the Early Middle Ages, the only Latin translations of Greek philosophical works were Boethius' translation of two of Aristotle's logical works, the *Categories* and *On Interpretation* (often referred to as the *ars vetus* or the Old Logic), as well as Chalcidius' (c.300) partial translation (about two-thirds) of Plato's *Timaeus*.

The later flood of Greek classics flowed into Europe through two primary regions, Spain and Sicily. The meager manuals of the encyclopedists were replaced by Latin translations of the original Greek genius, e.g. Euclid in geometry, Ptolemy in astronomy, Galen in medicine, and Aristotle in logic, natural science and metaphysics. In twelfth century Spain, traveling scholars such as Gerard of Cremona translated the Greek classics in a most roundabout fashion. The Greek classics had been preserved in Arabic translation during the Early Middle Ages while Europe was in an intellectual decline. Gerard and his colleagues were assisted by Iberian Jews who translated the Arabic versions of the Greek works into the current Spanish idiom. Then Christian translators would translate the Spanish into Latin. Hence we have the circuitous route of Greek original, Arabic translation, Spanish translation, and finally Latin translation.

In Sicily, manuscripts were translated directly from Greek into Latin during the twelfth century because the Italian merchants had never lost touch with their Greek trading partners in the Byzantine Empire. Since both types of translation were the result of either Spanish scholars drawn to philosophy and natural science, or Sicilian scholars influenced by the Italian need for mathematics in its commerce and navigation, the books translated generally belonged to the quadrivium rather than the trivium.

In conclusion, it is interesting to note how the trivium and quadrivium vied for preeminence during medieval and Renaissance times. In the Early Middle Ages, scholars focused on the trivium. Unfortunately these encyclopedists' knowledge of the quadrivium (as the attached lists show) was rather primitive. By contrast, during the Twelfth Century Renaissance European culture emphasized philosophy and science at the expense of literature. Finally, history reversed itself again and during the Italian Renaissance translations of classical literature flourished. And again, after the fall of Constantinople in 1452, Greek scholars fled to Western Europe, especially to Italy.

In addition to the battle between the trivium and quadrivium, the arts within the trivium were themselves locked in internecine conflict. William of Sherwood (1200/1210–1266/1271) may have waxed ecstatic about "grammar, which teaches one how to speak correctly; rhetoric, which teaches one how to speak eloquently; and logic, which teaches one how to speak truly" (*Introduction to Logic*, 1.1). However, these three arts carried on a virtual war with each other from Roman times through the High Middle Ages.

Rhetoric was the queen of the trivium during the classical Latin age of Cicero. This preeminence extended to the beginning of the Early Middle Ages because of the emphasis placed on rhetoric by Augustine and by Martianus. However, with the complete collapse of Western classical civilization, the sophisticated use of rhetorical oratory in politics became obsolete. Rhetoric often was reduced to a series of manuals on the proper techniques of letter writing.

Following the demise of rhetoric, grammar became the queen of the trivium, especially in monastic and cathedral schools. This emphasis on grammar was a response to the need to produce liturgical works and books in monasteries as well as the need to produce trained clerks and notaries in a secular world that was predominantly illiterate. Cathedral schools in particular focused on the Latin literary classics of Virgil and Ovid (as well as the Vulgate translation of the Bible) to teach proper grammar. Education became synonymous with literary education.

During the twelfth century, hitherto unpublished logical works of Aristotle (referred to as the *ars nova* or the New Logic) flooded Western Europe and dialectic, much to the chagrin of the grammarians, became the queen of the trivium. An entire debate poem by Henri d'Andeli personified this medieval battle between logic or dialectic (championed by Aristotle and Boethius) and grammar (championed by Donatus and Priscian [authors of medieval grammar manuals] as well as Homer, Virgil, and Ovid). Charles Homer Haskins describes the battle in his groundbreaking work, *The Renaissance of the Twelfth Century*:

> The *artes* have vanquished the *auctores* [authoritative poets]. In the *Battle of the Seven Liberal Arts* (c.1250) Donatus and Priscian still represent grammar in the sense of literary studies, but they fight a losing battle. Logic, indeed, has now encroached upon the method as well as the sphere of grammar: not only is less time given to grammar, but it must be studied in a logical rather than a literary fashion.[101]

While grammar and literature dominated the curriculum of cathedral schools, dialectic and debate came to dominate the curriculum of the nascent universities in the twelfth and thirteenth centuries. As Edward Grant explains so clearly in his book *The Foundations of Modern Science in the Middle Ages* the rigor of logic in the twelfth century was a precursor to the rigor of the quadrivium and ultimately to the rigor of scientific method in the sixteenth century.

Remember, following each list are bibliographic references to the relevant primary sources (A) that are listed in chronological order by the author's lifetime and secondary sources (B) that are listed in alphabetical order by the author's name.

---

101. Charles Homer Haskins, *The Renaissance of the Twelfth Century* (Cambridge, MA: Harvard University Press, 1955), pp. 136-137.

Seven Liberal Arts

trivium	Greek origin	description
1. grammar	from *gramma* (letter)	the art of cultivated speech
2. rhetoric	from *rhētōr* (orator)	the art of persuasive speech (particularly in civil court cases)
3. logic/dialectic	from *lekton* (spoken)	the rules of argumentation
quadrivium		
4. arithmetic	*arithmos* (number)	the science of numbers
5. music	from *mousikē**	the science of measure in relation to sound
6. geometry	from *metron* (measuring) and *ge* (earth)	the science of measurement (at first measuring earth [surveying] and then the heavens)
7. astronomy	*astronomia*	the science of the movement of heavenly bodies

*"*Mousikē* originally (in ancient Greece) referred to any art over which the Muses presided, but especially music or lyric poetry set and sung to music."

Liddell and Scott, *Greek-English Lexicon*

NOTE: "Grammar . . . extended far beyond the realm it claims today. . . . Quintilian suggests *literatura* as the proper translation of the Greek *grammatike*, and *literatura*, though it does not mean 'literature', included a good deal more than literacy. It included all that is required for 'making up' a 'set book': syntax, etymology, prosody, and the explanation of allusions. . . . *Scholarship* is perhaps our nearest equivalent."

C. S. Lewis, *The Discarded Image*, p. 187

A. Plato, *Republic*, 522c ff.
   Martianus Capella, *The Marriage of Philology and Mercury*, books III-IX
   Cassiodorus, *An Introduction to Divine & Human Readings*, book II
   Isidore of Seville, *Etymologies*, books I-III
   Dante, *Convivio*, II.xiii
B. Grant, Edward, *The Foundations of Modern Science in the Middle Ages*, pp. 42-47
   Lewis, C. S., *The Discarded Image*, pp. 185-197
   Wagner, David, ed. *The Seven Liberal Arts in the Middle Ages*

The Seven Liberal Arts (continued)

<u>trivium</u>	<u>celestial sphere (following Dante)</u>
1. grammar	Moon
2. logic/dialectic	Mercury
3. rhetoric	Venus

<u>quadrivium</u>

4. arithmetic	Sun
5. music	Mars
6. geometry	Jupiter
7. astronomy/astrology	Saturn

    A. Plato, *Republic*, 522c ff.
       Martianus Capella, *The Marriage of Philology and Mercury*, books III-IX
       Cassiodorus, *An Introduction to Divine & Human Readings*, book II
       Isidore of Seville, *Etymologies*, books I-III
       Dante, *Convivio*, II.xiii
    B. Grant, Edward, *The Foundations of Modern Science in the Middle Ages*, pp. 42-47
       Lewis, C. S., *The Discarded Image*, pp. 185-197
       Wagner, David, ed. *The Seven Liberal Arts in the Middle Ages*

The Three Philosophies
(the liberal arts prepare students for these higher sciences)

<u>area of study</u>	<u>celestial sphere</u> (following Dante)
1. natural philosophy (physics)	Stars or the *Stellatum*
2. moral philosophy (ethics)	*Primum Mobile*
3. theology (metaphysics)	*Empyrean*

A. Plato, *Republic*, 522c ff.
   Martianus Capella, *The Marriage of Philology and Mercury*, books III-IX
   Cassiodorus, *An Introduction to Divine & Human Readings*, book II
   Isidore of Seville, *Etymologies*, books I-III
   Dante, *Convivio*, II.xiii
B. Grant, Edward, *The Foundations of Modern Science in the Middle Ages*, pp. 42-47
   Lewis, C. S., *The Discarded Image*, pp. 185-197
   Wagner, David, ed. *The Seven Liberal Arts in the Middle Ages*

Symbols of the Seven Liberal Arts

trivium	historical personification	other symbols
1. grammar	Donatus	writing instruments
2. logic/dialectic	Aristotle	scorpion or snake, scales
3. rhetoric	Cicero	scroll, book

quadrivium		
4. arithmetic	Pythagoras	abacus, tablet with figures
5. music	Boethius	musical instruments
6. geometry	Euclid	compass, square
7. astronomy	Ptolemy	astrolabe, celestial globe

A. See the Royal Portal or west front of Chartres Cathedral
B. Calter, Paul, *Squaring the Circle*, p. 450

Donatus, West Portal, Chartres Cathedral

Grammar – Major Topics (following Cassiodorus)

1. the spoken word = vibration of the air perceptible to the ear
2. the letter = smallest part of a spoken word
3. the syllable = a group of letters or single vowel that can be measured as a unit
4. feet = a measure of syllables and of quantity
5. accentuation = artistic pronunciation of a word
6. punctuation = clear pausing in well-regulated pronunciation
7. parts of speech = noun, pronoun, verb, adverb, participle [adjective], conjunction, preposition, interjection
8. figures of speech = transformations of words for purposes of adornment
9. etymologies = true or probable origin of words
10. orthography = art of composing correctly; applies to speaking and writing

   A. Martianus Capella, *The Marriage of Philology and Mercury*, book III
     Cassiodorus, *An Introduction to Divine and Human Readings*, II.i.2
     Isidore of Seville, *Etymologies*, I.v ff.
   B. Wagner, David, ed., *The Seven Liberal Arts in the Middle Ages*, pp. 58-95

Grammar, West Portal, Chartres Cathedral

Rhetoric – The Five Parts (following Cicero)

1. invention = devising arguments that are true or appear true in order to make a case appear credible

2. arrangement = proper order and distribution of the arguments devised

3. proper expression = adaption of suitable words to the argument

4. memorization = lasting comprehension of the arguments and the language of the arguments

5. delivery = harmony of voice and gesture in deference to the dignity of the argument

   A. Cicero, *De Oratore*, I.xxxi.142-143 (see also Cicero's *De Inventione*, I.ix)
      Martianus Capella, *The Marriage of Philology and Mercury*, book V
      Cassiodorus, *An Introduction to Divine and Human Readings*, II.ii.2
   B. Wagner, David, ed. *The Seven Liberal Arts in the Middle Ages*, pp. 96-124

Dialectic – Grammar & Argument (following Hugh of St. Victor)

1. Grammar (includes material in Aristotle's *Categories* and *On Interpretation*)

2. Argument

a. Demonstrative arguments = arguments leading to a necessary conclusion (these arguments are discussed in Aristotle's *Posterior Analytics*)

b. Dialectical arguments = arguments leading to a probable conclusion; also defined as arguments that are readily believable and can be used to defeat an opponent in debate (includes material in Aristotle's *Topics)*

c. Sophistical arguments = arguments where premises are ambiguous, e.g. fallacies like equivocation (these arguments are discussed in Aristotle's *On Sophistical Refutations)*

NOTE: See the Logic chapter for information on the Divisions of Argumentation.

A. Martianus Capella, *The Marriage of Philology and Mercury*, book IV
Cassiodorus, *An Introduction to Divine and Human Readings*, II.iii
Hugh of St. Victor, *The Didascalicon: A Medieval Guide to the Arts*, III.1
B. Wagner, David, ed., *The Seven Liberal Arts in the Middle Ages*, pp. 125-146

Dialectic, West Portal, Chartres Cathedral

Arithmetic – Four Different Divisions of Numbers (following Cassiodorus)

1. Odd and even numbers:

   Odd number = a number that cannot be divided into two equal parts (e.g. 3, 5, 7, 9)

   Even number = a number that can be divided into two equal parts (e.g. 2, 4, 6, 8)

2. Abundant, deficient, or perfect numbers:

   Abundant number = a number whose sum of its factors is greater than itself (e.g. the sum of the factors of 12, $1 + 2 + 3 + 4 + 6 = 16$)

   Deficient number = a number whose sum of its factors is less than itself (e.g. the sum of the factors of 8, $1 + 2 + 4 = 7$)

   Perfect number = a number whose sum of its factors is equal to itself (e.g. the sum of the factors of 6, $1 + 2 + 3 = 6$)

3. Absolute or relative numbers:

   Absolute number = numbers when not considered in relationship to other numbers (e.g. 3, 4, 5, 6)

   Relative number = numbers when considered in relationship to other numbers (e.g. 4 compared to 2, 6 compared to 3, and 8 compared to 4 are all considered "doubles")

4. Discrete or continuous numbers:

   Discrete number = numbers considered as separate units (e.g. 3 is separate from 4, just as 5 is separate from 6)

   Continuous number = numbers considered as connected units (e.g. 3 would be considered continuous within a stream of numbers if it was understood to be the measurement of a magnitude in a line, plane, or solid)

NOTE: See next page for primary and secondary references.

Arithmetic – Four Types of Mathematics (following Hugh of St. Victor)

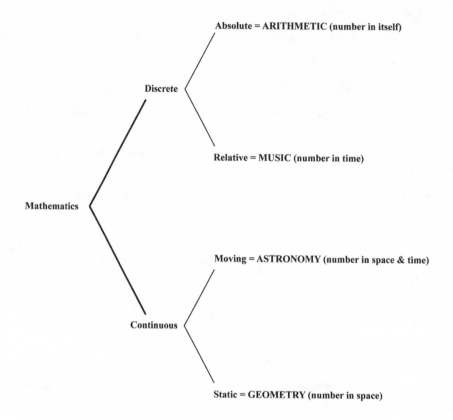

Absolute = ARITHMETIC (number in itself)

Discrete

Relative = MUSIC (number in time)

Mathematics

Moving = ASTRONOMY (number in space & time)

Continuous

Static = GEOMETRY (number in space)

A. Nicomachus, *Introduction to Arithmetic*, I.iii-xxiii
   Martianus Capella, *The Marriage of Philology and Mercury*, book VII
   Cassiodorus, *An Introduction to Divine and Human Readings*, II.iv.3-6
   Isidore of Seville, *Etymologies*, III.i-vii
   Hugh of St. Victor, *Didascalicon: A Medieval Guide to the Arts*, II.6
B. Calter, Paul, *Squaring the Circle: Geometry in Art & Architecture*, p. 8
   Wagner, David, ed., *The Seven Liberal Arts in the Middle Ages*, pp. 147-168

Music (following Cassiodorus)

Three Divisions of Music

1. harmonics (distinguishes treble sounds from bass sounds)
2. rhythmics (studies whether sounds are agreeable or disagreeable)
3. metrics (studies measure of poetry – iambic, elegiac, heroic, etc.)

Three Types of Instruments

1. percussion instruments (bells & objects struck by a rigid piece of metal)
2. stringed instruments (harps & other artfully fashioned cords)
3. wind instruments (trumpets, pipes & other objects blown full of breath)

    A. Martianus Capella, *The Marriage of Philology and Mercury*, book IX
       Cassiodorus, *An Introduction to Divine and Human Readings*, II.v.4-6
       Isidore of Seville, *Etymologies*, III.xviii-xxi
    B. Wagner, David, ed., *The Seven Liberal Arts in the Middle Ages*, pp. 169-195

Music, West Portal, Chartres Cathedral

Boethius' Classification of Music

1. *divina musica* (divine music; harmony within God)

2. *musica mundana* (world music; harmony within nature)

    a. music/motion of the heavenly spheres

    b. binding of the four earthly elements

    c. variation of the four seasons

3. *musica instrumentalis* (external music; assists in curing human souls and bodies)

    a. percussion

    b. string

    c. wind

4. *musica humana* (human music; harmony within human beings)

    a. harmony of the body and soul

    b. harmony of the parts of the soul (reason, spirit, appetite)

    c. harmony of the elements within the body

    A. Boethius, *The Consolation of Philosophy*
    B. Chamberlain, David, "Philosophy of Music in the *Consolatio* of Boethius"

Geometry (following Martianus)

Geometric Figures (cf. Euclid's Elements, I, definitions; XI, definitions)

geometric entities	description	figure in arithmetic
point	that which has no parts	the monad
line	breadthless length	the dyad
surface/plane	length and breadth only	the triad
solid	length, breadth, and depth	the tetrad

A. Euclid, *Elements*
Martianus Capella, *The Marriage of Philology and Mercury*, VI (708-722)
Cassiodorus, *An Introduction to Divine and Human Readings*, II.vi
Isidore of Seville, *Etymologies*, III.xi-xii
B. Wagner, David, ed., *The Seven Liberal Arts in the Middle Ages*, pp. 196-217

Geometry (continued)

Plane Figures (Euclid, I, definitions)

I. Straight Line Figures

Trilateral Figures (Euclid, I, definition 20):

Equilateral Triangle (3 equal sides) =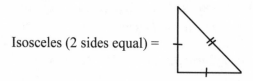

Isosceles (2 sides equal) =

Scalene (no sides equal) =

Geometry (continued)

Quadrilateral Figures (Euclid, I, definition 22):

Square (equilateral, right-angled) =

Oblong (right-angled, not equilateral) =

Rhombus (equilateral, not right-angled) =

Rhomboid (opposite sides and angles equal to
one another, but neither equilateral nor right-angled) =

Trapezium (any quadrilateral figures other than above) =

Medieval Literacy

Geometry (continued)

Multilateral Figures (Euclid I, definition 19)

Two examples of multilateral figures include:

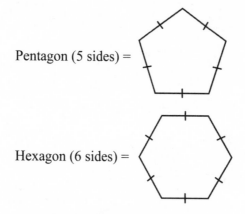

Pentagon (5 sides) =

Hexagon (6 sides) =

II. Curved Line Figures

Perfect circles (equal length lines from circumference to center) =

Elliptical figures (plane figure contained by one line) =

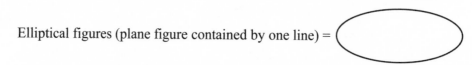

III. Mixed Figures (figures with curved and straight lines)

Figures like semi-circles, etc. =

Geometry (continued)

Solid Figures (Euclid, XI, definitions)

Simple Classification

1. pyramid (imposed on the surface of a triangle) =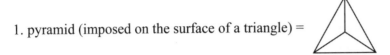

2. cone or cylinder (imposed on the surface of a circle) =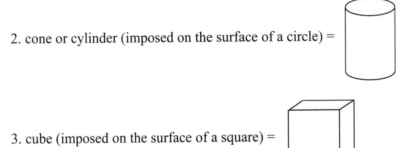

3. cube (imposed on the surface of a square) =

A. Euclid, *Elements*
   Martianus Capella, *The Marriage of Philology and Mercury*, VI (708-722)
   Cassiodorus, *An Introduction to Divine and Human Readings*, II.vi
   Isidore of Seville, *Etymologies*, III.xi-xii
B. Wagner, David, ed., *The Seven Liberal Arts in the Middle Ages*, pp. 196-217

Astronomy (following Martianus)

Four Elements of the Geocentric Universe

1. earth (heaviest element)
2. water
3. air
4. fire (lightest element)
(5.) aether (celestial element)

The Sphere of the Fixed Stars: The Constellations

1. the northern constellations

> 35 constellations in total

2. the southern constellations

3. the Zodiac (which keeps the constellations separate)

The Planets

1. Moon (orbits the Earth)

2. Mercury, "the Twinkler" (orbits the Sun)

3. Venus, "the Light-bringer" (orbits the Sun)

4. Sun (orbits the Earth)

5. Mars, "the Fiery" (orbits the Earth)

6. Jupiter, "the Blazer" (orbits the Earth)

7. Saturn, "the Shiner" (orbits the Earth)

A. Martianus Capella, *The Marriage of Philology and Mercury*,
VIII (814, 838 & 850 ff.)
Cassiodorus, *An Introduction to Divine and Human Readings*, II.vii.2
Isidore of Seville, *Etymologies*, III, xlii ff.
B. Wagner, David, ed., *The Seven Liberal Arts in the Middle Ages*, pp. 218-247

The Ten Celestial Circles (incorporeal lines dividing the universe)

1. Horizon (observer's "latitude") Celestial circle with no fixed location; a "horizontal" circle with respect to the observer's perspective looking out into space

2. Meridian (observer's "longitude") Celestial circle with no fixed location; perpendicular to horizon; a "vertical" or overhead circle with respect to the observer's perspective

3. Equinoctial (celestial equator) Perpendicular to the axis of the world and equidistant between the north and south poles; passes through east & west points of the horizon

4. Ecliptic (Zodiac) Sun's annual path through the Zodiac; inclined at an angle of 23 degrees to equator; changes orientation with respect to the horizon

5. Equinoctial Colure Passes through the equinoxes and celestial poles; changes orientation with respect to the horizon

6. Solstitial Colure Passes through the solstices and celestial poles; changes orientation with respect to the horizon

7. Tropic of Cancer (summer tropic) Parallel to the equator (23.5 degrees N) and tangent to the ecliptic at the summer solstice

8. Tropic of Capricorn (winter tropic) Parallel to the equator (23.5 degrees S) and tangent to the ecliptic at the winter solstice

9. Celestial Arctic Circle Parallel to the equator (66.5 degrees N); everything north of this circle is the Arctic proper

10. Celestial Antarctic Circle Parallel to the equator (66.5 degrees S); everything south of this circle is the Antarctic proper

A. Plato, *Timaeus*, 36c-e
Macrobius, *Commentary on the Dream of Scipio*, I.xv.8-19
Martianus Capella, *The Marriage of Philology and Mercury*, VIII (818-837)
Sacrobosco, *On the Sphere*, chapter II
B. Heilbron, J. L., *The Sun in the Church: Cathedrals as Solar Observatories*, p. 63

Latin Mnemonic Verse (for remembering the seven liberal arts)

Gram. loquitur, Dia. verba docet, Rhet. verba colorat
Mus. canit, Ar. numerat, Geo. ponderat, Ast. colit astra

[Grammar speaks, Dialectic teaches truths, and Rhetoric colors words
Music sings, Arithmetic counts, Geometry weighs, and Astronomy tends to the stars]

NOTE: Translation courtesy of Abbot Elias Dietz, OSCO.

A. No particular author.
B. Lewis, C. S., *The Discarded Image*, p. 186

The Liberal Arts Curriculum of Ancient Athens

1. gymnastics (*gymnastikē*): included running, high jumping, boxing, discus throwing and javelin throwing (gymnastics teachers were called pedotribes)

2. music (*mousikē*): included choir, dance and recitation of lyric poetry (children were taught by cither players or music masters)

3. grammar (*grammata*): included reading and writing (the teacher was literally a humble "teacher of letters")

NOTE: For a long time, grammar was the least prestigious subject in Greece. Early Athenian aristocracy emphasized gymnastics and military training. Even the bookish Plato held music in higher esteem than grammar and said that, "Anyone who cannot take his place in a choir [i.e. as both singer and dancer] is not truly educated" (*Laws* 654a-b).

NOTE: "To sum up this complex development [of ancient education] in a simple formula, it might be said that the history of ancient education reflects the progressive transition from a "noble warrior" culture to a "scribe" culture. . . . Its origins are to be found in a society impregnated with the warrior spirit, which nevertheless managed to produce the central pivot around which the whole of Greek education was to be organized – and this was a book, Homer's *Iliad*, though it is true that it was entirely devoted to celebrating the deeds of heroes. . . . It was not until long afterwards, when the Christian Faith decided to organize culture and education around the Book of Books – the Bible, the source of all knowledge and life – that the literary man of antiquity finally became a scribe."

H. I. Marrou, *History of Education in Antiquity*, p. xiv

A. Aristotle, *Politics*, 1337b
B. Knowles, David, *The Evolution of Medieval Thought*, pp. 53-55
   Liddell and Scott, *Greek-English Lexicon*
   Marrou, H. I., *A History of Education in Antiquity*, pp. 42-43

The Liberal Arts Curriculum of the Philosopher-King in Plato's *Republic*

Ages 5-15   Music and gymnastic (trivium)

Ages 15-20   Gymnastic and military service (gymnastics)

Ages 20-30   Math, geometry, astronomy (quadrivium)

Ages 30-35   Five year course in dialectic (philosophy)

Ages 35-50   Affairs of state (practical political and military experience)

Age 50+   Rulers take turns ruling and spend most of their time in contemplation

NOTE: This curriculum refers to what an ideal ruler should study according to Plato. Over the doors of Plato's school, the Academy, were written the words, "Let no one without geometry enter here."

A. Plato, *Republic*, 537a ff.
   Averroes, *Averroes on Plato's Republic*, 77.12 ff.
B. Grube, G.M.A., *Plato's Thought*, p. 240

The Liberal Arts Curriculum of the Medieval University (c.1100-1500)

Trivium (in Latin, "where three roads meet") or the "lower" arts:

1. grammar (e.g., Donatus' *Ars Major* and *Ars Minor* and Priscian's *Institutes*)
2. rhetoric (e.g., Cicero's *De Inventione*)
3. logic (e.g., Peter of Spain's *Summulae Logicale*)

Quadrivium (in Latin, "where four roads meet") or the "higher" arts:

4. arithmetic (e.g., Boethius' *Arithmetica*)
5. geometry (e.g., Euclid's *Elements*)
6. astronomy (e.g., Sacrobosco's *On the Sphere* and Ptolemy's *Almagest*)
7. music (e.g., Boethius' *De Musica* and Augustine's *De Musica*)

Three Philosophies:

1. natural philosophy or science (e.g., Aristotle's *Physics* and *On the Soul*)
2. moral philosophy (e.g., Aristotle's *Nicomachean Ethics*)
3. metaphysics (e.g., Aristotle's *Metaphysics*)

Approximate Stages:

Ages 5-13:	Grammar school (Latin grammar and literature)
Ages 14-17:	Bachelor of arts (3-4 years study in the trivium and natural philosophy)
Ages 18-21:	Master of arts (2+ years of study in the quadrivium, natural philosophy, moral philosophy, and metaphysics; the master of arts was a prerequisite for study in the higher faculties of law, medicine, or theology)
Ages 22-35	Doctorate in one of the three professions of law, medicine, or theology (a theology doctorate could take an additional 12 years after the master of arts; some statutes forbade awarding the doctorate in theology to anyone under the age of 35 years)

NOTE: The High Middle Ages focused on the Seven Liberal Arts (popular textbooks noted) and the Late Middle Ages focused on the Three Philosophies.

    A. Charters & primary sources cited in Helene Wieruszowski's *Medieval University*

    B. Artz, Frederick, *The Mind of the Middle Ages: An Historical Survey*, pp. 308-316

    Grant, Edward, *The Foundations of Modern Science in the Middle Ages*, pp. 33 ff.

    Grant, Edward, *God and Reason in the Middle Ages*

Types of Medieval Schools (not including Latin grammar schools)

types	approach	curriculum
1. monastic schools	*lectio divina* and biblical exegesis	Biblical exegesis and biblical commentaries of the Fathers. *Lectio divina* = spiritual reading leading to contemplation.
2. cathedral schools	literary and biblical exegesis	Alcuin: "liberal studies and the holy word."
3. universities	scholastic disputation	Advanced liberal arts (emphasis on dialectics) and the professions. Divided into four faculties of (1) arts, (2) law, (3) medicine, and (4) theology.

types	milestones	description
1. monastic schools	c.529	St. Benedict founds Monte Cassino.
	c.787	Charlemagne orders schools to be established in every bishopric and monastery in his kingdom.
	c.910	Monastery of Cluny
	c.1113	Monastery of St. Victor
2. cathedral schools (with famous scholars)	c.732	School of York (Alcuin)
	c.850	School of Laon (Anselm of Laon)
	c.972	School of Rheims (Gerbert)
	c.990	School of Chartes (Fulbert)
	c.1119	School of Notre Dame (Abelard)
3. universities (with famous subjects)	c.1088	University of Bologna (canon law)
	c.1150	University of Paris (theology)
	c.1167	University of Oxford (natural science)
	c.1218	University of Salamanca (civil law)
	c.1231	University of Salerno (medicine)

A. Charters & primary sources cited in Helene Wieruszowski's *Medieval University*

B. Artz, Frederick, *The Mind of the Middle Ages: An Historical Survey*, pp. 314-319

Southern, R. W., *The Making of the Middle Ages*, pp. 185-218

PART TWO: KNOWLEDGE

VI. Logic

Aristotle is the master of those who know.

Dante, *Inferno,* IV.131

Experience taught me a manifest conclusion, that, whereas logic furthers other studies, so, if it remains by itself, it remains bloodless and barren, nor does it quicken the soul to yield fruit of philosophy, except the same conceive elsewhere.

John of Salisbury, *Metalogicon,* ii.10

In no branch of study was Aristotle more the master than in the realm of logic. While Plato used logic, Aristotle formalized it, defined its uses, and established its boundaries. The philosopher of science, Alfred North Whitehead, once said that the history of Western philosophy was merely a series of footnotes to Plato. It might also be said that for well over two thousand years, the science of logic was merely a series of footnotes to Aristotle. And while the mathematical logic of the philosophers Alfred North Whitehead and Bertrand Russell has expanded the scope of logic, nothing has altered the fundamental tenets set down by Aristotle twenty-four centuries ago.

The most famous logician of the Middle Ages, Peter Abelard (1079-1142), summed up the scope of logic and its debt to Aristotle in the third paragraph of his *Glosses on Porphyry*:

Moreover in writing logic the following order is extremely necessary that since arguments are constructed from propositions, and propositions from words, he who will write logic perfectly, must first write of simple words, then of propositions, and finally devote the end of logic to argumentations, just as our prince Aristotle did, who wrote the *Categories* on the science of words, the *On Interpretation* on the science of propositions, the *Topics* and the *Analytics* on the science of argumentation.[102]

Lest modern students think that medieval logic was totally bloodless, they best keep in mind that the logician who penned these words, Peter Abelard, was not only the greatest medieval logician, but also its most notorious lover. As celebrity tutor to the beautiful Heloise, when she was discovered to be pregnant Abelard was summarily "wounded where he had sinned" and both he and Heloise ended up living monastic lives, he as an unsuccessful abbot and she as a remarkably successful abbess.

In spite of his erotic calamities, Abelard's summation of Aristotle's science of words, propositions, and arguments led to medieval logic's famous "three acts of the intellect." Each of these verbal expressions corresponds to a particular mental act.[103]

---

102. Peter Abelard, *Glosses of Peter Abelard on Porphyry* in Richard McKeon's *Selections from Medieval Philosophers* (New York: Charles Scribner's Sons, 1958), p. 209.

103. Peter Kreeft, *Socratic Logic.* Third edition (South Bend, IN: St. Augustine's Press, 2008), pp. 28-29.

Verbal Expression	Mental Act
Words (or terms)	Conceiving (or simple apprehension)
Propositions	Judging
Arguments (or syllogisms)	Reasoning (or deductive inference)

The science of words is the science of arriving at an adequate definition of something. For example, first we have a sense perception of something. "I see a man I recognize as Socrates." Second, we form a mental image from that sense perception. "I have a picture of a short, ugly, smiling Socrates in my imagination." Third, we create a concept by abstracting from the sensible image to form an idea. "I have the concept of the human being called Socrates." Now that we know Socrates to be a man we can push the analysis further by inquiring what a human is? Things can be defined in terms of their extension (or how many examples of a particular class exist). Or things can be defined in terms of their comprehension or meaning. While Aristotle's tongue-in-cheek definition of the human being as a featherless biped is true, it does not provide much useful information. Defining the human being as a rational animal is more precise. Humanity is a species of the genus animal, a species separate from other animals due to the specific difference of rationality. Ultimately then we define Socrates as a particular member of the class of rational animals.

The science of propositions analyzes the relationship between words or terms. In a categorical proposition one term is said to belong to or not belong to another term and the intellect judges whether this relationship is true or false. Strictly speaking the categorical proposition contains three elements (a subject-term, a predicate-term, and a copula). The copula (the verb "to be") unites the two terms. There are four logical forms of categorical proposition. The first form is the universal affirmative form. "All human beings [subject] are [copula] rational animals [predicate]." The second form is the universal negative. "No human beings are rational animals." The third form is the particular affirmative. "Some human beings are rational animals." And the fourth form is the particular negative. "Some human beings are not rational animals." Medieval logicians were particularly enamored of the logical relationships between these four forms in terms of contradictories (forms opposed in quality [affirmative or negative] and quantity [universal or particular]), contraries (forms opposed in quality), and alternation (forms opposed in quantity). See the chart on the Traditional Square of Opposition for more information.

The science of arguments in its formal aspect is based on how propositions relate to each other, especially in the standard categorical syllogism. This classic type of argument typifies the third act of the intellect, deductive reasoning. Just as in a categorical proposition there are three terms (subject, predicate, and copula), so in a categorical syllogism there are three propositions (major premise, minor premise, and conclusion). Furthermore, within these three propositions there are three, and only three, terms (a major term, a minor term, and a middle term). Consider the classic example.

All human beings are mortal.	[major premise]
Socrates is a human being.	[minor premise]
Therefore, Socrates is mortal.	[conclusion]

The predicate of the conclusion (mortal) is the major term and the major premise is always the premise containing this term. The subject of the conclusion (Socrates) is the minor term and the minor premise is always the premise containing the minor term. The remaining term, the middle term, appears in both premises, but never in the conclusion.

The medievals delighted in an intricate analysis of all possible forms of the categorical syllogism (summarized in the Latin poem included in this chapter). The heart of the analysis centered on finding the basic rules for determining whether a syllogism was valid or invalid. Unlike the science of propositions, the science of argumentation is not concerned with truth or falsity, but with validity and deductive inference. If all human beings are mortal and Socrates is a human being, then we can correctly infer that Socrates is mortal. If all human beings are blondes and Socrates is a human being, we could correctly infer that Socrates was blonde. This argument would be valid, but the major premise ("all human beings are blondes") would not be true.

The six rules and two corollaries for determining a valid syllogism fall under four headings.[104]

Essential Structure

1. A syllogism must have three and only three terms.
2. A syllogism must have three and only three propositions.

Distribution of Terms

3. No term that is undistributed in the premises may be distributed in the conclusion.
4. The middle term must be distributed at least once.

Negative Propositions

5. No syllogism can have two negative premises.
6. If either premise is negative, the conclusion must be negative.

Two Corollaries

7. No syllogism may have two particular premises.
8. If a syllogism has a particular premise, it must have a particular conclusion.

Please note that the word "distributed" refers to the quantity of a term. A term is distributed when it refers to all members of the class of things referred to by the term. Hence in the proposition, "all human beings are mortal," the subject-term is distributed. In the proposition, "some human beings are mortal," the subject-term is not distributed.

Armed with these three acts of the intellect, the formal rules applied to each act, and a methodology for translating ordinary sentences into proper categorical form, medieval logicians attacked each other with great vigor in their disputations or public debates. While medieval scholasticism is usually characterized as "bloodless and barren," it tended to be quite passionate and combative in actual practice. C. S. Lewis describes his logic tutor, Mr. Kirkpatrick ("the Great Knock") with more passion than any of the friends and teachers he mentions in his autobiography. Of logic itself, Lewis notes that most boys would not have liked Kirk's ruthless dialectic, but "to me it was red beef and strong beer."[105] The medievals could not have described their passion for logic any better.

---

104. Kreeft, *Logic*, p. 243.
105. Lewis, *Joy*, p. 136.

By way of addendum, it should be noted that the medievals distinguished formal logic (the study of the forms of argumentation) from material logic (the study of the content of argumentation). The content of argumentation is virtually indistinguishable from philosophy *per se*, and so *Medieval Literacy* delays mention of these matters to the next chapter on Philosophy. There mention is made of such famous material logic lists as the Tree of Porphyry as well as Aristotle's categories and predicables. Just as the science of words today (linguistics) leads to endless debates among analytic philosophers, so the science of words in medieval times led to sharp debates, particularly in regard to the problem of universal terms. Much of medieval philosophy exhausted itself on this problem of universals that will be discussed further in the chapter on Philosophy.

Remember, following each list are bibliographic references to the relevant primary sources (A) that are listed in chronological order by the author's lifetime and secondary sources (B) that are listed in alphabetical order by the author's name.

Three Laws of Thought

1. The Principle of Identity = If any statement is true, then it is true.

2. The Principle of Contradiction = No statement can be both true and false.

3. The Principle of Excluded Middle = Any statement must be either true or false.

    A. Aristotle, *Topics*, 152a (for Principle of Identity)
       Aristotle, *Metaphysics*, 996b (for Principle of Contradiction)
       Aristotle, *Metaphysics*, 1011b (for Principle of Excluded Middle)
    B. Kneale, William and Martha, *The Development of Logic*, pp. 42-46
       Kreeft, Peter, *Socratic Logic*, pp. 220-221
       "Laws of Thought," *The Encyclopedia of Philosophy*, vol. 4

Outline of Aristotle's *Organon* (his works on logic)

Formal Logic

1. *Categories* = analysis of terms (definitions) to distinguish clear from unclear terms; the classification of predicates represents actual modes of being in the world beyond the mind

2. *On Interpretation* = analysis of propositions (statements) to distinguish true from false statements

3. *Prior Analytics* = analysis of arguments (syllogisms) to distinguish valid from invalid arguments

Material Logic

4. *Posterior Analytics* = analysis of scientific method and demonstrative arguments (arguments that are certain)

5. *Topics* = analysis of dialectical arguments (arguments that are probable)

6. *On Sophistical Refutations* = analysis of sophistical arguments (arguments that are ambiguous)

NOTE: Before the avalanche of Latin translations of the Greek classics in the twelfth century (see Introduction to the chapter on the Seven Liberal Arts), the only logical works of Aristotle in Latin were the *Categories* and *On Interpretation*. These two works were referred to as the Old Logic (*ars vetus*) in contradistinction to the four other works that appeared in the twelfth century and were referred to as the New Logic (*ars nova*). Arabic tradition included Aristotle's *Rhetoric* and *Poetics* within the *Organon*.

    A. Aristotle, see above works
       John of Salisbury, *Metalogicon*, books III and IV
    B. Kneale, William and Martha, *The Development of Logic*, pp. 23 ff.

Three Acts of the Intellect

1. Conceiving = simple apprehension of things; formation of concepts or terms that can be clear or unclear

> Example of a term: "Socrates"
> Example of a term: "mortal"
> Example of a term: "human"

2. Judging = putting two terms or concepts together to form a proposition that can be true or false

> Example of a true proposition: Socrates is mortal.
> Example of false proposition: All dogs are large.

3. Reasoning = putting two propositions (and three terms) together and inferring a conclusion that can be a valid or invalid argument

> Example of a valid argument: All humans are mortal.
> <u>Socrates is a human.</u>
> Therefore, Socrates is mortal.

> Example of an invalid argument: All tigers are mammals.
> <u>All mammals are animals.</u>
> Therefore, all animals are tigers.

A. Abelard, Peter, *Glosses of Peter Abelard on Porphyry* (3rd paragraph) in Richard McKeon's *Selections from Medieval Philosophers*, p. 209 ff.
B. Kreeft, Peter, *Socratic Logic*, pp. 28 ff.

Definition: Types of Definition

1. nominal definition = definition by other words without the essential meaning or of words that mean the same thing (synonymous definition)

   Example: Bashful means shy.

2. causal definition = definition by naming the cause or causes of the thing defined (often one of Aristotle's four causes)

   Example: Pneumonia is a disease caused by the pneumococcus.

NOTE: Modern textbooks often refer to this as the operational definition or the definition by performance of an experimental procedure

   Example: A solution is acid if and only if litmus paper turns red when dipped into it.

3. essential definition = definition of a thing by classifying it according to its genus and difference

   Example: Ice [species] means frozen [difference] water [genus].
   Doe [species] means female [difference] deer [genus].
   Daughter [species] means female [difference] offspring [genus].

NOTE: For further information about the medieval use of terms like genus, species, difference, property and accident, see the section on "Aristotle's Five Predicables" on page 172 in the Philosophy chapter.

A. Aristotle, *Posterior Analytics*, 93b28 ff.
B. Joseph, Miriam, *The Trivium*, pp. 81 ff.

Proposition: The Components of a Proposition

Socrates is mortal.

Socrates = the subject in this example [subject abbreviated by S]

is = the copula that connects the subject and predicate

mortal = the predicate in this example [predicate abbreviated by P]

Abbreviation: S is P.

    A. Aristotle, *On Interpretation*, 17a
    B. Joseph, Miriam, *The Trivium*, pp. 90 ff.

Proposition: The Traditional Square of Opposition

A = universal affirmative   universal negative = E
All chickens are brown.   No chickens are brown.

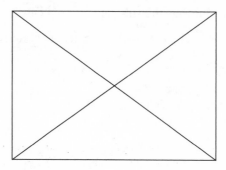

I = particular affirmative   particular negative = O
Some chickens are brown.   Some chickens are not brown.

types of propositions	example
A = universal affirmative statements	All chickens are brown.
E = universal negative statements	No chickens are brown.
I = particular affirmative statements	Some chickens are brown.
O = particular negative statements	Some chickens are not brown.

NOTE: A and I come from the Latin word, *affirmo*; E and O come from the Latin word, *nego* (note first two vowels in each word). Affirmative and negative refer to a statement's QUALITY. Universal and particular refer to a statement's QUANTITY.

Proposition: The Traditional Square of Opposition (continued)

1. Contradictory opposition

For statements opposed in both quantity and quality, if one of those statements is true, the other must be false and vice-versa). For example, if the A statement, "all swans are white," is true, then the O statement, "some swans are not white," must be false.

2. Contrary opposition

A and E statements opposed in quality cannot both be true. For example, the statements, "all swans are white" and "no swans are white" cannot both be true.

3. Subcontrary opposition

I and O statements opposed in quality cannot both be false. For example, the statements, "all swans are white" and "some swans are white" cannot both be false.

4. Relations of subalternation and superalternation

If a universal statement is true, then the corresponding particular statement must also be true. If a particular statement is false, then the corresponding universal statement must also be false. In the Square of Opposition, you "descend with truth and ascend with falsity."

For example, if the A-statement, "all swans are white," is true, the I-statement, "some swans are white," must also be true. If the I-statement, "some swans are white," is false, then the A-statement, "all swans are white," must also be false.

    A. Aristotle, *On Interpretation*, 17a ff.
       Aristotle, *Prior Analytics*, 25a ff.
       Martianus Capella, *The Marriage of Philology and Mercury*, IV (396-403)
       William of Sherwood, *Introduction to Logic*, 1.16
    B. Kreeft, Peter, *Socratic Logic*, pp. 174 ff.

Argument: The Components of a Categorical Syllogism

The Two Premises

1. Major Premise (which contains the predicate of the conclusion)
2. Minor Premise (which contains the subject of the conclusion)
(3.) Conclusion

The Three Terms	Position in the Syllogism	Example
1. Major Term = P	Predicate of the conclusion	animals
2. Minor Term = S	Subject of the conclusion	dogs
3. Middle Term = M	Appears only in the premises	mammals

Sample Syllogism (form)	Sample Syllogism (content)
All M is P.	All mammals are animals.
All S is M.	All dogs are mammals.
All S is P.	Therefore, all dogs are animals.

    A. Aristotle, *Prior Analytics*, 25b30 ff.
       William of Sherwood, *Introduction to Logic*, 3.4
    B. Kreeft, Peter, *Socratic Logic*, pp. 215 ff.
       Joseph, Miriam, *The Trivium*, pp. 130 ff.

Argument: Mood and Figure in a Categorical Syllogism

Mood

Mood arises from the disposition of the propositions according to quality and quantity, hence AAA refers to three universal, affirmative propositions in a given syllogism (refer back to the Traditional Square of Opposition).

Example: AAA syllogism = All mammals are animals.
<u>All dogs are mammals.</u>
All dogs are animals.

AII syllogism = All immoral companions should be avoided.
<u>Some immoral companions are intelligent persons.</u>
Some intelligent persons should be avoided.

Figure

Figure arises from location of the terms in the syllogism; hence if M is the middle term, P is the major term, and S is the minor term, the four possible figures are:

Figure One	Figure Two	Figure Three	Figure Four
M is P	P is M	M is P	P is M
<u>S is M</u>	<u>S is M</u>	<u>M is S</u>	<u>M is S</u>
S is P	S is P	S is P	S is P

NOTE: Figure four was not discovered until after the Middle Ages. At this time, the fifth, sixth, seventh, eighth, and ninth moods of Figure One were grouped together as Figure Four.

A. Aristotle, *Prior Analytics*, 25b30
William of Sherwood, *Introduction to Logic*, 3.5-8
B. Kreeft, Peter, *Socratic Logic*, pp. 257-258
Joseph, Miriam, *The Trivium*, pp. 130 ff.

Argument: Valid Syllogisms Using Latin Mnemonic Verse

Barbara, Celarent, Darii, Ferio	AAA, EAE, AII, EIO
Cesare, Camestres, Festino, Baroco	EAE, AEE, EIO, AOO
Darapti, Disamis, Datisi, Felapton, Bocardo, Ferison	AAI, IAI, AII, EAO, OAO, EIO
Bramantip, Camenes, Dimaris, Fesapo, Fresison	AAI, AEE, IAI, EAO, EIO

NOTE: The first three vowels of each word stand for the mood of a syllogism. Thus, Barbara = an AAA syllogism and Darii = an AII syllogism. Line one of the poem shows all possible moods (AAA-1, EAE-1, AII-1, EIO-1) for valid figure one syllogisms. Line two shows all possible moods (AEE-2, EAE-2, AOO-2, EIO-2) for valid figure two syllogisms, etc.

Example of a valid "Barbara" or AAA-1 syllogism

All M is P	All mammals are animals.
All S is M	All dogs are mammals.
All S is P	Therefore, all dogs are animals.

Example of a valid "Cesare" or EAE-2 syllogism

No P is M	No fish are mammals.
All S is M	All whales are mammals.
No S is P	Therefore, no whales are fish.

NOTE: William of Sherwood is the originator of this particular version of the Latin mnemonic poem.

    A. William of Sherwood, *Introduction to Logic*, 3.9
    B. Kreeft, Peter, *Socratic Logic*, p. 258
       Joseph, Miriam, *The Trivium*, p. 159
       Kneale, William and Martha, *The Development of Logic*, p. 232

Three Types of Arguments (Material Division)

1. Demonstrative Arguments = arguments with true premises leading to a necessary conclusion; Aristotle describes how philosophers and mathematicians think in his *Posterior Analytics* that deals with truth in the purest, theoretical sense

Example: All humans are mortal.
             <u>Socrates is a human.</u>
             Therefore, Socrates is mortal.

[the premises are certain and the structure of the argument is valid]

2. Dialectical Arguments = arguments with probable premises leading to a probable conclusion; Aristotle catalogs probable arguments in his *Topics*; cf. Plato's remark that natural sciences are "the science of the probable," even the law of gravity is only a highly statistical probability; dialectical arguments are sincere reasoning for practical results, but not pure truth

Example: The Moors have weapons.
             Therefore, the Moors have iron.

[based on historical and sense experience provided by the missing major premise: "All people who have weapons, have iron," this argument is only probable, not certain]

3. Sophistical Arguments = arguments with ambiguous premises and the arguer is not sincere; arguments aimed at victory in politics or the courtroom (analyzed in *On Sophistical Refutations*)

Example: Murder is a terrible crime.
             Therefore, the defendant in court today must be guilty

[fallacy of irrelevant conclusion; see Sophistical Arguments below]

   A. Aristotle, *Topics*, 100a
      Hugh of St. Victor, *The Didascalicon: A Medieval Guide to the Arts*, II.30
      John of Salisbury, *Metalogicon*, ii.3
      William of Sherwood, *Introduction to Logic*, 4.1
   B. Wagner, David, ed., *The Seven Liberal Arts in the Middle Ages*, pp. 125 ff.

Sophistical Arguments

Verbal Fallacies (*in dictione*)

1. Equivocation = ambiguity in a single term (e.g. obtuse)

Some triangles are obtuse.
<u>Whatever is obtuse is ignorant.</u>
Therefore, some triangles are ignorant.

2. Amphiboly = ambiguity in sentence structure

I stood on the veranda, watching the fireworks go up in my pajamas (Groucho Marx).

3. Composition = ambiguity due to combining words wrongly

A man is capable of walking, when he is sitting. Therefore, he is capable of walking when he is sitting.

4. Division = ambiguity due to separating words wrongly

Five is two and three; therefore five is two and is three.

5. Accent = ambiguity due to a shift in accent resulting in a shift in meaning

Anything that ought to be suspended [*pendere*] ought to be hanged.(short accent, 2nd e)
A just man ought to be esteemed [*pendere*]. (long accent, 2nd e)
Therefore, a just man ought to be hanged.

6. Figure of Speech = mistaken inference from grammatical form (e.g., using a term as a noun in a premise and as an adjective in the conclusion)

What you bought yesterday, you ate today.
You bought something-raw [*crudum*] yesterday.
Therefore, you ate raw [*crudum*] today.

A. Aristotle, *On Sophistical Refutations*
   William of Sherwood, *Introduction to Logic*, chapter 6
B. Ross, W. D., *Aristotle*, pp. 57-58

Sophistical Arguments (continued)

Non-Verbal Fallacies *(extra dictionem)*

1. Accident = general rule misapplied to a specific case

Freedom of speech is a natural right. Therefore, it's OK to yell "fire" in a theater.

2. Consequent = fallacy which argues that since the consequent follows from the antecedent, the antecedent must follow from the consequent

Whenever it rains the ground is wet. Therefore, whenever the ground is wet, it must have rained.

3. In a Certain Respect and Absolutely = when a term is used in a qualified sense in a premise and in an unqualified sense in the conclusion, and vice-versa

Socrates is a dead man.
Therefore, Socrates is a man.

4. Irrelevant Conclusion (*ignoratio elenchi*) = conclusion drawn that is not supported by the premises

Murder is a terrible crime. Therefore, the defendant in court today must be guilty.

5. Begging the Question (*petitio principii*) = assuming as a premise for an argument the very conclusion one is trying to prove

Murder is morally wrong. Therefore, abortion is morally wrong. [This argument assumes that abortion is a form of murder which is what the very debate is about.]

6. False Cause (*non causa pro causa*) = imagined and untrue causal connection

There are more laws on the books today than ever before, and more crimes are being committed than ever before. Therefore, to reduce crime we must eliminate the laws.

7. Treating More Than One Question as One = just like it says!

 Are all things good or not good? [This question can't be answered as such since there are some things in the world that are good and some that are not.]

    A. Aristotle, *On Sophistical Refutations*
       William of Sherwood, *Introduction to Logic*, chapter 6
    B. Ross, W. D., *Aristotle*, pp. 58-59

VII. Philosophy

> Have the carpenter, then, and the tanner certain functions or activities, and has man none? Is he born without a function? Or as eye, hand, foot, and in general each of the parts evidently has a function, may one lay it down that man similarly has a function apart from all of these? What then can this be?
>
> Aristotle, *Nicomachean Ethics*, 1097b

Aristotle's four causes provide the most convenient and concise introduction to premodern philosophy. According to Aristotle there are four primary kinds of causes and no thing can be fully understood unless all of the four causes bringing that thing about are known. These causes include: (1) a material cause, (2) a formal cause, (3) an efficient cause, and (4) a final cause. Take a desk for example. The material cause of the desk is the wood, that "out of which" the desk is made. The formal cause is the engineer's sketch or blueprint of the desk, the "into which" the wood or matter is formed. The efficient cause is the carpenter or agent that brings the desk into existence, "by which" the desk is made. And the final cause is "to write on," the purpose or need that the desk fulfills "for the sake of which" the wood was put into the shape of a desk by the carpenter.

The change from basic materials into finished product is literally a "transformation" of lumber into a desk. Lumber itself entails a transformation of the wood from a tree (matter) into the form of lumber. Matter in the Aristotelian sense is not raw material *per se*, but any potentiality capable of transformation. The wood from trees can be transformed into various types and shapes of lumber and this new form of lumber can be transformed itself into other forms like desks, chairs and the like. With human artifacts like desks, it is easier to understand all four causes. The final cause is always the human need that the artifact fills. As the old saying goes, "necessity is the mother of invention."

Natural objects also entail four causes. Take for example, a natural event suggested by Henry Veatch, "the Sun shining on the stone sill of a window."[106] This event entails a change in quality from the stone sill being not warm to the stone sill becoming warm. The material cause of this natural event is a stone sill that is cold or not warm. This sill has the potential to become something else, that is, to become warm. The formal cause of this event is a warm stone sill. The sill has been literally transformed from cold into warm. The efficient or agent cause of this warming is the sun. And the final cause of the event is that the sill becomes warm. It is the nature of the stone sill to become warm when the Sun shines on it.

Note that this natural purpose does not entail any conscious purpose as in human events like the making of a desk, with the purpose of having something to write on. As Veatch says, "There is no reason at all why the final cause of an efficient action should

---

106. Henry Veatch, *Aristotle: A Contemporary Appreciation* (Bloomington: Indiana University Press, 1974), p. 47.

necessarily be an end in the sense of conscious purpose."[107] Everything in nature tends towards an end that is simply the result of the natural process in question. During autumn the maple leaf changes from green to yellow as part of its natural tendency. The final cause of the change is for the leaf to become yellow.

For human beings and for human institutions, the notion of final causality generally entails a more discernible conscious purpose (although clearly activities like human sexual reproduction, while tending toward the natural end of new offspring for the species, are not always conscious or deliberate). According to Aristotle humans are political animals that naturally form political institutions. Take for example the government of the United States of America. Following somewhat loosely an example given by Veatch's teacher John Wild,[108] the material cause of the United States would be the rational individuals who make up the country. The formal cause would be the union of these individuals to perform certain duties necessary for the common good. The efficient cause could be viewed in various ways. In a temporal sense, the Founding Fathers were the efficient cause of the United States.

However, one might also consider the Constitution as both the ongoing efficient and formal cause of the country. The Constitution articulates how individuals are transformed into citizens to promote the common good. And the final cause would be the common good itself. As articulated in the Declaration of Independence this common good includes the promotion of "life, liberty, and the pursuit of happiness" among the citizenry. Of course the common good also entails a willingness of individual citizens to sacrifice their own life, liberty, and happiness for the good of the whole. As this example shows, the four causes are not separate realities. The Constitution could be both an efficient and formal cause. And the citizens could be understood as both an efficient and a material cause, and indeed as a final cause since they partake in the common good that the U.S. democracy promotes.

Aristotle was most concerned to discover the final cause of human existence itself. As mentioned in the epigraph to this chapter, he found it inconceivable that carpenters and tanners (not to mention eyes, hands, and feet) all would have a specific purpose and human existence in general would not. He argues that everything in nature has a particular function (or ecological niche in today's parlance). "Nature makes nothing in vain." The function of an eye is sight. The virtue of an eye is 20-20 vision. And the vice of an eye is blindness.

For Aristotle it is obvious that all humans seek happiness.[109] How to attain happiness is the difficult issue. As this book mentioned earlier in chapter four on Psychology, becoming a happy person presupposes becoming a good person, and as Aristotle never tires of saying, "It is no easy task to be good" (*Nicomachean Ethics*, 1109a). Becoming good requires moral skill. For Aristotle the purpose of human *being* is the cultivation of moral skill or virtue. Moral skill is the perfection of human functioning. Stated otherwise, virtue : a human being :: skill : an artisan. Or, virtue : a human being :: instinct : an animal. The perfection of natural human functions might include physical strength and grace, moral courage, and rational deliberation. "Living intelligently" might be a broad

---

107. Veatch, *Aristotle*, p. 48.

108. John Wild, *Introduction to Realistic Philosophy* (New York: Harper and Brothers, 1948), p. 188.

109. Cf. the discussion of Veatch, *Aristotle*, pp. 103 ff.

final cause of human existence for Aristotle.

However, since human beings vary in their degrees of intelligence and physical stature, he argued that they are far from equal. He would not be popular today, arguing that women were fit by nature to produce babies and men were fit by nature to fight wars. Furthermore, he argued that a carpenter's intellectual virtue is a far cry from a philosopher's intellectual virtue. As was discussed in the introduction to chapter four on Psychology, only philosophers (according to Aristotle) can become fully human.

In fact, he argued that the final cause for the highest human beings (the philosophers) is a life of contemplation – a life lived in rapt wonderment at the beauty and complexity of the universe. Since for Aristotle the universe is eternal (with no beginning and no end), his god is not "outside" the universe but is the heart and soul of the universe. Contemplation is a participation in the divine activity of "thought [god] thinking itself" (*Metaphysics*, 1074b). As god is perfect and perfection, by definition, is unchanging, Aristotle's god, the Un-Moved Mover, does not create motion by a material push (propulsion), but by an immaterial pull (attraction). His god is the final rather than the efficient cause of the universe. As a consequence of this logic, in Aristotle's theology there is no place for divine creation (something cannot come from nothing) or for divine providence (god only dwells on his own perfection).

It took a great deal of creative energy on the part of medieval theologians to reconcile the passive god of Aristotle (the world's final cause) with the active God of the Bible (the world's efficient cause) who is busy creating and redeeming the world. In addition to this tension, Aristotle's formal causes (for example, a stone sill's becoming *warm* as mentioned earlier), when understood as abstract concepts (for example, warmness), created endless arguments among medieval philosophers. The debate over the ontological status of these abstractions came to be known as the problem of universals, a conflict that practically lead to bloodshed in medieval universities. If the formal cause of a desk is its "deskness," where exactly does this mental "blueprint" reside? Inside the mind? Outside the mind? Or do these universals exist at all?

Porphyry (233–c.303) set the terms of the debate in his famous *Isagoge* or Introduction to Aristotle's *Categories* and then conveniently backed out of the argument.

> I shall beg off saying anything about (a) whether genera and species [universal concepts] are real or are situated in bare thoughts alone, (b) whether as real they are bodies or incorporeals, and (c) whether they are separated or in sensibles and have their reality in connection with them (*Isagoge*, 2).[110]

Porphyry, in effect, threw a grenade into the Middle Ages, a time bomb that exploded centuries after his own death.

Extreme medieval realists like Anselm believed (following Plato) that universals had an existence of their own – they were real. The individual things we observe in the world (desks, horses, etc.) are material copies of the immaterial forms of "deskness" or "horseness." On the other hand, medieval nominalists like William of Occam argued that universals were just names (with no ultimate reality) for the family resemblance we observe among the multitude of material objects. Moderate realists like Thomas Aquinas

---

110. An entire translation of the *Isagoge* can be found in Paul Vincent Spade, ed., *Five Texts on the Mediaeval Problem of Universals* (Indianapolis, IN: Hackett Publishing Co, 1994). This passage cited can be found on page 1 of Spade's text.

(following Aristotle) took a more nuanced position (see the list on "The Ontological Status of Universal Concepts" on page 175 of this chapter). Medieval universities were hotbeds of controversy between the realists and the nominalists as well as between the Averroists who held to a pagan reading of Aristotle (no divine creation, no divine providence) and the Thomists who sought to reconcile Aristotelian thought with the dynamic, providential, and creator God of the Bible.

One final comment needs to be made regarding the medieval fascination with number symbolism. Today number symbolism has little place outside the occult world of Tarot cards and astrology. But for the medievals the symbolism of numbers was a natural by-product of formal causality. There is a clear affinity between the science of numbers and formal causes. The very word, form, brings to mind a geometrical figure or shape. As today we believe the universe to be composed of tiny material atoms (and sub-atomic particles), the medievals believed the universe to be composed of immaterial shapes or forms that accounted for the design we see in the universe and its parts. Form was the principle of intelligibility and matter was the principle of individuality. Numbers were viewed as forms carried to the highest degree of abstraction. For example, behind the form, "triangle," was the more abstract form of "three" or "threeness." Plato and his medieval followers (like Boethius) believed the world to be composed of immaterial forms. Aristotle and his medieval followers (like Abelard) were somewhere between the realists and the nominalists. They believed that universal concepts were real but had no independent existence. These concepts, like metaphysical parasites, only existed as embedded in individual creatures.

The reader should take special note of the list on page 159 called "The Path of Philosophy." Western (European) philosophy originates on the Ionian coast of western Asia Minor before the time of Socrates. After its flourishing during the classical age of Greece and up until the flourishing of scholasticism at the University of Paris in the thirteenth century, philosophy sojourns outside of Europe proper – in Egypt, in Iraq, and in Andalusia (Islamic medieval Spain). Three books that tell the story of this sojourn in particularly engaging (if admittedly a tad romantic) fashion are Thomas Cahill's *Mysteries of the Middle Ages*, María Rosa Menocal's *The Ornament of the World: How Muslims, Jews, and Christians Created a Culture of Tolerance in Medieval Spain*, and Richard Rubenstein's *Aristotle's Children: How Christians, Muslims, and Jews Rediscovered Ancient Wisdom and Illuminated the Dark Ages*. These three books describe the flood of Greek classics flowing into Europe during the High Middle Ages, a story summarized on page 96 in the introduction to chapter five on the Seven Liberal Arts.

However, note that this story of philosophy sojourning outside of Europe fails to account for the flourishing of the works of Boethius, Pseudo-Dionysius, and John Scotus Erigena (and their Christian Platonism) during the Early Middle Ages.

Remember, following each list are bibliographic references to the relevant primary sources (A) that are listed in chronological order by the author's lifetime and secondary sources (B) that are listed in alphabetical order by the author's name.

PREMODERN CLASSIFICATIONS OF PHILOSOPHY

Classification of Philosophy in Aristotle

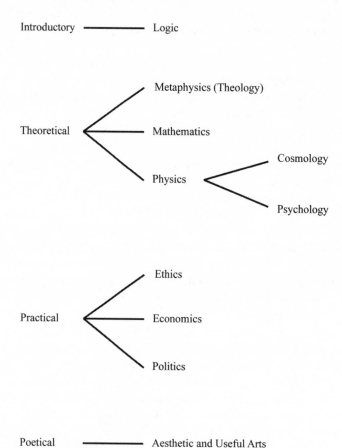

NOTE: "All knowledge is theoretical, practical, or poetical" (Aristotle, *Topics*, 145a).

    A. Aristotle, *Metaphysics*, 1025b25
      Aristotle, *Topics*, 145a
    B. Weisheipl, James A., "Classification of the Sciences in Medieval Thought,"
      Mediaeval Studies 27 (1965)

Classification of the Sciences in Al-Fārābi

I. The Linguistic Sciences (chapter one):

1. the science of single terms
2. the science of compound expressions
3. the science of the laws of single terms
4. the science of the laws of compound expressions
5. the science of orthography
6. the science of locution
7. the science of prosody and versification

II. Logic (chapter two):

1. rules of single terms (Aristotle's *Categories*)
2. rules of propositions (Aristotle's *On Interpretation*)
3. rules of general discourse (Aristotle's *Prior Analytics*)
4. rules of demonstrative arguments (Aristotle's *Posterior Analytics*)
5. rules of dialectical arguments (Aristotle's *Topics*)
6. sophistic reasoning (Aristotle's *On Sophistical Refutations*)
7. rhetorical arguments, oratory, and eloquent address (Aristotle's *Rhetoric*)
8. rules of poetic versification (Aristotle's *Poetics*)

NOTE: The medieval Arabic tradition expanded Aristotle's *Organon* to include eight rather than six of Aristotle's works. See page 128 in chapter six on Logic for more information.

III. Mathematics (chapter three):

1. arithmetic
2. geometry
3. optics
4. astronomy
5. music
6. dynamics
7. mechanics

NOTE: Note the inclusion of the four liberal arts of the quadrivium. See page 98 in chapter five on The Seven Liberal Arts for more information.

Classification of the Sciences in Al-Fārābi (continued)

IV. Physics and Metaphysics (chapter four):

Physics:

1. the principles that simple and compound natural bodies have in common
   (Aristotle's *Physics*)
2. the simple bodies (four elements) and the fifth heavenly element
   (Aristotle's *On the Heavens*)
3. the generation and corruption of natural bodies and elements
   (Aristotle's *Generation and Corruption*)
4. the principles of accidents and affections pertaining to the elements exclusively
   (first three books of Aristotle's *Meteorology*)
5. the bodies compounded from the simple elements
   (fourth book of the *Meteorology*)
6. the types of bodies made up of similar parts, like minerals and stones
   (attributed to Aristotle's *The Book of Minerals* which does not appear in ancient
   lists of Aristotle's books)
7. the varieties of plants
   (attributed to *The Book of Plants* which is not from Aristotle)
8. what animals have in common
   (Aristotle's *Book of Animals* and *De Anima*)

Metaphysics:

1. ontology: the study of existing entities insofar as they exist
   (book VII of Aristotle's *Metaphysics*)
2. epistemology: the first principles of particular sciences
   (book IV of the *Metaphysics*)
3. theology: the study of immaterial entities
   (owes more to Plotinus than Aristotle here)

V. Political Science, Jurisprudence, and Theology (chapter five):

Political Science:

1. politics (Aristotle's *Politics* was not translated into Arabic)
2. ethics (Aristotle's *Nicomachean Ethics*)

Jurisprudence (*fiqh*):

1. the part dealing with fundamental beliefs
2. the part dealing with particular actions

Theology (*kalām*):

1. the part dealing with beliefs
2. the part dealing with actions

PREMODERN CLASSIFICATIONS OF PHILOSOPHY (CONTINUED)

Classification of the Sciences in Al-Fārābi (continued)

NOTE: Nothing shows the vast extent of Islamic learning in the Early Middle Ages as clearly as Al-Fārābi's *Enumeration of the Sciences*. During this period in the West, the only Latin translation of Greek philosophical works available were Boethius' translation of two of Aristotle's logical works, the *Categories* and *On Interpretation* (often referred to as the *ars vetus* or the Old Logic), as well as Chalcidius' partial translation (about two-thirds) of Plato's *Timaeus*. At the time of Al-Fārābi (c.870-950) almost the entire Aristotelian corpus was available to Islamic scholars. As R. W. Southern notes concerning the Early Middle Ages, "A comparison of the literary catalogues of the West with the list of books available to Moslem scholars makes a painful impression on a Western mind" (citation below).

> A. Al-Fārābi, *The Enumeration of the Sciences* (only chapter five is translated into English and can be found in Joshua Parens and Joseph C. Macfarland, *Medieval Political Philosophy: A Sourcebook*, 2nd edition, pp. 18-23)
> B. Fakhry, Majid, *Al- Fārābi, Founder of Islamic Neoplatonism*, pp. 40-51
> Southern, R. W., *Western View of Islam in the Middle Ages*, p. 9.

Classification of Philosophy in Hugh of St. Victor

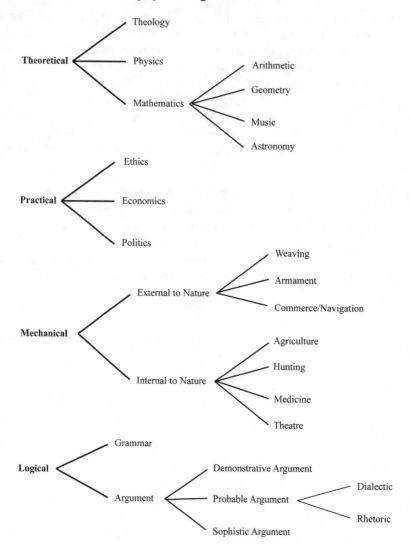

A. Hugh of St. Victor, *The Didascalicon: A Medieval Guide to the Arts*, III.1
B. Weisheipl, James A., "Classification of the Sciences in Medieval Thought," *Mediaeval Studies* 27 (1965), p. 66

PREMODERN CLASSIFICATIONS OF PHILOSOPHY (CONTINUED)

The Tree of Knowledge (School of Hugh of St. Victor)

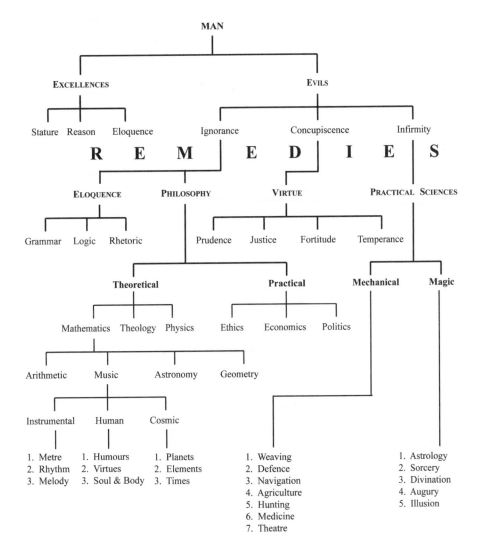

SOURCE: Reprinted with the kind permission of John Wiley & Sons Ltd. from R. W. Southern, *Medieval Humanism and Other Studies* (New York: Harper and Row, 1970), chart I.

PREMODERN SCHOOLS OF PHILOSOPHY

Pre-Socratic Philosophers

1. Thales: Water is the most basic element in the world; all things are filled with gods.

2. Anaximander: The "boundless" is the cause of all things.

3. Anaximenes: Air is the basic element in the universe.

4. Heraclitus: Fire is the basic element in the world; all natural phenomena are in a constant process of change ("you cannot step into the same river twice").

5. Xenophanes: One God is the cause of all things (as opposed to the polytheism of Homer and Hesiod).

6. Parmenides: Change is an illusion and a self-contradictory notion; while we perceive change the world is unchanging ("being is").

7. Zeno: Change and motion are illusions (see the famous "Paradoxes" by this student of Parmenides).

8. Empedocles: The world is composed of four elements (earth, air, fire, and water) and two sources of motion (love and strife).

9. Anaxagoras: Mind is the cause of all things.

10. Pythagoras: The essence of the universe is number and mathematical ratios.

NOTE: Pythagoras was the first Greek philosopher to say he was not a wise man but a lover (*philia*) of wisdom (*sophia*), that is, a philosopher.

NOTE: The atomists (Leucippus, Democritus and Epicurus) believed that the world consisted of indivisible bodies (atoms) moving in empty space.

> A. Diogenes Laertius, *Lives and Opinions of Eminent Philosophers*
> Cicero, *De Natura Deorum,* I.x ff.
> B. Burnet, John, *Early Greek Philosophy*
> Jones, W. T., *The Classical Mind*, 2nd edition, pp. 8-39

PREMODERN SCHOOLS OF PHILOSOPHY (CONTINUED)

The Golden Age of Greek Philosophy

1. Socrates: Turned from the naturalistic explorations of the pre-Socratics to self-knowledge and ethical speculation.

2. Plato: Argued that the sensible world reflected the more real world of Ideas (founded the Academy).

3. Aristotle: Organized formal logic as well as the natural sciences (founded the Lyceum).

    A. Cicero, *De Natura Deorum*
    B. Artz, Frederick, *The Mind of the Middle Ages*, pp. 10 ff.
      Jones, W. T., *The Classical Mind*, 2nd edition, pp. 108 ff.

PREMODERN SCHOOLS OF PHILOSOPHY (CONTINUED)

Hellenistic Schools of Philosophy

1. The Epicurean School: Followers of the Greek atomist, Epicurus, and the Roman atomist, Lucretius, preached salvation through atheism (overcoming fear of the gods leads to peace of mind).

2. The Stoic School: Roman followers of the Greek philosopher, Zeno (who founded the Stoa), taught an ascetic obedience to nature's order (natural law) as a means to peace of mind. These followers included Seneca, Epictetus, and Marcus Aurelius.

3. The Skeptic School: Critics of the dogmatism of the other schools of philosophy. Skeptics sought peace of mind by accepting that there is no conclusive evidence for any beliefs. Skeptics included Cicero (who held to a "modified" skepticism) and Sextus Empiricus.

(4). The Neo-Platonic School: Followers of Plotinus taught that rational argument led to a mystical vision of God that transcended all bodily experience. These followers included Porphyry and Proclus. For a brief summary of the cosmology of this school, see page 54.

    A. Cicero, *De Natura Deorum* (for schools up to his time)
    B. Artz, Frederick, *The Mind of the Middle Ages*, pp. 22 ff.
      Jones, W. T., *The Classical Mind*, 2nd edition, pp. 312 ff.

PREMODERN SCHOOLS OF PHILOSOPHY (CONTINUED)

Medieval Schools of Philosophy (University of Paris, 13th c.)

1. Christian Platonism: Alexander of Hales and his student, Bonaventure, taught traditional Platonic and Augustinian philosophy.

2. Latin Averroism: Siger of Brabant and Boethius of Dacia taught Averroes' strict interpretation of Aristotle. This interpretation:
    a) denied the creation of the world (affirmed its eternity),
    b) denied the immortality of individual human souls, and
    c) denied the active providence of God.

3. Christian Aristotelianism: Albert the Great and his student, Thomas Aquinas, reconciled Aristotle with biblical faith. This reconciliation:
    a) affirmed the creation of the world,
    b) affirmed the immortality of individual human souls, and
    c) affirmed the active providence of God.

NOTE: The Islamic theological tradition (see next page on Al-Ghazālī) is slightly different from Christian Aristotelianism in its *emphasis* on the resurrection of the body along with the immortality of the soul (not that the Christian tradition *denied* either).

    A. Averroes, *On the Harmony of Religion and Philosophy*, II (9.20)
    B. Artz, Frederick, *The Mind of the Middle Ages*, pp. 261 ff.
        Knowles, David, *The Evolution of Medieval Thought*, pp. 213-251
        Rubenstein, Richard, *Aristotle's Children*, p. 210

PREMODERN SCHOOLS OF PHILOSOPHY (CONTINUED)

The Three Major Heresies of Philosophers According to Al-Ghazālī

1. the assertion of the eternity of the world (Part One, 1st through 4th Discussions)

2. the assertion that God only knows universals, not particulars, and that there is no active Providence of God (Part One, 13th Discussion)

3. the assertion of the immateriality of the soul and consequent denial of a bodily resurrection (Part Two, 20th Discussion)

NOTE: By comparing this list with the previous list of Medieval Schools of Philosophy, it can be seen that Al-Ghazālī (1058-1111) set a high bar for religious orthodoxy and put philosophy (both Islamic and Western) on the defensive. Medieval philosophy was deeply influenced by the three major heresies outlined in Al-Ghazālī's *The Incoherence of the Philosophers*. In this work, Al-Ghazālī condemns seventeen philosophical doctrines as heretical innovations and three others (the ones above) as totally opposed to Islamic belief.

A. Al-Ghazālī, *The Incoherence of the Philosophers*
   Averroes, *The Harmony of Religion and Philosophy*, II (9.20)
B. Fakhry, Majid, *Islamic Philosophy, Theology and Mysticism: A Short Introduction*, p. 71

PREMODERN SCHOOLS OF PHILOSOPHY (CONTINUED)

Major Medieval Arabic Scholars

scholar	description	major work
1. Al-Kindī c.801–c.873	The first Arab philosopher. He defended Islamic dogma through the use of reason, but believed revelation to be superior to reason.	*Refutation of the Arguments of Atheists*
2. Al-Fārābi c.870-950	Founder of Arab neo-Platonism; also called the "second Aristotle." The first famous Arab philosopher.	*The Enumeration of the Sciences*
3. Ibn Sina (Avicenna) 980-1037	Champion of Arab neo-Platonism; also called the "third Aristotle." Read Aristotle's *Metaphysics* 40 times till Al-Fārābi's commentary enlightened him as to its meaning. Greatest physician of his day.	*Book of Healing*
4. Al-Ghazālī 1058-1111	Sufi mystic and harsh critic of Arab neo-Platonism and the works of Al-Fārābi and Avicenna.	*The Incoherence of the Philosophers*
5. Ibn Rushd (Averroes) 1126-1198	The greatest commentator on Aristotle among the Arabs. He defended philosophy against Al-Ghazālī and criticized Al-Fārābi and Avicenna for their divergence from Aristotle's teachings.	*On the Harmony of Religion and Philosophy*
6. Ibn 'Arabī 1165-1240	Sufi mystic who described mystical reality in neo-Platonic terminology.	*The Gems of Wisdom*

NOTE: Averroes was highly respected by Thomas Aquinas who referred to him simply as The Commentator in his *Summa Theologica*. However, his thought among the Latin medieval scholars remained controversial because of his alleged theory of "double-truth," where reason and revelation could never be harmonized nor could the truth of either be found to be superior to the truth of the other.

    A. See major works as listed.
    B. Fakhry, Majid, *A History of Islamic Philosophy*, 3rd edition

PREMODERN SCHOOLS OF PHILOSOPHY (CONTINUED)

Major Medieval Jewish Scholars

scholar	description	major work
(1.) Philo 15/10 BCE- 40/50 CE	Founder of medieval philosophy according to Harry Wolfson. Reconciled Judaism and philosophy by interpreting the Pentateuch allegorically.	*Torah* commentaries
2. Saadia ben Joseph 882-942	First philosophical account of Jewish dogma. First formulation of ten articles of faith that Maimonides expanded to 13.	*Book of the Doctrine of the Faith and the Grounds of Knowledge*
3. Solomon ibn Gabirol (Avicebron) c.1020-1060	Spanish Neoplatonist who shifted Jewish philosophy from the Islamic East to the Islamic West.	*Fons Vitae* (Source of Life)
4. Shlomo Yitzhaki (Rashi) 1040-1105	A Frenchman, born in Troyes, he is considered by many to be Judaism's greatest teacher.	*Torah* and *Talmud* commentaries
5. Judah Halevi 1085-1140	Spanish Jewish physician, poet and philosopher. *The Kuzari* is an *apologia* for Judaism in the form of a Platonic dialogue.	*The Kuzari*
6. Maimonides 1135-1204	Greatest Jewish scholar of the Middle Ages. Physician, merchant, lawyer, philosopher, and theologian. Famous "confession of faith" in 1168 expresses 13 tenets of Judaism.	*Guide of the Perplexed*

A. See major works as listed.
B. Artz, Frederick, *The Mind of the Middle Ages*, pp. 161-163

PREMODERN SCHOOLS OF PHILOSOPHY (CONTINUED)

Major Medieval Christian Scholars

scholar	description	major work
1. Augustine 354-430	The greatest Christian Platonist.	*City of God*
2. Boethius c.480-c.525	The greatest scholar of the "seminal period" to know Greek philosophy and logic.	*Consolation of Philosophy*
3. Pseudo-Dionysius 6th c.	Syrian monk whose Greek works reintroduced neo-Platonism into Latin Christendom.	*The Celestial Hierarchy*
4. John Scotus Erigena c.810-c.877	Rare scholar in the Early Middle Ages to know Greek. Irish monk, philosopher, and theologian.	*On the Division of Nature*
5. Anselm c.1033-1109	Celebrated the ontological proof for the existence of God.	*Proslogium*
6. Peter Abelard 1079-1142	The greatest and most combative logician of the Middle Ages.	*Sic et Non*
7. Bernard of Clairvaux 1091-1153	Arch-enemy of Abelard. Known for his mysticism.	*Sermons on the Song of Songs*
8. Peter Lombard c.1100-1161	Theologian who developed a scholastic, as distinct from a monastic, approach to Scripture.	*Four Books of Sentences*
9. Bonaventure 1221-1274	Most famous Franciscan medieval scholar.	*The Soul's Journey to God*
10. Thomas Aquinas c.1225-1274	Most famous Dominican medieval scholar. Master of the scholastic method.	*Summa Theologica*
11. Siger of Brabant c.1240-c.1280s	Latin Averroist condemned for heresy.	*De Aeternitate Mundi*
12. Roger Bacon c.1214-1294	British (and Franciscan) critic of scholastic method and advocate of experimental science.	*Opus Majus*

PREMODERN SCHOOLS OF PHILOSOPHY (CONTINUED)

Major Medieval Christian Scholars

scholar	description	major work
13. Duns Scotus c.1265-1307	Scottish (and Franciscan) metaphysician who championed the primacy of the will over the intellect.	*A Treatise on God as First Principle*
14. William of Occam c.1288-c.1348	British (and Franciscan) scholar who championed nominalism.	*Summa Logicae*

A. See major works as listed.

B. Jones, W. T., *The Medieval Mind*, 2nd edition

PREMODERN SCHOOLS OF PHILOSOPHY (CONTINUED)

The Path of Philosophy

1. Athens (Greece): The Classical Greek Phase

Socrates (d. 399 BCE; the founder of moral philosophy)
Plato (d. 348/347 BCE; student of Socrates, wrote philosophical dialogues)
Aristotle (d. 322 BCE; student of Plato, systematized logic)

2. Alexandria (Egypt): The Hellenistic Phase

Plotinus (d. 270; mystical Platonist)
Porphyry (d. 303; Plotinus' biographer, author of *Introduction to Aristotle's Categories*)
Augustine (d. 435; Christian Platonist)
Proclus (d. 485; last proponent of classical Greek pagan thought)

3. Baghdad (Iraq): The Arab-Islamic Phase One

Al-Kindī (d. 866; first Arab philosopher)
Al-Fārābi (d. 950; the "second Aristotle")
Avicenna (d. 1037; the "third Aristotle")
Al-Ghazālī (d. 1111; greatest medieval Islamic theologian, fierce critic of philosophy)

4. Cordova (Spain): The Arab-Islamic Phase Two

Averroes (d. 1198; the last great Arab philosopher)
Maimonides (d. 1204; greatest Jewish scholar of the Middle Ages)
Ibn 'Arabī (d. 1240; learned Sufi mystic)

5. Paris (France): The Latin Phase

Bonaventure (d. 1274; Christian Platonist)
Thomas Aquinas (d. 1274; Christian Aristotelian)
Siger of Brabant (d. c.1280s; Latin Averroist)

NOTE: For the philosophers on the Ionian coast of western Asia Minor before Socrates, see the earlier list on page 150, Pre-Socratic Philosophers. Note also that Christian Platonism was alive and well in the Early Middle Ages through Boethius, Pseudo-Dionysius, and John Scotus Erigena.

    A. See philosophers as listed.
    B. Fakhry, Majid, *Averroes: His Life, Works, and Influence*, pp. ix ff.
      Lewis, C. S., *Studies in Medieval and Renaissance Literature*, p. 45

Pythagorean Number Symbolism

Square Numbers (sequence of the sums of successive odd numbers)

1

1 + 3 = 4 (a square number)

1 + 3 + 5 = 9 (a square number)

Etc.

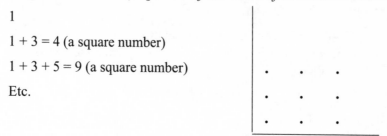

Oblong Numbers (sequence of the sums of successive even numbers)

2

2 + 4 = 6 (an oblong number)

2 + 4 + 6 = 12 (an oblong number)

Etc.

Triangle Numbers (sequence of the sums of successive whole numbers)

1

1 + 2 = 3 (a triangle number)

1 + 2 + 3 = 6 (a triangle number)

1 + 2 + 3 + 4 = 10 (a triangle number)

Etc.

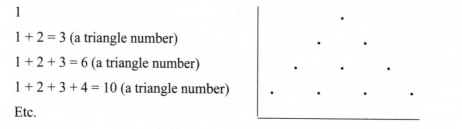

Pythagorean Number Symbolism (continued)

1 = Monad: The monad represents the point in geometry and is the symbol of unity. It is the source of all numbers. Other symbols include God and creation.

1 = .

2 = Dyad: The dyad represents the line in geometry and is the symbol of duality and diversity. It is the first female number (all even numbers were considered feminine in antiquity). Other symbols include Adam and Eve, the pairs of creatures in the Ark, and the two-fold nature of Christ (human and divine).

2 = . .   (oblong number)

3 = Triad: The triad represents the plane in geometry and is the symbol of divinity and of the harmony of unity and diversity. It is the first male number (all odd numbers were considered masculine in antiquity). Other symbols include the Trinity, the three theological virtues, and the three Magi.

3 =   .
     .   . (triangle number)

4 = Tetrad: The tetrad represents the solid in geometry and is the symbol of earth and its elements and the seasons. It is the first feminine square number (2 x 2). Other symbols include the evangelists and the cardinal virtues.

4 = . .
     . . (square number)

5 = Pentad: The pentad is the masculine marriage number because it is the first female number (2) *plus* the first male number (3). It is incorruptible because all multiples of 5 end in 5. Other symbols include the five senses, the wounds of Christ, the five books of Moses (the Torah), the points of a star, and the five geographic zones. Mary in Latin (*Maria*) has 5 letters.

5 = ...   (rectilinear number)

6 = Hexad: The hexad is the female marriage number because it is the first female number (2) *times* the first male number (3). It is the first perfect number because it equals the sum of its divisors (1 + 2 + 3). The second perfect number is 28 (1 + 2 + 4 + 7 + 14). Other symbols include the six ages of the world and the six days of creation.

6 = . . .
    . . . (oblong number)

Pythagorean Number Symbolism (continued)

7 = Heptad: The heptad is the virgin number because 7 has no factors and is not a factor of any number in the decad. It is the sum of the divine number (3) plus the earth number (4). Other symbols include the days of the week, the seven sorrows of Mary, the planets, the sacraments, the seven deadly sins, the seven tones of a musical scale, and the seven petitions in the Our Father.

7 = ... (rectilinear number)

8 = Octad: The octad is the first feminine cube (2 x 2 x 2). The first masculine cube is 27 (3 x 3 x 3). Other symbols include the Resurrection and regeneration (seven days of creation followed by the time of grace), and the Beatitudes.

8 = ...
    . . . .   (oblong number)

9 = Ennead: The ennead is the first masculine square (3 x 3). It is an incorruptible number because it reproduces itself when multiplied (e.g. 9 x 9 = 81 and 8 + 1 = 9). Other symbols include the nine choirs of angels.

9 = . . .
    . . .
    . . .   (square number)

10 = Decad: The decad is the Sacred Tetractys and the Symbol of the Universe. It is the sum of the archetypal numbers (1 + 2 + 3 + 4 = 10). Other symbols include the Ten Commandments and the lost tribes of Israel.

10 =   .
        . .
      . . .
    . . . . (triangle number)

NOTE: Pythagoreans distinguished *arithmetic* (number theory and number symbolism) from *logistic* (the art of computation used in mundane business matters).

A. Nicomachus, *Introduction to Arithmetic*, II.viii-xii
   Iamblichus, *The Theology of Arithmetic*
   Cassiodorus, *An Introduction to Divine and Human Readings*, II.iv.6-8
B. Calter, Paul, *Squaring the Circle: Geometry in Art & Architecture*, pp. 4-7
   Hopper, Vincent Foster, *Medieval Number Symbolism*, pp. 33-49

Pythagorean Table of Opposites

Limit	Unlimited
Odd	Even
One	Plurality
Right	Left
Male	Female
At Rest	Moving
Straight	Crooked
Light	Darkness
Good	Bad
Square	Oblong

NOTE: Odd numbers were considered masculine; even numbers feminine. Odds were considered stronger than evens because (a) unlike an odd number, when an even number is halved it has nothing in the center, (b) odd plus even always give odd, and (c) two evens can never produce an odd, while two odds produce an even. Because the birth of a son was considered more fortunate than the birth of a daughter, odd numbers became associated with good luck. "The gods delight in odd numbers," wrote Virgil in his *Ecologue*, viii.

Paul Calter, *Squaring the Circle*, pp. 5-6

A. Aristotle, *Metaphysics*, 986a
B. Calter, Paul, *Squaring the Circle*, p. 5

Pythagoras, West Portal, Chartres Cathedral

The Sacred Tetractys $(1 + 2 + 3 + 4 = 10)$

	Monad		
	[1]		

Odd & Even:

	Dyad	Triad	
	[2]	[3]	

Squares:

Tetrad	Pentad	Hexad
[2x2=4]	[2x3=6]	[3x3=9]

Cubes:

Heptad	Octad	Ennead	Decad
[2x2x2=8]	[2x2x3=12]	[2x3x3=18]	[3x3x3=27]
[8=earth]	[12=water]	[18=air]	[27=fire]

A. Iamblichus, *The Theology of Arithmetic*
B. Calter, Paul, *Squaring the Circle*, p. 7
   Hopper, Vincent Foster, *Medieval Number Symbolism*, p. 42

Plato's Lambda

progressions of body					progressions of soul
Point		1			The Monad
Line	2		3		First Even and Odd
Plane	4			9	First Even and Odd Squares
Solid	8			27	First Even and Odd Cubes

NOTE: These seven numbers are in the shape of the Greek letter, λ, lambda. According to Macrobius (II.ii.17): "The fabrication of the World-Soul, as we may easily see, proceeded alternately: after the monad, which is both even and uneven, an even number was introduced, namely, two; then followed the first uneven number, three; fourth in order came the second even number, four; in the fifth place came the second uneven number, nine; in the sixth place the third even number, eight; and in the seventh place the third uneven number, twenty-seven. Since the uneven numbers are considered masculine and the even feminine, God willed that the Soul which was to give birth to the universe should be born from the even and uneven, that is from the male and female; and that, since the Soul was destined to penetrate the solid universe, it should attain to those numbers representing solidity in either series."

> A. Plato, *Timaeus*, 35b-c
> Macrobius, *Commentary on the Dream of Scipio*, I.vi.45-47 and II.ii.17
> Hugh of St. Victor, *Didascalicon*, II.4-5
> B. Calter, Paul, *Squaring the Circle*, p. 22

The Platonic Solids

figure	description	corresponding element
1. tetrahedron	4 faces of equilateral triangles	fire
2. hexahedron (cube)	6 faces of squares	earth
3. octahedron	8 faces of equilateral triangles	air
4. icosahedron	20 faces of equilateral triangles	water
5. dodecahedron	12 faces of pentagons	the cosmos

NOTE: In a further attempt (as in Plato's lambda) to explain how the universe "devolved" from the immaterial world to the material world, in the *Timaeus* Plato describes the four basic elements as being comprised of four different geometric shapes. These geometric shapes or "atoms" combine with each other to produce physical forms. According to Plato the fifth sacred geometric form, the dodecahedron, symbolizes the spherical universe itself.

Since squares can be reduced to two triangles when divided diagonally, and since the triangle is the first geometric entity to have depth (points and lines are not tangible), Plato concludes that the universe is composed of triangles and that the triangle is the fundamental property of all sense objects.

A. Plato, *Timaeus*, 53c ff.
B. Calter, Paul, *Squaring the Circle*, pp. 295-304

The Platonic Solids (continued)

Tetrahedron (4 equilateral triangles):

NOTE: The tiniest and most mobile structure with the sharpest edges belongs to fire.

Hexahedron (6 squares):

NOTE: The structure which is the most immobile belongs to earth.

Octahedron (8 equilateral triangles):

NOTE: The structure in-between fire and earth in terms of mobility belongs to air.

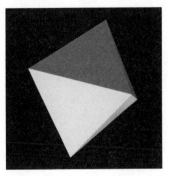

The Platonic Solids (continued)

Icosahedron (20 equilateral triangles):

NOTE: The largest structure and the least mobile of the first four elements belongs to water.

Dodecahedron (12 pentagons):

NOTE: The structure that most nearly approaches a sphere (i.e. the universe).

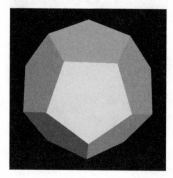

SOURCE: Compiled by Mark Grote.

Plato's Cave

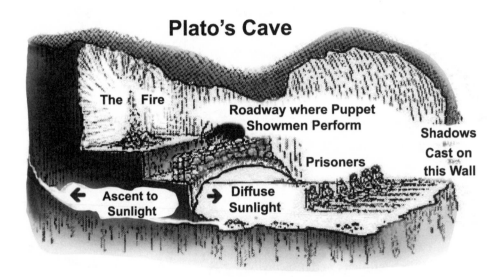

Plato's Divided Line and the Image of the Cave

objects in the cave	objects on the divided line	
Natural objects	Forms (Form of the Good)	
		THE SUN
Reflections of natural objects	Mathematical objects	
- - - - - - - - - - - - -	- - - - - - - - - - - - - - - - - -	- - - - -
Artifacts in front of fire	Physical objects	
		THE FIRE
Images of artifacts on cave wall	Images	

NOTE: Every society is a cave where the citizens that are shackled to the floor of the cave mistake the shadows on the cave wall for reality. The shadows are projected by each society's propagandists (e.g., poets, politicians, etc.). Each potential philosopher must be forcibly dragged out of the cave by his or her teacher to see reality outside the cave. Plato's "divided line" represents the ascent to truth that is part of his doctrine of Ideas. According to this theory, things that we perceive with our senses in the world are only pale and imperfect reflections of the eternal, immaterial Ideas in which they participate. For example, a desk is only an imperfect reflection of the Idea of "deskness" in the mind of the artisan who creates it. The story of the cave is a metaphor for Plato's theory of knowledge that corresponds to the "divided line."

    A. Plato, *Republic*, 514a ff.
       Averroes, *Averroes on Plato's Republic*, 74.15 ff.
    B. Jones, W. T., *The Classical Mind*, 2nd edition, pp. 126-138

Plato's Divided Line in Detail

mental object	mental faculty	
B -----------------	-----------------	
Forms (*archai*)	Intuition (*noēsis*)	
E ----------------	----------------	knowledge (*epistēmē*) of the intelligible world
Math objects (*mathēmatica*)	Thought (*dianoia*)	
C =============	=============	=============
Physical objects/artifacts (*zōa*)	Trust (*pistis*)	
D -----------------	-----------------	opinion (*doxa*) about the visible world
Images (*eikones*)	Imagination (*eikasia)*	
A ----------------	----------------	

NOTE: Proportions = AD:DC::CE:EB::AC:CB

A. Plato, *The Republic*, 509d ff.
B. Frederick Copleston, *A History of Philosophy*, vol. I, part III, chapter 19
   Jones, W. T., *The Classical Mind*, 2nd edition, pp. 126-138.

Aristotle's Four Causes

cause	example of a desk
1. material (intrinsic) cause	lumber
2. formal (intrinsic) cause	blueprint of the desk
3. efficient (extrinsic) cause	carpenter
4. final (extrinsic) cause	for writing, etc.

NOTE: Note that according to Aristotle's hylomorphic theory, form is the principle of intelligibility and matter is the principle of individuation.

    A. Aristotle, *Physics*, 194b ff.
       Aristotle, *Metaphysics*, 983a ff.
    B. Adler, Mortimer, *Aristotle for Everybody: Difficult Thought Made Easy*, pp. 39-48
       Copleston, Frederick C., *A History of Philosophy*, vol. I, part IV, chapter 29
       Veatch, Henry, *Aristotle: A Contemporary Appreciation*, pp. 41-49

Aristotle, West Portal, Chartres Cathedral

Aristotle's Five Predicables
(most fundamental distinctions defining things)

Example: "Human beings are rational animals."

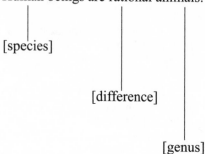

[species]

[difference]

[genus]

1. Genus/Genera = a broader classification (e.g. animals in above example)

2. Species = a narrower classification/sub-class of a genus (e.g. human beings in above example)

3. Difference = a characteristic which increases the meaning or definition of a class of things and decreases the number of things so defined (e.g. rational in above example)

- -

4. Property = a characteristic that is found in ALL the individuals of a species and not found in individuals of any other species (e.g. "capable of laughter" is a property of humans and only of humans).

5. Accident = a characteristic found in some members of a species, but not in all and found in other species (e.g. baldness is an accident of humans found in other species)

NOTE: Genus, species, difference, property, and accident are universal terms (universals) used in describing things in the world (particulars).

A. Aristotle, *Topics*, 101b38 ff.
Porphyry, *Isagoge*
Abelard, *Glosses of Peter Abelard on Porphyry*
B. Copleston, Frederick C., *A History of Philosophy*, vol. I, part IV, chapter 28
Kreeft, Peter, *Socratic Logic*, pp. 56 ff.
Ross, W. D., *Aristotle*, p. 55-56

Aristotle's Ten Categories
   (broadest classifications or genera in the universe)

categories	example	grammatical examples (parts of speech)
1. substance	man or house	nouns and pronouns
2. quantity	three yards long	adjectives
3. quality	white	adjectives
4. relation	double	prepositions and conjunctions
5. place	in the market-place	adverbs
6. time	last year	adverbs
7. posture	lies, sits	
8. habit (state)	armed, with shoes	
9. action	cuts	verbs
10. passion	is cut, is burnt	verbs

  A. Aristotle, *Categories*, 1b25 and *Topics*, 103b20-25
     Porphyry, *Isagoge*, 30
     Abelard, *Glosses of Peter Abelard on Porphyry*
  B. Copleston, Frederick C., *A History of Philosophy*, vol. I, part IV, chapter 28
     Kreeft, Peter, *Socratic Logic*, p. 55
     Ross, W. D., *Aristotle*, pp. 22-25

The Tree of Porphyry

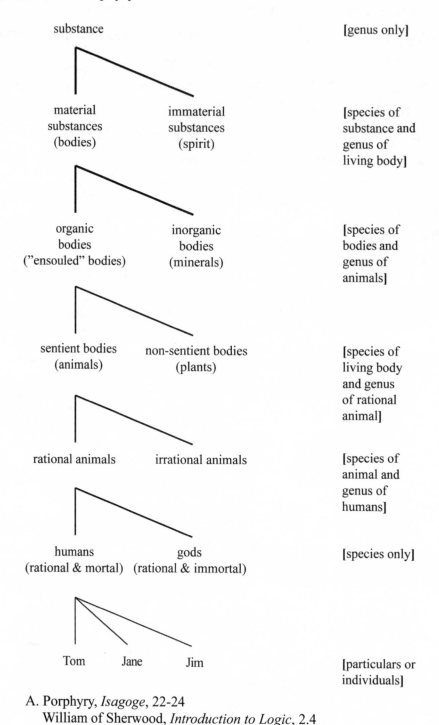

substance   [genus only]

material substances (bodies)   immaterial substances (spirit)   [species of substance and genus of living body]

organic bodies ("ensouled" bodies)   inorganic bodies (minerals)   [species of bodies and genus of animals]

sentient bodies (animals)   non-sentient bodies (plants)   [species of living body and genus of rational animal]

rational animals   irrational animals   [species of animal and genus of humans]

humans (rational & mortal)   gods (rational & immortal)   [species only]

Tom   Jane   Jim   [particulars or individuals]

A. Porphyry, *Isagoge*, 22-24
   William of Sherwood, *Introduction to Logic*, 2.4
B. Kreeft, Peter, *Socratic Logic*, p. 61

The Ontological Status of Universal Concepts

1. extreme realism = *universalia ante rem*

The doctrine that universal concepts (e.g., humanity or horseness) have separate and independent existence from the particular examples of the concepts (e.g., Socrates or Barbaro). According to the doctrine of realism, universals are independent, immaterial entities. Proponents of this position included Plato and Anselm.

2. nominalism = *universalia post rem*

The doctrine that universals are simple conventions used to describe particulars which share a "family" resemblance with each other. According to the doctrine of nominalism universals are mere linguistic conveniences with no real existence. Proponents of this position included Roscelin and William of Occam.

3. moderate realism = *unversalis in re*

The doctrine that universals exist within the particulars as a common likeness and exist in the human intellect as a concept formed from the focus of the intellect on that likeness. According to the doctrine of conceptualism, universals are neither entirely independent entities or entirely subjective mental states. They are mental abstractions reflecting real similarities among particulars. Proponents of this position included Aristotle, Abelard, and Thomas Aquinas.

- A. Aristotle, *Categories* and *Topics*
  Boethius, *Second Commentary on Porphyry's Isagoge*
  Abelard, *Glosses of Peter Abelard on Porphyry*
  John of Salisbury, *Metalogicon*, ii.17-20
- B. Artz, Frederick, *The Mind of the Middle* Ages, pp. 255-258
  Jones, W. T., *The Medieval Mind*, 2nd edition, pp. 185-196

The Ontological Argument for the Existence of God (paraphrase)

1. We have the concept of a greatest conceivable being which is God.

2. A greatest conceivable being existing in our mind is different from a greatest conceivable being existing in our mind and in reality.

3. A greatest conceivable being existing only in our mind is less than a greatest conceivable being existing in our mind and in reality.

4. A greatest conceivable being existing only in our mind is thus absurd, because no greatest conceivable being can be less than anything. If it were it would not be a greatest conceivable being.

5. Therefore, a greatest conceivable being exists in reality.

    A. Anselm, *Proslogion*, 2-3
    B. Copleston, Frederick, *History of Philosophy*, vol. II, part III, chapter 15

Thomas' Five Ways (proofs for existence of God)

First Way: Argument from Motion (paraphrase)

1. It is evident to the senses that some things are in motion.

    a. Motion is the transformation from potential energy to actual or kinetic energy. A thing at rest is potentially in motion

    b. A series of dominoes standing next to each other is potentially in motion and actually at rest.

2. Nothing moves from potentiality (e.g. wood is potentially hot) to actuality (e.g. fire is actually hot) by itself, but must be moved by some other thing actually in motion.

    a. Nothing comes from nothing. Nothing happens without a cause.

    b. A domino at rest can only be moved by something actually moving.

3. Since nothing moves itself except by some other thing, and this thing is moved by some other thing, and so on, we are left with an infinite regress of movers.

4. An infinite regress is impossible.

5. In order for there to be a casual process at all, there must be a mover which itself is not moved and this Unmoved Mover "everyone understands to be God."

NOTE: The Unmoved Mover is outside the stars and planetary spheres (see Cosmology chapter). Aristotle says: "There is, then, something which is always moved with an unceasing motion, which is motion in a circle; and this is plain not in theory but also in fact. Therefore the first heaven [the outer sphere] must be eternal. . . . And since that which is moved and moves is intermediate, there is something which moves without being moved, being eternal . . . . The final cause, then, produces motion as being loved, but all other things move by being moved" (*Metaphysics*, 1072a-b). Dante ends the *Paradiso* (XXXIII, 145) with a tribute: "The love that moves the Sun and the other stars."

    A. Aristotle, *Physics*, 241b24 ff.
       Aristotle, *Metaphysics*, 1072a21 ff.
       Thomas Aquinas, *Summa Theologica*, I, q. 2, a. 3
    B. Copleston, Frederick, *History of Philosophy*, vol. II, part V, chapter 34
       Kenny, Anthony, *The Five Ways: Saint Thomas' Proofs of God's Existence*,
          pp. 6-33
       Kreeft, Peter, *A Shorter Summa*, pp. 58-59

Thomas' Five Ways (continued)

Second Way: Argument from Efficient Causation (paraphrase)

1. It is evident to the senses that there is an order of efficient causation in the world (see the list of Aristotle's four causes in this chapter – material, formal, efficient, final).

2. Nothing can be the efficient cause of itself, but must have an efficient cause independent of itself. If this were not so, then a thing could be prior to itself, which is logically impossible.

3. Since the proximate cause of something (e.g. parents are the proximate of children) is dependent on remote or intermediate causes (e.g. grandparents are a remote cause of children) and remote causes are ultimately dependent on a first cause, without a first cause there could be no remote or proximate causes and no effects in the world.

4. It is clearly not the case that there are no causes and effects in the world.

5. There must be, in order for there to be a casual process at all, a first efficient cause which causes other things but is not itself caused. This is the First Cause "everyone gives the name of God."

    A. Aristotle, *Metaphysics*, 994a-b
       Maimonides, *The Guide of the Perplexed*, I.69
       Thomas Aquinas, *Summa Theologica*, I, q. 2, a. 3
    B. Copleston, Frederick, *History of Philosophy*, vol. II, part V, chapter 34
       Kenny, Anthony, *The Five Ways: Saint Thomas' Proofs of God's Existence*,
          pp. 34-45
       Kreeft, Peter, *A Shorter Summa*, pp. 60-61

Thomas' Five Ways (continued)

Third Way: Argument from Contingency (paraphrase)

1. We find in nature things that are possible to exist and possible not to exist. In other words, we find contingent beings that did not always exist in the past and will not always exist in the future. Everything we observe goes in and out of existence.

2. It cannot be the case that all things in the world are contingent (that all things are possible not to exist).

  a. What is possible not to exist once did not exist.
  b. If all things are possible not to exist, then at one time nothing existed.
  c. If at one time nothing existed, then nothing would now exist.
  d. It is obviously false that nothing now exists.

3. Since it is impossible that all things in nature exist contingently, then there must be something that exists necessarily.

4. But every necessary thing has its necessity caused by itself or caused by another. As has been stated in previous arguments, it is impossible to have an infinite regress of necessary beings whose necessity is caused by another.

5. We cannot help but conclude that there is some Being who exists necessarily of itself and not by another. This Necessary Being "everyone speaks of as God."

  A. Maimonides, *The Guide of the Perplexed*, II.1
     Thomas Aquinas, *Summa Theologica,* I, q. 2, a. 3
  B. Copleston, Frederick, *History of Philosophy*, vol. II part V, chapter 34
     Kenny, Anthony, *The Five Ways: Saint Thomas' Proofs of God's Existence*,
         pp. 46-69
     Kreeft, Peter, *A Shorter Summa*, pp. 61-62

Thomas' Five Ways (continued)

Fourth Way: Argument from Degrees of Perfection (paraphrase)

1. Human beings are able to make comparative judgments about worldly creatures or beings (e.g. beauty contests).

2. These judgments correspond to the varying degrees of perfection or value that exist in all beings. Some beings are more and some are less good than others, more and less beautiful, etc.

3. These comparative judgments cannot continue in an infinite regress (A more beautiful than B, B more beautiful than C, C more beautiful than D, etc.). We are only able to make judgments of value, to judge that something is more or less beautiful, because we have in our mind a standard of the greatest value or the most beautiful. In other words, better implies best.

4. The maximum value in any universal concept (e.g. truth, beauty, goodness, etc.) is the cause of all the lesser values.

5. There must be something that is to all being the cause of their being, goodness, and every other perfection and this "we call God."

    A. Aristotle, *Metaphysics*, 993b
       Thomas Aquinas, *Summa Theologica*, I, q. 2, a. 3
    B. Copleston, Frederick, *History of Philosophy*, vol. II, part V, chapter 34
       Kenny, Anthony, *The Five Ways: Saint Thomas' Proofs of God's Existence*,
          pp. 70-95
       Kreeft, Peter, *A Shorter Summa*, pp. 62-63

Thomas' Five Ways (continued)

Fifth Way: Argument from Design (paraphrase)

1. We observe inorganic objects (beings lacking intelligence) operating in nature towards a specific end (e.g. small bodies of water always flow downstream toward larger bodies of water).

2. Since the inorganic beings in nature always (or almost always) act the same way, it is obvious that they do not act randomly or according to chance.

3. Whatever lacks intelligence cannot move towards an end (or purpose) unless it is directed by a being endowed with knowledge and intelligence (e.g. an arrow moves towards its target as directed by the archer).

4. Therefore, some Intelligent Being exists by whom all natural things are directed towards their natural ends, and this being "we call God."

> A. Thomas Aquinas, *Summa Theologica*, I, q. 2, a. 3
> B. Copleston, Frederick, *History of Philosophy*, vol. II, part V, chapter 34
>   Kenny, Anthony, *The Five Ways: Saint Thomas' Proofs of God's Existence*, pp. 96-120
>   Kreeft, Peter, *A Shorter Summa*, p. 63

Thomas' Transcendentals (properties that necessarily accompany being)

1. unity (*unum*)

2. truth (*verum*)

3. goodness (*bonum*)

4. thing (*res*)

5. something, otherness (*aliquid*)

   A. Thomas Aquinas, *On Truth*, 1.1
   B. "Transcendentals," *New Catholic Encyclopedia*, 2nd edition, vol. 14

Divine Attributes (properties that necessarily accompany God)

attribute	Aristotle's *Metaphysics*	Thomas' *Summa Theologica*
1. aseity (self-existence)	1072b	I, q. 2, a.3
2. simplicity (immateriality)	1073a	I, q. 3
3. goodness	1072b	I, q. 6
4. infinity	1073a	I, q. 7
5. omnipresence		I, q. 8
6. immutability	1073a	I, q. 9
7. eternity	1073a	I, q. 10
8. unity (indivisibility)	1073a	I, q. 11
9. omniscience		I, q. 14, a. 12
10. omnipotence	1073a	I, q. 25, a. 3

NOTE: These divine attributes are not a medieval list *per se*, but are attributes (for the most part) common both to the pagan god of Aristotle and the Christian God of St. Thomas. In Aristotle, god's omniscience is problematic because his god does not know earthly things that are, in a physical and metaphysical sense, beneath it. There is also no Providence in Aristotle's god; a god that only contemplates itself. The same issue applies to omnipresence. Compare the Christian God where "the Word became flesh" (John 1:14) and is present or incarnate throughout creation. As noted below, Maimonides discusses these same attributes, but only in negative terms as a way of emphasizing God's utter transcendence. For example, God is not subject to death, God is not a body, God is not powerless, God is not ignorant, etc.

    A. Aristotle, *Metaphysics*, 1072b-1073a
       Maimonides, *Guide of the Perplexed*, I.58
       Thomas Aquinas, *Summa Theologica*, I, q. 2 ff.
    B. "God in Philosophy," *New Catholic Encyclopedia*, 2nd edition, vol. 6

VIII. Theology

It is the ascent to what *is* which we shall truly affirm to be philosophy.

Plato, *Republic*, 521c

Descend that you may ascend, and ascend to God.

St. Augustine, *Confessions*, IV.12

Introducing medieval theology is an overwhelming, not to mention hubristic, exercise. One modest approach is to say a couple things about medieval theological method. How did the medievals approach theology? It might be argued that their method of humility distinguishes them from the ancients and their method of allegory distinguishes them from the moderns. Theology existed long before the medievals came on the historical scene. Plato was perhaps the first thinker to systematize theology when he composed rational rules for our speeches about the gods (*theologia*) in the *Republic* (379a). However, the method of theology changed radically with the advent of the Christian revelation and its unusual emphasis on both the dignity and the equality of all human beings.

In antiquity the metaphor for theology (and philosophy) was always one of "ascent." In Plato's famous myth of the Cave (*Republic*, 514a ff.), the budding young philosopher is torn from his chains of ignorance and forced to ascend up and out of the Cave into the light where his sensitive eyes move from the reflections of natural objects in a pond, to those objects themselves and finally to the heavens and the source of all life – the Sun or the Good. Plato defines philosophy as the "ascent to what *is*" (521c). The philosopher is moved by intellectual *eros*, the love of the lower for the higher.

Furthermore, this path to divinity was a one-way street – straight up. Aristotle's god was too dignified to condescend to mere mortals. His "thought thinking itself" neither thought about human beings nor was moved by their suffering and prayers. The status of humanity in the cosmic scheme of things greatly increased after the Christian God descended into human flesh (divine Incarnation) to assist and save suffering humanity (anticipated by the divine intervention and descent into Egypt to rescue the Chosen People from their bondage). This Incarnation of the deity disrupted the ancient cosmic and social hierarchy.

Medieval poets and theologians began imitating the "descent" of the Incarnation of Christ where the "Word became flesh" (John 1:14). While medieval Christianity did not do away with the metaphor of ascent, it radically altered the method of ascent. As St. Augustine puts the matter in his famous dictum, "Descend that you may ascend, and ascend to God" (*Confessions*, IV.12). In Dante's journey to enlightenment, he begins by ascending a hill (metaphor for philosophy) toward the Sun but is pulled back by Virgil to take a more circuitous route to enlightenment. Like Christ himself, he must descend into Hell before he can ascend into the heavens. The metaphor of descent expresses punishment for sin, but also compassion for the sinner. Dante is saved from his exile by the compassion of his beloved Beatrice who "descends" from her place in Heaven to commission Virgil to lead Dante on the journey down into Hell and up to Purgatory and finally Heaven. The

Christian path to truth entails a descending love or *agapē* (compassion of the higher for the lower) as a prelude to the ascent of the soul. As a fine Dante commentator remarks:

> Although human nature is basically rational, it is also fallen, spiritually sick and weak, and it cannot recover from the consequences of this state through its own strength. In Dante's theology, the soul must humbly seek its strength from Christ. . . . The journey into Hell is also a journey towards humility.[111]

While Virgil is Dante's initial guide, his final guide into Heaven is St. Bernard of Clairvaux, author of the famous work, *On the Steps of Humility and Pride*.

In less poetic language St. Bernard notes that in the ascent to truth, humility and compassion precede contemplation.

> These are the three steps of truth. We ascend the first by striving to be humble, the second by compassion, the third in the ecstasy of contemplation. In the first, Truth is discovered to be severe; in the second, holy; in the third, pure. Reason leads to the first, in which we think about ourselves. Affection leads to the second, in which we think about others. Purity leads to the third, in which we are lifted up to see what is out of sight. (*On the Steps of Humility and Pride*, VI.19)

The proud contemplation of the ancient philosopher gave way to the humble contemplation of medieval monks and poets.

According to medieval Christian theology, human reason was weakened (but not destroyed) by the pride and sin of Adam. "After the Fall, not only was the belief in the events of the Bible necessary to salvation, but Adam and Eve and their descendents lost their ability to clearly see God's signs in nature."[112] Before the Fall, signs of God's activity in nature were "clearly legible." After the Fall, reason needed to be assisted by Scripture and purified by charity in order to function properly. And so St. Augustine recommended his famous metaphor of descent in theology ("descend that you may ascend"). While logic and dialectic (per Peter Abelard) had their place in medieval theology, this seat of honor had to be shared with emotion, humility, and charity (per Bernard of Clairvaux).

A major difference between medieval and modern theology centers on the medieval trust in allegory as a path to God. The Greek word *allēgoria* comes from a word meaning "to speak elsewhere than in the agora or public marketplace."[113] The word, allegory, carries the connotation of speaking secretly. Isidore of Seville referred to allegory as "other-speech" (*Etymologies*, I.xxxvii.22) and ancient grammarians referred to allegory by the formula, *aliud dicitur, aliud intelligitur* (one thing is said, another understood). While modern literary theory tends to distrust allegory as at best a form of irony and at worst a form of lying (that is, saying one thing and meaning another), the medievals could not avoid thinking allegorically. They viewed historical and natural events as significant beyond themselves because they viewed the entire world as significant beyond itself. The world is God's allegory. To refer back to the chart on page 10 in the Introduction:

---

111. Marguerite Mills Chiarenza, *The Divine Comedy: Tracing God's Art* (Boston: Twayne Publishers, 1989), p. 35.

112. Chiarenza, *Divine*, p. 119.

113. "Allegory," *The Dante Encyclopedia*, p. 24.

history	status of nature	explanation
the ancients (500 BCE to 500)	nature as divine (sacred object)	Nature is "full of gods" (Thales). Nature is eternal and perfect in the heavenly realm.
the medievals (500-1500)	nature as sacrament (sacred symbol)	Nature is neither divine nor eternal, but a product of divine activity. Like a sacrament, creation reveals and conceals God.
the moderns (1500-today)	nature as raw material (desacralized)	Nature has no spiritual status, but is merely raw material to be used for "the relief of man's estate" (Francis Bacon).

The world is a symbol that both reveals and conceals its speaker, God. The world is a word spoken by God. God said, "let there be light and there was light" (Genesis 1:3).

Stated otherwise, the medievals believed that God's invisible nature could be perceived through the visible nature created by God (Romans 1:20). However, in addition to speaking through the "book of Creation," God also speaks through the "book of Scripture." As a result of the Fall, as we have already noted, men and women needed an additional book, the "book of Scripture," in order to understand the world (if only imperfectly) and in order to achieve salvation.

The method of the allegorical interpretation of Scripture has its roots in Scripture itself. The sole occurrence of the word allegory in the New Testament occurs in Paul's interpretation of the story of Abraham's two sons. Abraham had one son by the slave woman, Hagar, and one by the free woman, Sarah. For Paul these two sons signify two different levels of meaning, one literal or historical and the other allegorical or spiritual. "Now this is an allegory: these women are two covenants" (Galatians 4:24). Hagar represents the Old Law and Sarah the New Law. In 2 Corinthians 3:6, St. Paul emphasizes the radical distinction between these two levels of interpretation: "For the letter [literal meaning] kills, but the spirit [allegorical meaning] gives life."

The early Christian theologians expanded on Paul's two-fold method by constructing a three-fold method of biblical interpretation based on Paul's division of human nature into body (sōma), soul (psychē), and spirit (pneuma) in I Thessalonians 5:23. As Origen argues, "Just as man, therefore, is said to consist of body, soul and spirit, so also does the holy scripture, which has been bestowed by the divine bounty for man's salvation" (On First Principles, IV.ii.4). In medieval times, this three-fold sense of literal (Jerusalem as the city of the Jews), moral (Jerusalem as the soul of the believer), and spiritual (Jerusalem as the City of God) interpretation developed into the four-fold sense that finds its classic exposition in Thomas' Summa Theologica. As an extension of the literal sense of Scripture, Thomas distinguishes three additional senses of Scripture.

Therefore, so far as things of the Old Law signify the things of the New Law, there is

186

the allegorical sense; so far as the things done in Christ, or so far as the things which signify Christ, are types of what we ought to do, there is the moral sense. But so far as they signify what relates to eternal glory, there is the anagogical sense. (*Summa Theologica*, I, q. 1, a.10)

Medieval school children learned a simple Latin poem to help them remember this four-fold sense of Scripture. *Littera gesta docet, quid credas allegoria, Moralis quid agas, quo tendas anagogia.* (The literal teaches what happened, allegory is what you believe, The moral is what you do, and anagogy is where you are heading.)[114]

Dante gives the most famous medieval example of this four-fold sense of Scripture in his philosophical work, *Convivio* (II.i). The literal or historical interpretation of the Exodus is the departure of the sons and daughters of Israel from Egypt. The allegorical sense of the Exodus is that the Exodus of the Old Covenant prefigures the redemption brought about by Christ in the New Covenant. The moral sense of the Exodus is the individual believer's "escape" from sin, the conversion of the soul from sin to grace. "In a sense deeply ingrained in the medieval reading of Scripture, each conversion from sin and each consequent salvation is an Exodus, a departure of God's people from Egypt."[115] Finally, the anagogic or eschatological sense of the Exodus relates to the departure of the soul from Earth to heavenly glory.

Dante clearly had these four senses in mind when he describes his boat ride in the *Divine Comedy* with over a hundred souls headed for Purgatory singing Psalm 113 in memory of the Exodus. As Dante recollects, "'*In exitu Israel de Aegypto*' they sang together with one voice, and went on, singing the entire psalm" (*Purgatorio*, II.46-48). For Dante, the mountain of Purgatory stands like a desert between the Hell of his fallen nature and the heavenly Jerusalem. It might be added that in the *Divine Comedy* Dante consciously blends the "allegory of the poets," where the fictitious events of the poets signify a true moral to the story as in Aesop's fables, from the "allegory of the theologians" where the true historical events of Scripture signify even deeper spiritual truths.

This idea of things signifying other things is not without significance. Granted, medieval allegorical interpretations were subject to abuse and exaggeration. However, compared to modern and postmodern methods of interpretation, medieval exegesis could appear almost rigorous. Medieval exegesis limited its interpretation to the four broad parameters of literal meaning, allegorical meaning, moral meaning, and anagogic meaning. Modern schools of deconstruction move from arguing like the medievals that a text has more than one meaning to arguing that it has an infinity of meanings. Texts signify whatever the reader reads into the text, based on his or her historical and political biases; they do not signify anything extra-textual.

According to deconstruction "theory," the very search for meaning in a book (the notion that words signify non-linguistic reality) is a theological delusion. The process of deconstruction destroys what literary critic George Steiner refers to as the age-old

---

114. This famous verse from the medieval schools is quoted by Nicholas of Lyra in the First Prologue to his *Postilla Litteralis*. This work can be found in J.-P. Migne, *Patrologie, Series Latina* (PL), vol. 113, col. 28. While the work has not been translated into English, the English translation of this particular verse can be found in the Introduction to James George Kiecker's translation of *The Postilla of Nicholas of Lyra on the Song of Songs*.

115. Chiarenza, *Divine*, p. 57.

"covenant between the word and the world."[116] This covenant is anathema to postmodern literary criticism, which posits that the very idea of "meaning" is fascist.

Meaning implies hierarchy and hierarchy is by definition politically oppressive. The search for meaning or for God creates binary oppositions that entail violent hierarchies wherein one of the terms is privileged over the other. For example:

1. Speech over writing
2. Being over non-being
3. Mind over body
4. Male over female
5. True over false
6. Nature over culture

One task of deconstruction is to "reverse the polarity of common binary oppositions like *male* and *female*, *day* and *night*, *light* and *dark*, and so on, so that the second term, rather than the first, is 'privileged' and regarded as the more desirable."[117] Ironically, deconstruction could create a new hierarchical system.

C. S. Lewis foresaw certain aspects of deconstruction and dismissed them under the nonsense word of "Bulverism."[118] As he notes in *The Discarded Image*: "Hardly any battery of facts could have persuaded a Greek that the universe had an attribute so repugnant to him as infinity; hardly any such battery could persuade a modern that it is hierarchical."[119] Like the Greeks, for the medievals it was unthinkable to view the universe as anything other than hierarchical. Everything in the universe signifies other things ultimately leading to God. The medievals accepted that, since the Fall of Adam, the world is no longer transparent. As Henri de Lubac says in *Medieval Exegesis*: "Without sin, the symbol of the world, in its unspoiled transparency, would have sufficed. Now, to decipher it, we need the help of Scripture."[120]

Scripture is needed to understand what the world signifies. De Lubac continues, "[Scripture] is like a great poem, with a pedagogical intent, whose inexhaustible significance leads us to the pure heights of the summit of contemplation."[121] Dante no doubt had the same intent when he penned his great poem, the *Divine Comedy*. In this chapter on Theology, we include special emphasis on what C. S. Lewis referred to as the three greatest achievements of the medievals, the great cathedrals, the *Summa Theologica* of Thomas Aquinas, and the *Divine Comedy* of Dante.

Before examining these theology lists, two issues need to be addressed. First, what principle distinguishes the lists in chapter seven, Philosophy, from this current chapter on Theology? For example, why include the proofs for the existence of God in the chapter on

---

116. George Steiner, *Real Presences* (Chicago: University of Chicago Press, 1991), p. 93.

117. Peter Barry, *Beginning Theory: An Introduction to Literary and Cultural Theory* (New York: Manchester University Press, 2009), p. 71. This task of reversal is only one interpretation of deconstruction. For a provocative argument that deconstruction leads to religion, see Gianni Vattimo's *After Christianity*.

118. Lewis, *God in the Dock*, pp. 271 ff.

119. Lewis, *Discarded*, p. 222.

120. Henri de Lubac, *Medieval Exegesis: The Four Senses of Scripture* (Grand Rapids, MI: William B. Eerdmans, 1998), vol. 1, p. 77.

121. De Lubac, *Medieval*, vol. 1, p. 77.

Philosophy rather than this chapter on Theology? In general this book follows a distinction by St. Thomas between two classes of revealed truths. As the Thomist Etienne Gilson explains: "The first one comprises a certain number of revealed truths which, though they be revealed, are nevertheless attainable by reason alone. Such are, for instance, the existence of God and His essential attributes, or the existence of the human soul and its immortality."[122] Following Thomas, the existence of God, the divine attributes, and the immortality of the soul are all dealt with in the chapter on Philosophy. Although these truths are attainable by the light of natural reason, they are also revealed so that all human beings (not just a small number of metaphysicians) might have access to these truths. The second group of revealed truths are "all that part of the Revelation which surpasses the whole range of human reason."[123] These truths include the Trinity, the Incarnation, and the Redemption, themes that are found in this chapter on Theology.

The study of this second group of revealed truths, theology proper, entailed the most extensive commitment of time and effort among the four faculties in medieval universities (the other three being the arts, law, and medicine). Completion of the most advanced degree in theology could take an additional 12 years of study after completion of the master of arts. While the numerous books of Aristotle may have ended up the major references for the first group of truths accessible to reason, Revelation was the preserve of two texts – Peter Lombard's *Sentences* and the Bible – for hundreds of years (1150 to 1500). As historian of science Edward Grant explains:

> The *Sentences* [of Peter Lombard] remained an enduring part of the university curriculum for approximately the same length of time as the works of Aristotle. Along with the Bible, it was one of the two basic textbooks of the faculty of theology. After hearing lectures on the Bible and the *Sentences* for a period of years, a student lectured on various books of the Bible and then became a "biblical bachelor" (*baccalaureus biblicus*), after which he became a "Sententiary bachelor" (*baccalaureus sententiarius*), lecturing on the *Sentences* of Peter Lombard.[124]

The "sentences" of Peter Lombard were a collection of patristic texts (texts of Church Fathers like Ambrose, Jerome, and Augustine) rearranged in a thematic structure following the Creed.

The first of the four *Books of the Sentences* treats of God and the Trinity; the second of creation and creatures; the third of the Incarnation, the Redemption, and the virtues; and the fourth of the seven sacraments and eschatology (see list on page 203 for a description of eschatalogy). Peter Lombard attempted to steer a middle course between respect for the ancient authorities (*auctoritates*) – the Church Fathers – and the use of logic and dialectic (*ratio*) – showing the influence of Peter Abelard. It might be noted that the vast majority of patristic quotes come from Augustine, giving his Platonic thought a place of prominence throughout the High and Later Middle Ages. Furthermore, it should be mentioned

122. Etienne Gilson, *Reason and Revelation in the Middle Ages* (New York: Charles Scribner's Sons, 1966), p. 82.

123. Gilson, *Reason*, p. 83.

124. Edward Grant, *God and Reason in the Middle Ages* (New York: Cambridge University Press, 2001), p. 210. Although the *Sentences* are not translated into English, an excellent account of its contents can be gleaned from Philipp W. Roseman's *Peter Lombard* (New York: Oxford University Press, 2004).

that despite the medieval obsession with the *Sentences* and the number of commentaries written on them, the basic text for theologians was "always the Bible."[125]

A second issue involves the decision to include lists on Islam. According to R. W. Southern in his *Western Views of Islam in the Middle Ages*:

> The existence of Islam was the most far-reaching problem in medieval Christendom. . . . As a theological problem it called persistently for some answer to the mystery of its existence: what was its providential role in history – was it a symptom of the world's last days or a state in the Christian development; a heresy, a schism, or a new religion; a work of man or devil; an obscene parody of Christianity, or a system of thought that deserved to be treated with respect? It was difficult to decide among these possibilities. But before deciding it was necessary to know the facts.[126]

Given the violent conflicts between all three Peoples of the Book today (Jew, Christian, and Moslem), it is even more important than it was in the Middle Ages to know the facts about Islam; hence the inclusion of Islamic lists in this chapter.

One other reason for the inclusion of Islamic lists is Dante's surprisingly positive attitude toward Islam in an age when the Christian view was so overwhelmingly negative. For instance, while Dante condemns numerous Popes to the nether regions of Hell, he relegates the Islamic warrior Saladin (*Inferno*, IV.129) and the Islamic scholars Avicenna and Averroes (*Inferno*, IV.143-144) to the comparatively milder region of Limbo, a region that includes heroes of pagan antiquity like Socrates and Plato (*Inferno* IV.135). Even more surprising, Dante places the infamous Latin Averroist Siger of Brabant within the famous Circle of the Sun in Paradise. See the list Souls of the Wise in the Circle of the Sun on page 234 as well as Dante's *Paradiso*, X.133-138. R. W. Southern believes that Dante's placement of these great Islamic figures (and Islamic sympathizers like Siger of Brabant) was his way of "acknowledging a debt of Christendom to Islam which went far beyond anything he could have expressed in words."[127] This debt of medieval Christendom to Islamic scholarship, while far from signaling agreement, has also been noted on page 96 in chapter five on the Seven Liberal Arts, and on page 143 in chapter seven on Philosophy.

Remember, following each list are bibliographic references to the relevant primary sources (A) that are listed in chronological order by the author's lifetime and secondary sources (B) that are listed in alphabetical order by the author's name.

---

125. James Weisheipl, *Friar Thomas D'Aquino: His Life, Thought and Works* (Washington, D.C.: The Catholic University of America Press, 1983), p. 110.

126. R. W. Southern, *Western Views of Islam in the Middle Ages* (Cambridge, MA: Harvard University Press, 1962), p. 3.

127. Southern, *Western*, p. 56.

The Neo-Platonic Triad

	Greek	Latin	description
1. The One/Good	*agathon*	*Deus*	Nothing can be predicated of the One "beyond being" (*hyperousia*).
2. The Divine Mind	*nous*	*mens*	Emanation of the One, the highest form of being.
3. The World-Soul	*psychē*	*anima*	Emanation of Mind, containing all particular souls including human souls.

NOTE: Both St. Paul and Plotinus spoke of a human triad of body (*sōma*), soul (*psychē*), and spirit (*pneuma*).

    A. Plato, *Republic*, 509b
      I Thessalonians 5:23
      Plotinus, *The Enneads*, V.i.7-8
      Macrobius, *Commentary on the Dream of Scipio*, I.vi.20 and I.xiv.6ff.
    B. Knowles, David, *The Evolution of Medieval Thought*, 2nd edition, pp. 22-26.

The Classical Spiritual World

beings	definition	place in cosmos
1. divine beings	rational aetherial animals (gods)	among the spheres (in aether)
2. daemonic beings	rational aerial animals (angels, demons)	between earth & moon (in air)
3. human beings	rational terrestrial animals (mortals)	on earth

NOTE: The Latin translation of Greek, *daimon* is *genius*.

    A. Plato, *Symposium*, 202e
    B. Dodds, E. R., *Pagan and Christian in an Age of Anxiety*
       Lewis, C. S., *The Discarded Image*, pp. 40-44

Three Pagan Theologies (according to the Roman writer, Varro)

1. natural theology: theology of the philosophers, monotheistic, only for the few

2. civil or political theology: theology of the priests, polytheistic, prescribes sacred rites and sacrifices that reinforce the laws of the city

3. mythical theology: theology of the poets, polytheistic, satisfies the multitude

    A. Augustine, *City of God*, VI.5
    B. Fortin, Ernest L., "St. Augustine," in Leo Strauss and Joseph Cropsey, eds., *History of Political Philosophy*, 3rd edition

Images of the Trinity in the Soul (Augustine)

1. memory (*memoria*) = the ability to understand and retain knowledge

2. intellect (*intelligentia*) = the content of one's learning based on a good memory and a studious will

3. will (*voluntas*) = the use of one's understanding (for good or evil) as well as one's tendency to rest in one's knowledge or aspire to further knowledge

    A. Augustine, *On the Trinity*, X.11
       Thomas Aquinas, *Summa Theologica*, I, q. 32, a.1
    B. "St. Augustine," *New Catholic Encyclopedia*, 2nd edition, vol. 1

Three Ages of the Bondage of the Will in Augustine

State of Innocence	→	Fall of Adam	→	State of Corruption	→	Christ	→	State of Redemption

- -

posse peccare		*non posse*	*non posse*
posse non peccare		*non peccare*	*peccare*

- -

able to sin		not able not	not able to
able not to sin		to sin	sin

NOTE: "Therefore the first liberty of the will was *to be able not to sin*, the last will be much greater, *not to be able to sin*."

Augustine

    A. Augustine, *Treatise on Rebuke and Grace*, chapter 33
    B. Russell, Jeffrey Burton, *A History of Heaven*, p. 85

Three Ages of the World According to Joachim of Fiore

ages	Latin title	description
1. Age of the Father (Old Testament times)	*ordo conjugatorum*	Began with Adam, flowered with Abraham, consummated in Christ (symbolized by the married state).
2. Age of the Son (early Christianity)	*ordo clericum*	Began with Hosea, flowered with Zachary (father of John the Baptist), consummated in Joachim's time (symbolized by the clerical state).
3. Age of the Holy Spirit (medieval times)	*ordo monachorum*	Began with St. Benedict and consummated at the end of the world (symbolized by the monastic state, "the saintly vanguard of redeemed humanity").

NOTE: Joachim was censored at the Fourth Lateran Council in 1215.

A. Joachim of Fiore, *The Book of Concordance*, II.1.4-9 in Bernard McGinn, *Apocalyptic Spirituality*, pp. 124-131
B. Eliade, Mircea, *The Myth of the Eternal Return*, p. 145
"Joachim of Fiore," *New Catholic Encyclopedia*, 2nd edition, vol. 7
Vattimo, Gianni, *After Christianity*, pp. 25 ff.

Three-Fold Punishment for Sin

punishment	restorative arts
1. the ignorance of the mind	theoretical arts restore lost knowledge
2. the lust of the flesh	practical arts restore lost virtue
3. the weakness of the body	mechanical arts ameliorate bodily weakness
	(logical arts insure clarity in pursuit of other arts)

NOTE: Hugh of St. Victor divides all knowledge (the arts) into four major categories of the mechanical arts, the practical arts, the liberal arts, and the logical arts. For this breakdown, see "Classification of Philosophy (Hugh of St. Victor)" on page 148 in chapter seven, Philosophy.

A. Hugh of St. Victor, *On the Sacraments of the Christian Faith*, I.viii.1
B. "Hugh of St. Victor," *New Catholic Encyclopedia*, 2nd edition, vol. 7

The Four Evangelists

evangelist	corresponding beast
Matthew	human/angel
Mark	lion
Luke	ox
John	eagle

A. Ezekiel 1:10
   Revelation 4:7
   Isidore of Seville, *Etymologies*, VI.ii.40
   Hugh of St. Victor, *Didascalicon*, IV.6
B. "Evangelists, Iconography of," *New Catholic Encyclopedia*, 2nd edition, vol. 5

The Four Horsemen of the Apocalypse

symbol	color of horse	description of rider
1. wild beasts	white horse	prince aiming a bow
2. warfare	red horse	warrior swinging a sword
3. famine	black horse	banker carrying measuring scales
4. plague/death	green horse	cadaver holding a pitchfork

    A. Revelation 6:1-8
    B. "Revelation, Book of," *New Catholic Encyclopedia*, 2nd edition, vol. 12

Albrecht Dürer *Apocalypse*, 1498

The Four Islamic Schools of Theology (*kalām*)

schools	description
1. Esoterics (*bātiniyah*)	The experience of God is more important than reason. Allegorical interpretation of the Qur'ān is based on mystical experiences (e.g., Heaven and Hell are interpreted as states of the soul).
2. Literalists (*hashwiyah*)	No interpretation of the Qur'ān is allowed. Only the literal meaning is accepted. Similar to Christian fundamentalists.
3. Mu'tazalītes	Theological liberals. The Qur'ān is the created word of God. God's justice and human free will are affirmed in his tradition.
4. Ash'arītes	Theological conservatives. The Qur'ān is the uncreated, eternal word of God. God acts miraculously in the world (denial of necessary causation). Al-Ghazālī was the pre-eminent member of this school.

A. Averroes, *Al-Kashf'an Manāhij al-Adillah* (not translated into English)
B. Fakhry, Majid, *Averroes*, p. 167

Four Islamic Sources of Law

source	description
1. Qur'ān	The primary source of Islamic jurisprudence, mostly passages from the Medinan period which make up about 10% of the Qur'ān.
2. Sunnah	The Prophet's own actions, customs, and rulings as understood from the massive *h□adīth* literature.
3. *ijmā*	The consensus of the community of legal scholars. The early consensus is gleaned from the rulings of the Prophet, his Companions, and their Successors.
4. *qiyās*	Analogical and syllogistic reasoning for situations not mentioned in the Qur'ān or in *h□adīth* literature. For example, since grapevine drinks (intoxicants) are forbidden, it is reasonable to assert that vodka is forbidden.

A. Averroes, *On the Harmony of Religion and Philosophy*, cf. I (1.8, 2.10) and II (8.7)

B. "Islam: An Overview," *Encyclopedia of Religion*, 2nd edition, vol. 7

Five Categories of Behavior in Islamic Law

legal category	definition	examples
Obligatory (*wājib*)	An activity, the neglect of which is punished and the doing of which is rewarded.	Prayer is an individual duty and *jihād* a collective duty.
Recommended (*mandūb*)	An activity, the neglect of which is not punished and the doing of which is rewarded.	Extra prayers and fasts or pious deeds beyond the five pillars of Islam.
Permitted (*mubāh*)	A morally indifferent activity of which there is no reward or punishment for performance or neglect.	Marriage to one of the People of the Book (i.e., Moslems, Jews, Christians).
Discouraged (*makrūh*)	An activity, the avoidance of which is rewarded, but the doing of which is not punished.	Divorce.
Prohibited (*mah□z□ūr*)	An activity, the avoidance of which is rewarded and the doing of which is punished.	Theft, adultery, drunkenness (*hudud* offenses).

A. Averroes, *On the Harmony of Religion and Philosophy*, I (1.9)
B. Ruthven, Malise, *Islam: A Very Short Introduction*, p. 85

Five Constituents of Islamic Faith (*īmān*)

1. belief in God

2. belief in angels

3. belief in revealed books

4. belief in God's messengers

5. belief in the Last Day (of Judgment)

    A. *Al-Qur'ān* 4:136
    B. "Islam: An Overview," *Encyclopedia of Religion*, 2nd edition, vol. 7

Five Pillars of Islam

1. confession of faith (*shahādah*)	"There is no god but God" (Q. 37:35) and "Muhammad is the messenger of God" (Q. 33:40).
2. prayer (*salāt*)	Prayers the Muslim must perform, facing Mecca (Q. 2:144), five times a day at daybreak, noon, mid-afternoon, sunset, and upon retiring.
3. almsgiving (*zakāt*)	Almsgiving or the duty to give to the poor based on one's wealth in order to ease the economic hardship of others and eliminate inequality (e.g., Q. 2:43).
4. fasting (*sawm*)	Fasting obligatory during the month of *Ramadan* between sunrise and sunset. Muslims must abstain from food, drink, and sexual intercourse at this time (Q. 2:185).
5. pilgrimage (*hajj*)	A pilgrimage made to Mecca at least once in one's lifetime for those that are physically and financially able to do so (e.g., Q. 2:196).

A. *Al-Qur'ān* (see specific passages above)
B. Feuerstein, Georg, *Spirituality by the Numbers*, pp. 99-101
　Ruthven, Malise, *Islam: A Very Short Introduction*, pp. 143-148

Mezquita Cathedral in Córdova

Eschatology (study of the last things)

1. death (due to sin: Genesis 2:17, Romans 5:12)

2. judgment (Matthew 25:31-33)

3. Heaven (Acts 7:55)

4. Hell (Matthew 25:41, Revelation 21:8)

5. second coming of Christ or *Parousia* (Matthew 24:30, Revelation 21:1)

NOTE: Catholic tradition argues for Purgatory by appealing to 2 Maccabees 12:38-46.

> A. The Bible
> B. "Eschatology," *The New Dictionary of Theology*

The Five Places of the Medieval Universe

1. Heaven (a place of only good and of the highest good)

2. Paradise (a place of only good, but not of the highest good)

3. the world (a place of good and evil)

4. Purgatory (a place of only evil, but not of the greatest evil)

5. Hell (a place of only evil and of the greatest evil)

> A. Hugh of St. Victor, *On the Sacraments of the Christian Faith*, I.viii.2
> B. "Hugh of St. Victor," *New Catholic Encyclopedia*, 2nd edition, vol. 7

Macrobius' Five Species of Dreams

With Divination

1. *Somnium* (dreams show truth in allegorical form; e.g. Pharaoh's dream of fat and lean cattle)

2. *Visio* (direct vision of the future)

3. *Oraculum* (venerable person appears to dreamer and foretells the future)

Without Divination

4. *Insomnium* (repeats preoccupations of the day, working, etc.)

5. *Visum* (dreams when half-awake, nightmares included here)

A. Macrobius, *Commentary on the Dream of Scipio*, I.iii.1-20
B. Lewis C. S., *The Discarded Image*, pp. 63-65

Six Ages of the World

1. Adam to Noah

2. Noah to Abraham

3. Abraham to David

4. David to the Exile in Babylon

5. The Exile in Babylon to Christ

6. Christ to the Second Coming

NOTE: "For we call the works of foundation the creation of all things; but the works of restoration, wherein the sacrament of redemption was fulfilled or was figured by which those things which had perished were restored. Therefore, the works of foundation are those which were made at the beginning of the world in six days; but the works of restoration, those which from the beginning of the world are made in six ages for the renewal of man."
Hugh of St. Victor, *On the Sacraments of the Christian Faith*, I, i, 28

A. Augustine, *City of God*, XXII.30
Isidore of Seville, *Etymologies*, V.xxxviii-xxxix
Hugh of St. Victor, *On the Sacraments of the Christian Faith*, I.i.28
B. Cook, William R. and Ronald B. Herzman, *The Medieval Worldview: An Introduction*, p. 84
Guardini, Romano, *The End of the Modern World*, p. 18

Six Days of Creation

Acts of distinction or separation

1. light (God separates light and dark)

2. sky (God separates the watery chaos below the earth from the waters above the heavens)

3. earth (God separates dry land from the seas and the earth puts forth vegetation)

Acts of adornment (creatures with local motion)

4. planets and stars (the lights that inhabit the heavens)

5. fish (in the seas) and birds (in the sky)

6. animals (that inhabit the earth) and humans (made in God's image; male and female)

A. Genesis 1:1 to 2:3
Hugh of St. Victor, *On the Sacraments of the Christian Faith*, I.i.24-25
Thomas Aquinas, *Summa Theologica*, I, q. 67 ff. (distinction) and I, q. 70 ff. (adornment)
B. Kass, Leon, *The Beginning of Wisdom: Reading Genesis*, p. 29 ff.

Seven Sacraments

sacrament	action	purpose	virtue
Baptism (Mt 3:11)	pouring of water on the head of recipient by bishop, priest, or deacon (or anyone in emergency)	to remove original sin	faith
Penance (Jn 20:22)	confession of one's sins to a bishop or priest	to heal the penitent	justice
Eucharist (Lk 22:19)	transformation of bread and wine into the body and blood of Christ by a bishop or priest	communion with God	charity
Confirmation	anointing with chrism by a bishop	to strengthen the grace of baptism	courage
Matrimony (Gn 2:18)	establishes a permanent bond between spouses by spouses themselves (priest only witnesses)	provides grace for the spouses in building up the Church through their family	temperance
Holy Orders (I Tim 3:2)	ordination of a priest by the laying on of hands by a bishop	confers on the priest the power to celebrate the sacraments and liturgy	prudence
Anointing of Sick (Jm 5:14)	anointing of the sick with oil by bishop or priest	healing and grace	hope

NOTE: "A sacrament is the sign of a sacred thing" (Hugh of St. Victor, *On the Sacraments of the Christian Faith* I.ix.2). Baptism, Confirmation, and the Eucharist have been called Sacraments of Initiation. Penance and Anointing have been called Sacraments of Healing. Holy Orders and Matrimony have been called Sacraments of Vocation.

    A. Thomas Aquinas, *Summa Theologica*, III, q. 65, a. 1.
    B. "Sacramental Theology," *New Catholic Encyclopedia*, 2nd edition, vol. 12

Seven Petitions in the Lord's Prayer (*Pater Noster*)

1. Hallowed be thy name

2. Thy kingdom come

3. Thy will be done on earth as it is in Heaven

4. Give us this day our daily bread

5. Forgive us our trespasses as we forgive those who trespass against us

6. Lead us not into temptation

7. Deliver us from evil

NOTE: Some sources condense the sixth and seventh petitions into one combined sixth petition, "lead us not into temptation, but deliver us from evil."

    A. Matthew 6:9-13 (Luke 11:2-4 provides a shorter version of the Lord's Prayer)
    B. "Lord's Prayer," *New Dictionary of Catholic Spirituality*
       "Lord's Prayer, The," *New Catholic Encyclopedia*, 2nd edition, vol. 8

Seven Corporal Works of Mercy

1. Feed the hungry

2. Give drink to the thirsty

3. Welcome the stranger

4. Clothe the naked

5. Visit the sick

6. Visit the prisoner

7. Bury the dead

    A. Matthew 25:31-46 (first six works)
       Tobit 1:17 (the seventh work about burying the dead)
    B. "Mercy, Works of," *New Catholic Encyclopedia*, 2nd edition, vol. 9

Eight Beatitudes

1. Blessed are the poor in spirit, for theirs is the kingdom of Heaven.

2. Blessed are the meek, for they shall possess the land.

3. Blessed are they who mourn, for they shall be comforted.

4. Blessed are they that hunger and thirst after justice, for they shall have their fill.

5. Blessed are the merciful, for they shall obtain mercy.

6. Blessed are the clean of heart, for they shall see God.

7. Blessed are the peacemakers, for they shall be called the children of God.

8. Blessed are they that suffer persecution for justice' sake, for theirs is the kingdom of Heaven.

    A. Matthew 5:1-11
    B. Feurstein, Georg, *Spirituality by the Numbers*, pp. 154-156

Nine Choirs of Angels (according to Pseudo-Dionysius)

Highest hierarchy: (contemplates the power of the Father)	Seraphim (Isaiah 6:2)
	Cherubim (Ezekiel 10:15)
	Thrones (Colossians 1:16)
Middle hierarchy: (contemplates the wisdom of the Son)	Dominations (Ephesians 1:21)
	Virtues (Ephesians 1:21)
	Powers (Ephesians 1:21)
Lowest hierarchy: (contemplates the love of the Holy Spirit)	Principalities (Ephesians 1:21) (guardians of nations)
	Archangels (Jude 9) (guardians of individuals, e.g., Michael)
	Angels (many Scripture passages) (guardians of individuals, e.g., Gabriel)

A. Pseudo-Dionysius, *On the Celestial Hierarchies*, chapters 6-9
   Isidore of Seville, *Etymologies*, VII.v
   Thomas Aquinas, *Summa Theologica*, I, q. 108, a. 5-6
   Dante, *Convivio*, II.v
B. "Angels," *New Catholic Encyclopedia*, 2nd edition, vol. 1
   Lewis, C. S., *The Discarded Image*, pp. 70-75

Twelve Tribes of Israel

	tribe	emblem
1.	Judah (east camp)	lion cub
2.	Isaachar	donkey
3.	Zebulun	ship
4.	Reuben (south)	rising sun
5.	Simeon	tower
6.	Gad	tent
7.	Ephraim (west)	bull
8.	Mannaseh	palm tree
9.	Benjamin	wolf
10.	Dan (north)	serpent
11.	Asher	olive tree
12.	Naphtali	doe

NOTE: During the forty years wandering in the wilderness, the Israelites set up camp in the form of a square with the Holy of Holies in the middle. The three first tribes above were to the east of the tabernacle, the next three to the south, etc. Some traditions claim the encampment pattern was based on the signs of the zodiac, although that correspondence has been lost.

A. Numbers 1:5-15 and 2:1-32
B. Feuerstein, Georg, *Spirituality by the Numbers*, pp. 188-189

Twelve Apostles

1. Peter   (originally Simon)

2. Andrew   (brother of Peter)

3. James   (son of Zebedee, brother of John, also called James the Greater)

4. John   (brother of James)

5. Philip

6. Bartholomew   (also called Nathaniel)

7. Thomas   (the twin)

8. James   (son of Alphaeus, also called James the Lesser)

9. Matthew   (tax collector)

10. Simon   (the Zealot)

11. Judas Iscariot (traitor to Jesus, later replaced by Matthias)

12. Thaddaeus   (Mark); Judas (Luke)

    A. Matthew 10:1-4
       Mark 3:13-19
       Luke 6:12-16
       Isidore of Seville, *Etymologies*, VII.ix
    B. Feuerstein, Georg, *Spirituality by the Numbers*, pp. 191-192

Thirteen Cardinal Tenets of Judaism

1.   The existence of God.

2.   The unique unity of God, which is an oneness unlike any other.

3.   God has no material being, and all biblical references to parts of God's body must be understood purely metaphorically.

4.   God is eternal.

5.   God alone deserves to be worshipped.

6.   The words of the prophets are messages from God.

7.   Moses was the greatest of the prophets, and he alone received God's word in full consciousness.

8.   Moses received the entire Torah directly from God.

9.   Nothing may ever be added or omitted from the Torah.

10. God is aware of all human behavior.

11. After death, God rewards the good and punishes the wicked.

12. God will send the Messiah.

13. Upon the coming of the Messiah, the dead will be resurrected in bodily form.

NOTE: The Torah refers to the first five books of the Hebrew Scriptures: Genesis, Exodus, Leviticus, Numbers, and Deuteronomy. These books contain the 613 commandments (*mitzvot*) according to rabbinical tradition, including 248 positive rules (corresponding to the number of bones in the body according to Aristotle) and 365 negative rules (corresponding to the number of days in the year).

> A. Maimonides, Moses, *A Maimonides Reader* (edited by Isadore Twersky), pp. 417-423
>
> B. Feuerstein, Georg, *Spirituality by the Numbers*, pp. 198-199

Maimonides, Bronze Statue in Córdova

MEDIEVAL EXEGESIS OF SCRIPTURE

St. Paul's Two Meanings of Scripture

interpretation	covenants	figures
1. literal	Old Law (Moses)	Hagar
2. allegorical (spiritual)	New Law (Christ)	Sarah

NOTE: St. Paul explains the story of Abraham's two sons, one by the slave woman, Hagar, and one by the free woman, Sarah. "Now this is an allegory: these women are two covenants" (Galatians 4:24). And his twofold interpretation is stated most dramatically in 2 Corinthians 3:6: "For the letter (*gramma*) kills, but the Spirit (*pneuma*) gives life."

> A. 2 Corinthians 3:6
> Galatians 4:24
> B. De Lubac, Henri, *Medieval Exegesis*, vol. 1, p. 225 ff.

Origen's Threefold Sense

interpretation	aspect of human nature (cf. 1 Thessalonians 5:23)
1. historical	body (*sōma*)
2. moral	soul (*psychē*)
3. spiritual/mystical	spirit (*pneuma*)

NOTE: "Just as man, therefore, is said to consist of body, soul and spirit, so also does the holy scripture, which has been bestowed by the divine bounty for man's salvation."

Origen

> A. Origen, *On First Principles*, IV.ii.4
> B. De Lubac, Henri, *Medieval Exegesis*, vol. 1, p. 143

MEDIEVAL EXEGESIS OF SCRIPTURE (CONTINUED)

Cassian's Three Spiritual Senses (cf. Proverbs 22:20)

interpretation	example of Jerusalem	theological virtue
(historical assumed)	city of the Jews	
1. allegorical	church of Christ (on earth)	faith
2. eschatological	heavenly City of God	hope
3. moral	soul of man	charity

A. Cassian, John, *Conferences*, XIV.8
B. "Exegesis, Biblical," *New Catholic Encyclopedia*, 2nd edition, vol. 5

Medieval Fourfold Sense (in the traditional order)

interpretation	example of the Exodus from Dante
1 historical (literal)	Departure of the sons of Israel from Egypt
2. allegorical (dogmatic)	Redemption brought about by Christ (New Covant)
3. moral (tropological)	Conversion of the soul from sin to grace
4. eschatalogical (anagogic)	Departure of the soul from earth to eternal glory

A. Thomas Aquinas, *Summa Theologica*, I, q. 1, a. 10
   Dante, *Convivio*, II.i
B. De Lubac, Henri, *Medieval Exegesis*, vol. 2, pp. 197 ff.

MEDIEVAL EXEGESIS OF SCRIPTURE (CONTINUED)

Latin Mnemonic Verse (for remembering the four levels of meaning)

Littera gesta docet,	The literal teaches what happened,
quid credas allegoria,	Allegory is what you believe,
Moralis quid agas,	The moral is what you do,
quo tendas anagogia.	Anagogy is where you are heading.

NOTE: This famous verse from the medieval schools is quoted by Nicholas of Lyra in the First Prologue to his *Postilla Litteralis*. This work can be found in J.-P. Migne, *Patrologie, Series Latina* (PL), vol. 113, col. 28. While the work has not been translated into English, the English translation of this particular verse can be found in the Introduction to James George Kiecker's translation of *The Postilla of Nicholas of Lyra on the Song of Songs*.

> A. Nicholas of Lyra, Introduction to *The Postilla of Nicholas of Lyra on the Song of Songs*, p. 15.
> B. De Lubac, Henri, *Medieval Exegesis*, vol. 1, p. 1
> Vattimo, Gianni, *After Christianity,* p. 28

Three Types of Truth in the Qur'ān (Averroes)

type of truth	class of people
1. demonstrative (certain truth)	philosophers
2. dialectical (probable truth)	theologians
3. rhetorical (poetic truth)	simple believers

NOTE: For a further description of the three types of truth see the list Three Types of Arguments (Material Division) on page 137 in chapter six on Logic. For a further description of the classes of people see the list The Tripartite Soul in Plato in chapter four on Psychology.

> A. Averroes, *On the Harmony of Religion and Philosophy*, II (15.1-15)
> B. Artz, Frederick, *The Mind of the Middle Ages*, pp. 160-161
> Gilson, Etienne, *Reason and Revelation in the Middle Ages*, pp. 42 ff.
> Knowles, David, *The Evolution of Medieval Thought*, 2nd edition, p. 182

OUTLINE OF MONASTICISM

Major Medieval Monastic Orders

	founder(s)	origin (date/place)	highlights
Benedictine Orders			
Benedictines	St. Benedict of Nursia	529 Monte Cassino, Italy	First monastic order based on famous *Rule of St. Benedict.*
Cluniacs	William of Aquitaine	910 Cluny, France	Revival of the strict observance of the Benedictine rule that became a huge monastic empire.
Cistercians	St. Robert of Molesme (expansion of order due to St. Bernard of Clairvaux)	1098 Citeaux, France	Austere reform of the Benedictine order in contrast to the Cluniac empire.
Eremitical Orders			
Camoldolese	St. Romuald	1022 Camoldoli, Italy	Severe ascetic regime, more like early desert monks than Benedictines.
Carthusians	Bruno of Cologne and Guigo the Carthusian	c.1080 Chartreuse, France	Group hermitage in the Alps where each monk lived and slept in his own cell.
Military Orders			
Knights Hospitallers (wore a white cross)	Raymond du Puy (initiated military role of monks)	1113 Jerusalem	Begun as a hospice for sick pilgrims, later became an order of soldier monks.
Knights Templar (wore a red cross)	Hugh de Payns (*Rule of the Temple* written by Bernard of Clairvaux)	1119 Jerusalem	Defended pilgrims on their way to the Holy Land. Lived a common life and took vows of poverty, chastity and obedience.

OUTLINE OF MONASTICISM (CONTINUED)

Major Medieval Monastic Orders (continued)

	founder(s)	origin (date/place)	highlights
Mendicant Orders			
Franciscans (Order of Friars Minor)	St. Francis of Assisi	1209 Assisi, Italy	Itinerant preachers. Total poverty, even common property not allowed.
Dominicans (Order of Preachers)	St. Dominic	1216 Spain	Itinerant preachers and scholars. Voluntary poverty. Competed with heretical Cathars in austerity and beliefs.
Augustinians	Pope Innocent IV	1243 Italy	Pope Innocent IV united several eremitical groups in Tuscany with the *Rule of St. Augustine.*
Other Orders			
Premonstrants	St. Norbert	1119 Premontre, France	Followed *Rule of St. Augustine.* Precursor of later more successful mendicant orders.
Carmelites	Berthold	c. late twelfth century Mt. Carmel in Palestine	Groups of hermits in Palestine formed a brief Rule but later migrated to Europe due to Moslems. Later became a Mendicant Order.

NOTE: Eremitical monks lead the solitary life of hermits (like the early desert Fathers) in contrast to cenobitical monks that lead a life in common. Mendicant orders refer to orders that are not primarily contemplative (as in all the other orders mentioned here) but have an active apostolate to preach and teach while maintaining a life of poverty, chastity, and obedience. Strictly speaking, "orders" are distinct from "congregations." For purposes of this chart, we have not distinguished between orders and congregations.

A. Rule of St. Augustine, Rule of St. Benedict, Rule of the Temple, etc.
B. Lawrence, C. H., *Medieval Monasticism*, 3rd edition

Outline of Monasticism (continued)

Medieval Heretical Sects

heresy	description	geographic center & dates
Cathars	Dualists who taught that all matter is evil. Suppression of this heresy led to the Inquisition.	Twelfth to late thirteenth or early fourteenth centuries in northern Italy and southern France.
Flagellants	Groups of laymen, whipping themselves in public as a form of penance. Especially popular as a result of the Black Death.	Thirteenth and fourteenth centuries, particularly in Germany and adjacent lands.
Fraticelli	Spiritual Franciscans who took a radical view of poverty in religious life.	Thirteenth and fourteenth centuries (particularly 1290s) in Italy and southern France.
Hussites	Bohemian reform movement challenging the papacy.	Fifteenth century in Bohemia (central Europe).
Joachimites	Harsh critics of the Papacy and followers of Joachim of Fiore's apocalyptic speculations.	Thirteenth century throughout Europe.
Lollards	Followers of John Wyclif who emphasized individual faith and the supremacy of Scripture.	Fourteenth and fifteenth centuries in England.
Waldensians	Popular preachers of poverty following Valdes, a former businessman of Lyons.	Twelfth century until modern times in France, Italy, Germany, and parts of Eastern Europe.

    A. William of Tudela, *The Song of the Cathar Wars*
      Wyclif, John, *The English Works of Wyclif Hitherto Unprinted*
    B. Lambert, Malcolm, *Medieval Heresy*, 3rd edition

OUTLINE OF MONASTICISM (CONTINUED)

Three Evangelical Counsels (vows of religious orders)

counsel (cf. Philippians 2:8)	renunciation (cf. I John 2:16)
1. poverty	of external wealth (lust of the eyes)
2. chastity	of carnal pleasure (lust of the flesh)
3. obedience	of the pride of life

    A. Thomas Aquinas, *Summa Theologica*, I-II, q. 108, a. 4
    B. "Evangelical Counsels," *New Dictionary of Theology*

Three Steps to Truth (St. Bernard of Clairvaux)

1. humility

2. compassion

3. contemplation

NOTE: "These are the three steps of truth. We ascend the first by striving to be humble, the second by compassion, the third in the ecstasy of contemplation. In the first, Truth is discovered to be severe; in the second, holy; in the third, pure. Reason leads to the first, in which we think about ourselves. Affection leads to the second, in which we think about others. Purity leads to the third, in which we are lifted up to see what is out of sight."

    A. Bernard of Clairvaux, *On the Steps of Humility and Pride*, VI.19
    B. "Bernard of Clairvaux," *Dictionary of the Middle Ages*, vol. 2

Three Stages of the Contemplative Life

1. the purgative stage

2. the illuminative stage

3. the unitive stage

    A. Pseudo-Dionysius, *The Celestial Hierarchy*, III.2
    B. Knowles, David, *The Evolution of Medieval Thought*, 2nd edition, p. 25

O<small>UTLINE OF</small> M<small>ONASTICISM</small> (<small>CONTINUED</small>)

Four Types of Monks (according to St. Benedict)

1.	cenobites	monks in community with a rule and abbot
2.	anchorites	hermits
3.	sarabites	monks living without a rule
4.	gyrovagues	nomads, bums

   A. St. Benedict, *Rule of St. Benedict*, chapter 1
   B. "Monasticism," *New Dictionary of Theology*

The Divine Office (prayer schedule for monks)

	office	time	name
1.	Matins/Vigils	middle of the night	from *vigilia*, wakefulness
2.	Lauds	before dawn	from *lauds*, praises
3.	Prime	early morning (1ˢᵗ Hour = 6 a.m.)	from *prima hora*, first hour
4.	Terce	mid-morning (3ʳᵈ Hour = 9 a.m.)	from *tertia*, third
5.	Sext	mid-day (sixth Hour = 12 p.m.)	from *sexta*, sixth
6.	None	mid-afternoon (ninth Hour = 3 p.m.)	from *nona*, ninth
7.	Vespers	evening	from *vesper*, evening
8.	Compline	before retiring	from *completorium,* completion

NOTE: Each office includes the chanting of psalms, the singing of hymns, and the reading of Holy Scripture.

   A. Psalm 118:164
     St. Benedict, *Rule of St. Benedict*
     Dante, *Convivio*, IV.xxiii
   B. "Divine Office," *Dictionary of the Middle Ages*, vol. 4
     Eco, Umberto, *The Name of the Rose*, pp. 7-8

Twelve Steps of Humility (St. Benedict)

1. Keep the fear of God always before our eyes (cf. Psalm 36:1-2).

2. Love not our will but Christ's (cf. John 6:38).

3. Submit to the abbot or prioress in all obedience (cf. Philippians 2:8).

4. Embrace obedience even if it is difficult or unjust (cf. Romans 8:36).

5. Do not conceal from the abbot or prioress any sinful thoughts (cf. Psalm 32:5).

6. Be content with the most menial treatment and labors (cf. Psalm 73:22-23).

7. Confess in speech and our hearts that we are inferior to everyone else (cf. Psalm 22:7).

8. Do only what is endorsed by the common rule of the monastery.

9. Remain silent, only speaking if asked a question (Proverbs 10:19).

10. Do not be ready and prompt to laughter (Sirach 21:23).

11. Speak gently and briefly, with modesty and without laughter.

12. Manifest humility in our bearing and our hearts everywhere we go (Luke 18:13).

NOTE: The first "twelve-step program" in Western culture is described by St. Benedict as follows: "Wherefore, brethren, if we wish to attain to the summit of humility and desire to arrive speedily at that heavenly exaltation to which we ascend by humility of the present life, then must we set up a ladder of our ascending actions like unto that which Jacob saw in his vision [Genesis 28:12], whereon angels appeared to him, descending and ascending. By that descent and ascent we must surely understand nothing else than this, that we descend by self-exaltation and ascend by humility."

St. Benedict, chapter 7 of *The Rule*

    A. St. Benedict, *Rule of St. Benedict*, chapter 7
    B. Chittister, Joan, *Rule of St. Benedict: Insight for the Ages*, pp. 61-75

OUTLINE OF MONASTICISM (CONTINUED)

Twelve Steps of Pride (St. Bernard of Clairvaux)

1. curiosity (*curiositos*)

2. frivolity (*levitas*)

3. foolish merriment (*inepta laetitia*)

4. boastfulness (*jactantia*)

5. claiming special status (*singularitas*)

6. conceit (*arrogantia*)

7. audacity (*praesumptio*)

8. self-justification (*defensio peccatorum*)

9. insincere confession (*simulata confesso*)

10. rebellion (*rebellio*)

11. freedom to sin (*libertas peccandi*)

12. habitual sinning (*consuetudo peccandi*)

    A. Bernard of Clairvaux, *On the Steps of Humility and Pride*
    B. "Bernard of Clairvaux, St.," *New Catholic Encyclopedia*, 2nd edition, vol. 2

OUTLINE OF THOMAS AQUINAS' SUMMA THEOLOGICA

Pars Prima, First Part (I) (the *exitus*/procession of all creatures from God)

I. God's existence and essential attributes (QQ. 1-26)

    A. Essential attributes:

        1. The simplicity of God (God is not a composite of parts)
        2. The perfection of God (God is pure goodness, pure truth, pure actuality)
        3. The infinity of God (God is everywhere, there is nothing outside of God)
        4. The immutability of God (God is eternal and unchanging)
        5. The unity of God (God is one, not many)

    B. Attributes as known by us:

        1. The omniscience of God (God is all-knowing)
        2. The love of God (God is all-loving, cf. I John 4:16)
        3. The providence of God (God cares for creation)
        4. The omnipotence of God (God is all-powerful)
        5. The beatitude of God (God is purely happy)

II. Trinity of Divine Persons (QQ. 27-43)

        1. The relation of the Father to the Son (paternity or fatherhood)
        2. The relation of the Son to the Father (filiation or sonship)
        3. The relation of the Father and Son to the Holy Spirit (spiration or breathing forth)
        4. The relation of the Holy Spirit to the Father and Son (procession)

III. Procession of creatures from God:

        1. Creation in general (QQ. 44-49)
        2. Creation of spiritual beings – angels (QQ. 50-64)
        3. Creation of corporeal beings – the universe (QQ. 65-74)
        4. Creation of spiritual/corporeal beings – humans (QQ. 75-102)

IV. Divine Providence (QQ. 103-119)

        1. How God moves things directly
        2. How angels move things (via the nine choirs of angels)
        3. How bodies move things (via the heavenly and other bodies)
        4. How human beings move things (via human acts)

OUTLINE OF THOMAS AQUINAS' SUMMA THEOLOGICA (CONTINUED)

Prima Secundae, First Part of Second Part (I-II)
(the *reditus*/return of creatures to God)

The end or goal of human life = happiness (QQ. 1-5)

The means of attaining that ultimate goal = human acts (QQ. 6-21)

I. Passions (QQ. 22-48)

    1. Four primary passions
    2. Passions of the concupiscible appetite
    3. Passions of the irascible appetite

II. Habits in general (QQ. 49-54)

    1. Formation of habits
    2. Increase of habits
    3. Corruption of habits

III. Habits in particular:

    A. Virtues (QQ. 55-70)

        1. Intellectual virtues
        2. Moral virtues
        3. Theological virtues

    B. Vices and Sins (QQ. 71-89)

    Internal causes of sin:
        1. Ignorance (sin on the part of reason)
        2. Malice (sin on the part of the will)
        3. Passion (sin on the part of appetite)

    External causes of sin:
        1. The devil
        2. Human beings and original sin

IV. Treatise on Law (QQ. 90-108)

    1. Eternal Law
    2. Natural Law
    3. Human Law
    4. The Old Law
    5. The New Law

V. Treatise on Grace (QQ. 109-114)

    1. Necessity of grace
    2. Divisions of grace
    3. Causes and effects of grace

OUTLINE OF THOMAS AQUINAS' SUMMA THEOLOGICA (CONTINUED)

Secunda Secundae, Second Part of Second Part (II-II)

I. Theological virtues (with vices and gifts):

1. Faith (QQ. 1-16)
2. Hope (QQ. 17-22)
3. Charity (QQ. 23-46)

II. Cardinal virtues (with vices and gifts):

1. Prudence (QQ. 47-56)
2. Justice (QQ. 57-122)
3. Courage (QQ. 123-140)
4. Temperance (QQ. 141-170)

III. Other issues:

1. Gratuitous graces (QQ. 171-178)
2. Active and contemplative life (QQ. 179-182)
3. States of life (QQ. 183-189)

Pars Tertia, Third Part (III)

Christ as the way to salvation (QQ. 1-59)

Sacraments as means of salvation (QQ. 60-65)

Baptism (QQ. 66-71)
Confirmation (Q. 72)
Eucharist (QQ. 73-83)
Penance (QQ. 84-90)

OUTLINE OF THOMAS AQUINAS' SUMMA THEOLOGICA (CONTINUED)

Supplementum, The Supplement (Suppl)

Penance continued (QQ. 1-28)
Last Anointing (QQ. 29-33)
Holy Orders (QQ. 34-40)
Matrimony (QQ. 41-68)

Treatise on the resurrection of humankind (QQ. 69-99)

NOTE: In the *Summa Theologica*, Thomas imitates a structure similar to the public debates or "disputations" of his day. His *magnum opus* adheres to the following pattern:

1. Question (e.g. "Does God exist?")
2. Objections (e.g. negative answers, in this case why God does not exist)
3. "On the contrary . . ." (e.g. arguments from authority [Scriptures, earlier scholars] answering the question in the affirmative)
4. "I answer that . . ." (e.g. philosophical arguments answering the question in the affirmative, in this case arguments for the existence of God)
5. Replies to the earlier series of objections

Each question and answer with objections and replies might run for pages. The *Summa*, just one of his many books, contains 611 such questions.

This methodology of Thomas was not his own invention but grew out of the medieval tradition of scholasticism, most succinctly described by M. D. Chenu. "The 'style' of the Scholastics in its development as well as in its modes of expression can be reduced, as if to its simple elements, to three procedures. These followed progressively one upon the other and typify, moreover, both their historical genesis and their progress in technique. First came the *lectio* [reading]; from the reading was developed the *quaestio* [question]; from the question, the *disputatio* [disputation]; and in *summas*, the 'article,' somewhat as the residue of the disputed question, became the literary component. The entire medieval pedagogy was based on the reading of texts, and in the universities, scholasticism gave this type of work institutional form and enlarged upon it."
M. D. Chenu, *Toward Understanding St. Thomas*, p. 80

A. Thomas Aquinas, *Summa Theologica*
B. Weisheipl, James, *Friar Thomas D'Aquino; His Life, Thought and Works*

OUTLINE OF DANTE'S DIVINE COMEDY

Inferno: The Nine Circles of Hell
    (technique of *contrapasso*, punishment mirrors sin)

circle in Hell	punishment (and particular characters)
Vestibule or Ante-Hell (canto III)	Home of the morally lukewarm (neutrals) who are beset by stinging flies and wasps

- - - - - River Acheron (canto III) = boundary of underworld and UPPER HELL - - - - -

| 1. Limbo (canto IV) | Home of virtuous heathens and the unbaptized who, without hope, live in longing to see God (Limbo houses the poets Homer, Horace, Ovid, Lucan, and Virgil, as well as the philosophers Socrates, Plato, and Aristotle, and the Arabs Avicenna, Averroes, and Saladin) |

First Category of Sin: Sins of Incontinence (circles 2-5)

2. The Lustful (canto V)	Sinners whirled around by great gusts of wind (Dido, Cleopatra, Paulo, and Francesca here)
3. The Gluttonous (canto VI)	Sinners half-buried in vile slush of ice and rain; torn by claws and teeth of three-headed dog of Hell
4. The Avaricious (canto VII)	Two raging mobs (hoarders and spendthrifts) push huge boulders against each other (more shades here than any other circle of Hell, especially priests, Popes, and cardinals); discussion of the Wheel of Fortune in this canto

- - - - - - - - - - - River Styx (canto VIII) = muddy river of fleshly sins - - - - - - - - - - - -

| 5. The Wrathful (canto VIII) | Sinners strike and bite each other and themselves in the slime and swamp portion of the River Styx – constantly swallow mud |

- - - - - - - - Wall and Gate of Dis (canto IX) = boundary of LOWER HELL - - - - - - - -

Special Category of Sin: Sin of Heresy (circle 6)

| 6. The Heretics (cantos X-XI) | In the iron-walled City of Dis, heretics are encased in red-hot tombs (Epicurean philosophers here); Dante meets his political enemy (Farinata) and childhood friend's father (Cavalcante) sharing a tomb; Virgil lectures on Hell's categories of sins taken from Book VII of Aristotle's *Ethics* |

- - - - - - - - - - - River Phlegethon (canto XII) = river of boiling blood- - - - - - - - - - -

OUTLINE OF DANTE'S DIVINE COMEDY (CONTINUED)

Second Category of Sin: Sins of Violence (circle 7)

7. The Violent

Ring 1: River of Boiling Blood (violence against neighbors) (canto XII)	Sinners immersed in river Phlegethon and attacked by Centaurs if they stick their head above the water (Alexander the Great, Attila the Hun here)
Ring 2: Dense Forest of Thorns (violence against self) (canto XIII)	Souls of suicides are souls encased in gnarled trees and thorn-bushes; Harpies eat their leaves (Frederick II's trusted minister, Pier della Vigna here)
	Gamblers and spendthrifts are torn to pieces by wild dogs
Ring 3: Ring of Burning Sand (violence against God/nature)	Blasphemers lying face up and naked on hot sand are pelted by flakes of fire; five rivers in underworld reviewed here (canto XIV)
	Sodomites wander naked in constant motion on burning hot sand (Dante's teacher, Brunetto Latini here) (canto XV-XVI)
	Usurers crouch on burning hot sand with heavy moneybags around their necks (canto XVII)

Third Category of Sin: Sins of Fraud (circles 8-9)

8. Simple Fraud

The Eighth Circle or Malebolge (evil ditch) contains a series of concentric moats that surround an inverted castle – the pit of Hell.

Bolge 1: Panderers/Seducers (canto XVIII)	Sinners naked and scourged by horned demons
Bolge 2: Flatterers (canto XVIII)	Sinners sunk in excrement that comes out of their mouths when they speak
Bolge 3: Buyers and Sellers of Church Offices (canto XIX)	Sinners buried upside down on top of each other in stone fonts; Dante laments, "Ah, Constantine, to what evil you gave birth" (Popes Nicholas III and Boniface VIII here)
Bolge 4: Sorcerers (canto XX)	Sinners with their heads twisted 180 degrees walk backwards, with tears running down their buttocks

<small><small>Outline of Dante's Divine Comedy (continued)</small></small>

Bolge 5: Buyers and Sellers of Political Offices (canto XXI-XII)	Sinners drowned in boiling tar and attacked by demons if they surface
Bolge 6: Hypocrites (canto XXIII)	Sinners walk in small circles wearing brilliantly colored lead robes that heat up if they stop walking (two Franciscan friars here)
Bolge 7: Thieves (cantos XXIV-XXV)	Sinners bitten by snakes with some turned into reptiles (several of Dante's hometown citizens here)
Bolge 8: False Counselors (cantos XXVI-XXVII)	Sinners wrapped in flames (Ulysses here, his major fraud being the Trojan horse)
Bolge 9: Schismatics (canto XXVIII)	Sinners hacked by demons with bloody swords; prophet Mohammad's body is cleft in two from chin to groin; headless troubadour Bertrand de Born carries his severed head, swinging it like a lantern
Bolge 10: Falsifiers	Alchemists (falsifiers of things) covered with scabs and leprous sores that itch horribly (canto XXIX)
	Impersonators (falsifiers in deeds) changed into vicious hogs with tusks (canto XXX)
	Counterfeiters (falsifiers in deeds) suffer eternal thirst (canto XXX)
	Liars (falsifiers in words) suffer fever so hot their body smokes (canto XXX)

- - - - - - - - - River Cocytus (canto XXXI) = river of ice/frozen floor of Hell - - - - - - - -

It is no enterprise undertaken lightly, describing the center of the universe.

Dante, canto XXXII

9. Treachery

Region 1: Caina (traitors to family) (canto XXXII)	Region named after Cain, brother of Abel and the world's first murderer. Sinners frozen in ice with only heads above ice and faces turned downward.
Region 2: Antenor (traitors to country) (canto XXXIII)	Region named after the Trojan (in non-Virgilian versions of the story) who betrayed Troy to the Greeks. Sinners' faces look straight ahead.

OUTLINE OF DANTE'S DIVINE COMEDY (CONTINUED)

Region 3: Ptolomea (traitors to guests) (canto XXXIII)	Region named after Ptolemy (I Maccabees 16:11-17) who slew three guests at a banquet. Sinners faces turned upward. Count Ugolino gnaws on the skull of Archbishop Ruggieri who imprisoned Ugolino and his children in a tower to starve to death. In desperation, Ugolino ate the bodies of his dead children.
Region 4: Judecca (traitors to rightful lords) (canto XXXIV)	Region named after Judas who betrayed Christ. Sinners entirely frozen in ice. Here are the traitors to Caesar (Brutus, Cassius) and to Christ (Judas).
Lucifer frozen in ice (canto XXXIV)	Lucifer has three faces parodying the Trinity:

1. Red face perverting Divine Love
2. Yellow face perverting Divine Omnipotence
3. Black face perverting Divine Wisdom

Lucifer's wings send forth freezing blasts of impotence, ignorance and hatred.

The mouth of each face is stuffed with one of the world's three greatest traitors, Brutus, Cassius, and Judas.

A. Dante, *Inferno*
B. Chiarenza, Marguerite Mills, *The Divine Comedy: Tracing God's Art*, pp. 19-55

OUTLINE OF DANTE'S DIVINE COMEDY (CONTINUED)

Purgatorio: The Seven Terraces of the Mountain of Purgatory

terraces in Purgatory (capital sins)	population
Ante-Purgatory (cantos I-IX)	Includes suicides (Cato), excommunicates (Manfred), and late-repentants (Belacqua)

- -

First Category of Sin: Sins of Misdirected Love

1. The Proud (cantos X-XII)	Shades weighed down by heavy burdens
2. The Envious (cantos XIII-XV)	Shades dressed in hair-shirts with eyelids sewn shut
3. The Wrathful (cantos XV-XVII)	Shades chanting "Agnus Dei"

Second Category of Sin: Sins of Deficient Love

4. The Slothful (cantos XVII-XIX)	Shades running in crowds non-stop, day and night

Third Category of Sin: Sins of Excessive Love

5. The Greedy (cantos XIX-XXII)	Shades lying with faces and bodies pressed to the Earth
6. The Gluttonous (cantos XXII-XXIV)	Starved skeletons that food makes even more hungry
7. The Lustful (cantos XXV-XXVII)	Shades singing hymns inside burning fire

- -

Earthly Paradise/Garden of Eden (cantos XXVIII-XXXIII)	Virgil leaves and Beatrice becomes Dante's guide

    A. Dante, *Purgatorio*
    B. Chiarenza, Marguerite Mills, *The Divine Comedy: Tracing God's Art*, pp. 56-92

Outline of Dante's Divine Comedy (continued)

Paradiso: The Nine Spheres of the Heavens

<u>spheres of the Heavens</u>   <u>population</u>

Earth – center of the universe

- -

1. Moon (faith)
   (cantos II-IV)

Spirits lacking faith (e.g. two nuns who failed in their vows and succumbed to political marriages)

2. Mercury (hope)
   (cantos V-VII)

Spirits lacking hope; devoted to fame (e.g. story of minor official told by Emperor Justinian)

3. Venus (love)
   (cantos VIII-IX)

Spirits of lovers

4. Sun (wisdom)
   (cantos X-XIII)

Spirits of the wise (Thomas Aquinas, a Dominican, tells the story of St. Francis while Bonaventure, a Franciscan, tells the story of St. Dominic)

5. Mars (courage)
   (cantos XIV-XVII)

Spirits of soldiers of Christ (Emperor Charlemagne)

6. Jupiter (justice)
   (cantos XVIII-XX)

Spirits of the just (Emperors Trajan & Constantine)

7. Saturn (temperance)
   (cantos XXI-XII)

Spirits of temperate contemplatives (St. Benedict)

8. Stars – the *Stellatum*
   (cantos XXII-XXVI)

Vicars of Christ (Sts. Peter [faith], James [hope], and John [love])

9. *Primum Mobile*
   (cantos XXVII-XXXIII)

Nine choirs of angels

- -

Empyrean
(canto XXXIII)

Blessed Virgin and God; The Celestial Rose
(Beatrice leaves and St. Bernard becomes the guide)

A. Dante, *Paradiso*
B. Russell, Jeffrey Burton, *A History of Heaven: The Singing Silence*, pp. 151 ff.

OUTLINE OF DANTE'S DIVINE COMEDY (CONTINUED)

Souls of the Wise in the Circle of the Sun

soul	dates	author
1. St. Thomas Aquinas	c.1225-1274	Dominican monk, professor at University of Paris and author of *Summa Theologica*
2. Albert Magnus	c.1206-1280	Thomas's teacher, professor at the University of Cologne with a special interest in natural science
3. Gratian	fl. 1140	Canon lawyer, Camoldolese monk and theology professor at the University of Bologna, author of *Decretum*
4. Peter Lombard	c.1100-c.1160	Author of popular text, *Book of Sentences* and professor at Notre Dame cathedral
5. King Solomon	d. 938-916 BCE	Builder of the Temple of Jerusalem and author of the Book of Proverbs
6. Pseudo-Dionysius	fifth or sixth c.	Mystical theologian and author of the *Celestial Hierarchies*
7. Orosius	c.380-c.418	Portuguese born historian and colleague of St. Augustine
8. Boethius	c.480-c.525	Consul of the Roman Empire and author of the influential *Consolation of Philosophy*
9. Isidore of Seville	c.560-636	Bishop of Seville, author of encyclopedic *Etymologies*
10. The Venerable Bede	c.672-735	Historian and author of the *Ecclesiastical History of the English Peoples*
11. Richard of St. Victor	d. 1173	Scottish born prior of the monastery of St. Victor, disciple of Hugh of St. Victor
12. Siger of Brabant	d. 1281-1284	Opponent of St. Thomas and leader of the heretical Latin Averroism

A. Dante, *Paradiso*, X.94-148
B. Dante, *Paradiso*, X (footnotes on pp. 245-250 in the Hollander translation)

OUTLINE OF DANTE'S DIVINE COMEDY (CONTINUED)

Representation of the Celestial Rose

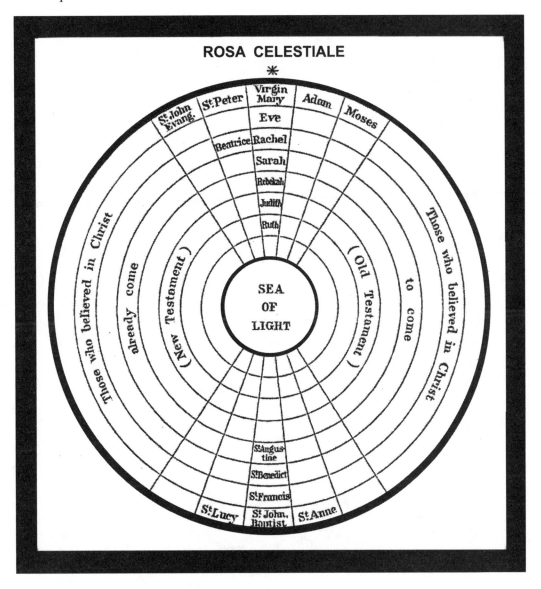

A. Dante, Paradiso, XXX.117 ff.

B. Russell, Jeffrey Burton, *A History of Heaven*, p. 182

OUTLINE OF DANTE'S DIVINE COMEDY (CONTINUED)

Representation of Dante's Universe

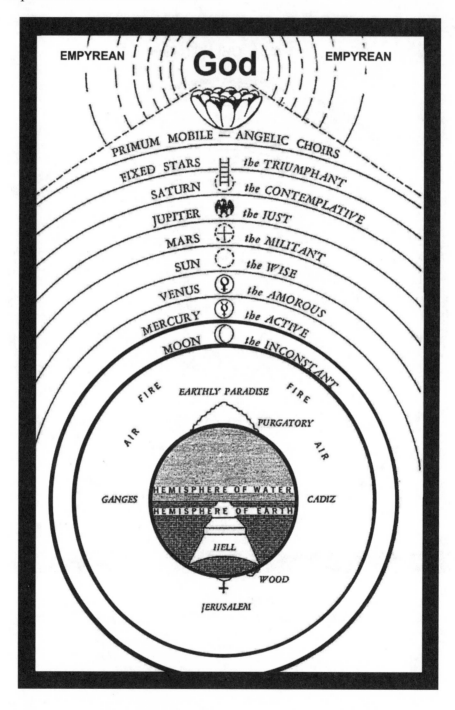

SOURCE: Compiled by Mark Grote.

BASIC LAYOUT OF A MEDIEVAL CATHEDRAL (CHARTRES CATHEDRAL)

(The Gothic Cathedral of Chartes. 1194 - 1260)

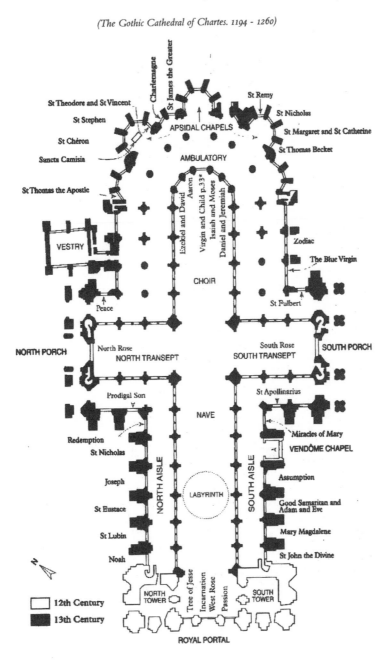

SOURCE: Reprinted with kind permission of Fons Vitae from Guilielmus Durandus' *The Rationale Divinorum Officiorum* (Louisville, KY: Fons Vitae, 2007), p. 2.

EPILOGUE

IX. Art and Literature:
Transition to Modernity

Art (*technē*) is the imitation (*mimesis*) of nature (*physis*).
Aristotle, *Physics*, 194a

THE DENIGRATION OF THE MECHANICAL AND FINE ARTS BEFORE THE MIDDLE AGES

Originality was not a medieval virtue. The medievals were quite content, even proud, to borrow their wisdom and narrative plots from classical Greece and Rome as well as the Hebrew and Christian Scriptures. They measured wisdom by its antiquity – the older the better. Just as the circular motions of the planets reflected God's eternity in a natural way, so the antiquity of human wisdom reflected God's eternity in an artistic fashion. The medievals not only revered art as an imitation of nature (like the ancient Greeks) but also as an imitation of God's creative activity – nature being God's primary work of art. The "book of nature" was considered one of the two books written by God, the other being the Bible.

In the premodern worldview, art (*technē* in Greek and *ars* in Latin) did not refer as it does today to the fine arts, but to a much broader activity – the imitation of nature's creative power through the making and using of artifacts. "The Greek *technē*, commonly translated as "art," "craft," or "skill," has behind it the Indo-European stem *techn-*, probably meaning "woodwork" or "carpentry.""[128] Arts as diverse as carpentry and dance fell under the classical category of art because both involved an imitation of nature. Given their imitative status all arts were, by definition, considered inferior to nature.

As the early lists in this chapter illustrate, the various arts were classified according to strict hierarchies. Liberal arts (*artes liberales*) like logic and geometry expressed the free exercise of the mind and were considered superior to vulgar arts (*artes vulgares*) like farming and carpentry that required the coerced exertion of the body. Unlike today, the usefulness of an art did not imply a higher status; in fact, the uselessness of an art demonstrated a freedom from economic necessity that implied a higher status.

Aristotle divided the vulgar arts into the cooperative and the constructive. The cooperative arts help nature produce things it can produce by itself. For example, agriculture assists nature in producing healthy plants. Medicine assists nature in producing healthy bodies. Teaching assists nature in producing healthy souls. The constructive arts produce things that nature cannot produce by itself. While carpentry produces houses and architecture produces cathedrals, nature does not spontaneously produces these kinds of artifacts. As Aristotle's distinction intimates, the more closely an art imitates nature, the higher the status of that art. Agriculture therefore is a more noble art than architecture in this classical scheme of things.

Arts were not only ranked according to how closely they imitated nature, but were

---

128. Carl Mitcham, *Thinking Through Technology: The Path between Engineering and Philosophy* (Chicago: University of Chicago Press, 1994), p. 117.

also classified according to their physicality. In ancient Greece, long before the rise of monasticism and St. Benedict's famous dictum, *ora et labora* (pray and work), physical work and the mechanical arts in particular were actually condemned as vices that ruined both the body and the soul. Consider this harsh condemnation of mechanical workers, particularly metal workers, by Socrates' disciple Xenophon in his *Oeconomicus* (IV.2):

> For indeed those [workers] that are called mechanical are spoken against everywhere and have quite plausibly come by a very bad reputation in the cities. For they utterly ruin the bodies of those who work at them . . . compelling them to sit still and remain indoors, or in some cases even to spend the whole day by a fire. And when the bodies are made effeminate, the souls too become much more diseased. Lack of leisure to join in the concerns of friends and the city is another condition of those who are called mechanical; those who practice them are reputed to be bad friends as well as bad defenders of their fatherlands.[129]

In antiquity manual labor was synonymous with slavery and, conversely, only slaves were fit for manual labor. Accordingly, the pagan philosopher Plotinus ranks the purely intellectual arts higher than the arts that produce physical objects.

However, the influence of Christianity, particularly monasticism, progressively raised the status of physical work and mechanical art until a point in the twelfth century where Hugh of St. Victor could include the mechanical arts in his grand classification of all the arts. This inclusion of mechanical arts would have been inconceivable in ancient Greece. In his new classification of the arts, Hugh added two categories of mechanical arts to the existing categories of liberal arts (trivium and quadrivium). Under mechanical arts external to nature (those that provide external cover to protect human fragility) he included weaving, armaments, and navigation. Under mechanical arts internal to nature (those whereby humans feed and nourish themselves), he included agriculture, hunting, medicine, and acting.

Unlike the liberal arts and the mechanical arts, the fine arts did not even merit recognition as a distinct class until modern times. Cicero included various fine arts within his category of the minor arts (*artes minores*), the bottom rung of his classification system; but he did not distinguish the fine arts from other minor arts. The fine arts were not recognized as a class until 1747 when Charles Batteux published *Les Beaux Arts réduits à un même principe* [The fine arts reduced to a single principle].[130] In this work he recognized seven fine arts (once again, echoing the seven liberal arts):

1. architecture
2. instrumental music
3. sculpture
4. painting
5. literature
6. drama
7. dance

---

129. Leo Strauss, *Xenophon's Socratic Discourse: An Interpretation of the Oeconomicus* (Ithaca, NY: Cornell University Press, 1970), p. 17.

130. Charles Batteux, *Les Beaux Arts réduits à un même principe* [The fine arts reduced to a single principle] (New York: Johanson Reprint Company, 1988).

While the medievals dismissed the fine arts as worthy of separate consideration, they did produce radical innovations in two fine arts – architecture (see page 237 on the "Basic Layout of a Medieval Cathedral" in chapter eight, Theology) and literature (a topic we will discuss shortly).

Another area of innovation in which they excelled is the aforementioned mechanical arts. Much of this innovation grew out of Christian doctrine; medieval technology out of the doctrine of the Incarnation wherein the Word became flesh (John 1:14), and medieval literature out of the doctrine of the equality of all souls before God (Galatians 3:28). Medieval technology will be discussed here only briefly. Suffice it to say that the ancient contempt for manual labor and acceptance of slavery made progress in the mechanical arts extremely unlikely. However, the physical world gained immense status with the doctrine of the Incarnation. Suddenly the material world was worthy of study.

Surprisingly, in medieval times science did not precede technology (which we now think of as "applied science"), but technology preceded science. The Middle Ages was a time of intense mechanical creativity. The historian of technology Lynn White, Jr. has documented numerous inventions that sparked astounding social changes (see his *Medieval Technology and Social Change*).[131] For example, the invention of the stirrup in the 730s transformed the technology of mounted shock combat to such an extent that a whole type of warrior, the knight, grew out of this change, and an entire system, feudalism, developed to support this extremely expensive system of warfare. Likewise the invention of the heavy plow in northern Europe (as opposed to the light scratch plow of Roman times) revolutionized agricultural output and led to the communal manor system, clearly documented by around 945. And the invention of the windmill in 1185 (Yorkshire) or earlier increased the spread of towns since towns no longer needed to be linked to rivers for their sources of power.

In *Medieval Technology and Religion*, White explicitly links religious movements like monasticism with progress in mechanical technology. Furthermore, he argues technological progress predated scientific progress in the West by centuries: "My fundamental proposition, then, is that the technological dominance of Western culture is not merely characteristic of the modern world; it begins to be evident in the Early Middle Ages and is clear by the Later Middle Ages."[132] White's scholarly work is a marvelous encyclopedia of other medieval inventions including cathedrals, watermills, rigid horse collars, nailed horseshoes, axle-cams, mechanical clocks, the mechanical crank, the flywheel, and the treadle, to name but a few.

THE GROWTH OF VERNACULAR LITERATURE IN THE TWELFTH CENTURY RENAISSANCE

The Middle Ages was not only a time of striking technological innovation, but of innovation in literature as well. During the twelfth century while Hugh of St. Victor idealized the mechanical arts in his book the *Didascalicon*, Chrétien de Troyes idealized courtly love in his romance *Lancelot* or *The Knight of the Cart*. Before examining the phenomenon of courtly romance and the elevated status of women in more detail, let us summarize the other achievements of the twelfth century. Although the *Renaissance of the Twelfth*

---

131. Lynn White, Jr., *Medieval Technology and Social Change* (New York: Oxford University Press, 1988).

132. Lynn White, Jr., *Medieval Religion and Technology* (Berkeley, CA: University of California Press, 1986), p. 80.

Century as popularized by Charles Homer Haskins is not accepted as gospel truth among all historians, there can be little doubt that the achievements of the twelfth century were at least as substantial as those of the Italian Renaissance.[133]

Highlights of the Twelfth Century Renaissance include:

1. The explosion in the mechanical arts and the elevation of their status as reflected in Hugh of St. Victor's classification of the arts.

2. A revival of the old Justinian legal code and the establishment of a comprehensive legal code (especially under Henry II of England).

3. The codification of canon law (Church law) under Gratian in his *Decretum*.

4. The birth of the universities out of the old cathedral schools and monastic schools.

5. The renewal of medieval rationalism under Peter Abelard, the master of logic.

6. The renewal of religious piety and emotionalism under the Cistercian, Bernard of Clairvaux, particularly the cult of the Virgin Mary.

7. The translation of Greek and Arabic classics into Latin.

8. The establishment of Gregorian chant for the Catholic liturgy.

9. The creation of vernacular literature on a mass scale including the glorification of chivalry in the *chanson de geste* and the glorification of courtly love in the *roman d'aventure* as well as the troubadour lyric.

It is this final achievement that we will examine in more detail.

The three major genres in medieval French literature (following the Old French tradition) are the *chanson de geste* (song of noble deeds), the troubadour lyric, and the *roman d'aventure* (courtly romance). The *chanson de geste* precedes the other two and, as in most things medieval, borrows heavily from classical literature in its subject matter, namely war. Valor and bravery in war had always been the subject of the epic in classical culture. In *the* Greek Epic, *The Iliad*, Homer opens with the line, "Sing the wrath, goddess, of Peleus's son Achilles," this poem being the story of Achilles' anger. In *the* Roman Epic, *The Aeneid*, Virgil opens with the line, "Of arms and the man I sing . . . through cruel Juno's unforgiving wrath." The phrase "of arms and the man" summarizes much of the content of most serious non-Biblical literature before the twelfth century Renaissance.

The *chansons de geste* comprised three literary cycles that were classified by the twelfth century French poet Jean Bodel in his *Chanson de Saisnes* (c.1200). As he says, "There are but three literary cycles that no one should be without: the matter of France, of Britain, and of great Rome." The Matter of France focused on martial valor during the conflict between the Franks and Saracens (Moors) at the time of Charlemagne, best typified in the epic poem *The Song of Roland* (c.1095). The Matter of Britain referred to the legendary Celtic history of the British Isles, particularly those pertaining to King Arthur and the Knights of the Round Table. One of the most famous examples of this semi-fictional history is Geoffrey of Monmouth's *History of the Kings of Britain* (c.1131). One should keep in mind, however, that the larger body of Arthurian myth comes more from France (starting with the work of Chrétien de Troyes) than from England. The Matter of Rome (that includes the Matter of Troy) celebrated episodes from the history and mythology of classical antiquity, particularly the exploits of Alexander the Great. *The*

---

133. Charles Homer Haskins, *The Renaissance of the Twelfth Century* (Cambridge, MA: Harvard University Press, 1955).

Romance of Alexander went through numerous editions including an Armenian edition in the fifth century, a French edition in the twelfth century, and a Middle English edition in the mid-fourteenth century.

Perhaps the most important change the medieval epic made to the classical epic was the gradual introduction of the chivalric ideal, most notably in *The Song of Roland*. The *chansons de geste* provide the clearest picture of this chivalric ideal. Roland is the embodiment of chivalry in legend, and Godfrey de Bouillon (leader of the First Crusade) the embodiment of chivalry in fact. Interestingly, the famous list of the giants of chivalry, the Nine Worthies (see page 264), makes no distinction between legendary and historical heroes. According to the ultra-Romantic nineteenth century scholar Leon Gautier, chivalry is "a German custom idealized by the Church."[134]

Gautier contrasts the violent Germanic coming-of-age customs in the Early Middle Ages with the gentler Roman coming-of-age customs. Roman youths on attaining manhood received togas as a symbol of their citizenship in the empire. Barbarian youths on coming of age received their first arms (a sword and shield) as a symbol of their citizenship in the tribe. Gautier argues that the code of chivalry was an attempt by the Church to civilize the German barbarian by transforming him into the Christian knight. He goes so far as to christen chivalry as the eighth sacrament (the baptism of the warrior), glorifying this ideal as "armed force in the service of the unarmed truth."[135] His list of the "Ten Commandments of the Code of Chivalry" on page 263 in this chapter provides a concise summary of this medieval ideal.

The Flowering of Chivalric Literature in the Middle Ages

Nowhere is the stark contrast between the Heroic Epic and the more civilized literature of troubadour lyrics and courtly romances made clearer than in Gautier's criticism of Arthurian romances. The Matter of Britain bridges the world of chivalry and the world of romance. As Gautier says:

> In the twelfth century – one is too apt to forget the date – the romance of the Round Table spread amongst us the taste for a less wild but also a less manly chivalry. The elegancies of love in them occupied the place formerly reserved for the brutality of war: and the spirit of adventure in them extinguished the spirit of the crusades. One will never know how much harm this cycle of the "Round Table" inflicted on us. It civilized us no doubt; but effeminated us.[136]

Gautier applauds the civilizing effect that the chivalric code had on German barbarism, but laments the effeminacy that courtly love brought to knightly behavior.

French medievalist Gaston Paris and C. S. Lewis are both responsible for the popularization of the term "courtly love" (*amour courtois*). Paris invented the word in 1883 and Lewis analyzed the concept in 1936 in the first chapter of his classic work *The Allegory of Love: A Study in Medieval Tradition*. Originally a product of troubadour poets in southern France in the eleventh century, the concept of courtly love grew into an institution and stable literary form (the Arthurian romance) in the whole of France in the twelfth century. The "first troubadour," Guillaume IX (1071-1127) gave women a new status when he

---

134. Leon Gautier, *Chivalry* (Avenel, NJ: Crescent Books, 1989), p. 11.
135. Gautier, *Chivalry*, p. 38.
136. Gautier, *Chivalry*, p. 24.

penned these famous words:

> I shall make a new song
> before the wind blows and it freezes and rains
> My lady is trying me, putting me to the test
> to find out how I love her.[137]

Here we have a role reversal where men and women change status and the warlike knight becomes the vassal of the aristocratic lady who tests her lover by treating him with contempt.

Lewis, who rarely finds pure originality in any piece of literature, comments on the radical novelty of courtly love: "Real changes in human sentiment are very rare – there are perhaps three or four on record – but I believe they occur, and that this [courtly love] is one of them. . . . There can be no mistake about the novelty of romantic love: our only difficulty is to imagine in all its bareness the mental world that existed before its coming."[138] This bareness refers to the classical world where women were mere property and true love, like martial valor, was the preserve of men. As Lewis continues:

> Love, in our sense of the word, is as absent from the literature of the Dark Ages as from that of classical antiquity. Their favourite stories were not, like ours, stories of how a man married, or failed to marry, a woman. They preferred to hear how a holy man went to Heaven or how a brave man went to battle. . . . The deepest of worldly emotions in this period is the love of man for man, the mutual love of warriors, who die fighting against all odds, and the affection between vassal and lord.[139]

Many scholars (particularly Peter Dronke) believe C. S. Lewis overstates his case. They argue that, while romantic love may not have been sanctioned by society or represented in literature until the twelfth century, it is coeval with humanity. Others take Lewis' assertion about the novelty of romantic love seriously, but see possible origins of romantic love further back in history in Muslim Spain (see for example, Roger Boase, *The Origin and Meaning of Courtly Love*).[140]

Regardless of origin, it is surprising that the songs of romantic love sung by male troubadours soon became the domain of women, particularly three strong-willed women of the twelfth century. Perhaps the first woman we know to spread the gospel of courtly love was the granddaughter of Guillaume IX, Duke of Aquitaine, the "first troubadour." Duchess Eleanor of Aquitaine (1122-1204) married the pious King Louis VII of France and insisted on accompanying him on the Second Crusade, about which they argued incessantly. After tiring of Louis, Eleanor found cause to annul the marriage and wedded Henry II of England. Eleanor virtually ruled England while her son with Henry II, Richard I, was off on the Third Crusade.

The second benefactress of courtly love was the daughter of Eleanor and King Louis VII, Countess Marie of Champagne (1145-1198). Marie was the major patron of roman-

137. Frederick Goldin, ed., *Lyrics of the Troubadours and Trouveres: An Anthology and a History* (Garden City, NY: Anchor Press, 1973), p. 41.

138. Lewis, *Allegory*, pp. 11, 4.

139. Lewis, *Allegory*, p. 9.

140. Roger Boase, *The Origin and Meaning of Courtly Love: A Critical Study of European Scholarship* (Manchester: Manchester University Press, 1977).

tic literature, commissioning Chrétien de Troyes to write the masterpiece of the genre, *Lancelot* or *The Knight of the Cart* (c.1170) and Andreas Capellanus to write the tongue-in-cheek handbook of courtly love, the *Art of Courtly Love* (c.1184), from which the rules of courtly love are listed below.

Finally, Queen Blanche of Castile (c.1185-1252), the daughter of Marie of Champagne, wife of Louis VIII, and mother of Louis IX continued the tradition. Like her grandmother, Eleanor, Blanche was a born ruler. She ruled France twice, once when her son Louis IX was underage and once when he was off looting the Byzantine Empire on the Fourth Crusade. Some have suggested the change in the status of women represented by these three ladies can be seen in the game of chess. Though hidden in the midst of "folk origin," apparently this game was first popular in the East where the "queen" was a male figure, the king's chief minister, who could only move diagonally one square at a time. In the twelfth century in the West, this piece turned into the queen and gradually became the most powerful piece on the chessboard, able to move in all directions for unlimited spaces.

This courtly love tradition was modified by raising the status of marriage to a sacrament at the Fourth Lateran Council in 1215. The Church propagated its own chaste version of courtly love by encouraging the cult of the Virgin Mary, a cult initiated by St. Bernard of Clairvaux. Eventually, the Church condemned the ideas of the courtly tradition as heretical in the early thirteenth century. But the ideals of courtly love were unstoppable. As Amy Kelly says in her biography of Eleanor of Aquitaine:

> The ideal of *l'amour courtois* which grew up in Poiters had, as has been well said, more than a little to do with freeing women from the millstone which the church in the first millennium hung about her neck as the author of man's fall and the facile instrument of the devil in the world. The court of Poitiers gave its high sanction to ideals which spread so rapidly throughout Europe that the "doctrine of the inferiority of woman has never had the same standing since."[141]

While Kelly's comments are understandable in their modern approbation of fair play, Lewis is more circumspect in his analysis of the courtly tradition.

Lewis neither attacks the Church for sexism nor the courtly tradition for heresy. He merely marvels at the flourishing of the tradition and accepts it as a typically medieval mixture of both pagan and Christian elements. Lewis emphasizes four characteristics of the courtly tradition:[142]

1. humility (the lady is the lord, and the knight is her vassal),
2. courtesy (the lady is cruel to test her lover, but her man must remain courteous),
3. adultery (true love by nature had to be outside of marriage since previously the notion of marriage was purely concerned with property and political convenience), and
4. the religion of love (as the Church worried, the courtly tradition had turned love into a religion).

According to Lewis, Chrétien de Troyes's *Lancelot* was the "flower of the courtly tradi-

---

141. Amy Kelly, *Eleanor of Aquitaine* (Cambridge, MA: Harvard University Press, 1950), p. 164.
142. Lewis, *Allegory*, p. 12 ff.

tion" due to its exemplification of these four characteristics.[143]

First, Lancelot becomes *The Knight of the Cart* by condescending to ride in a cart in his search for Guinevere. During the time of King Arthur when the action of this romance takes place, medieval villages often had only one cart, one that condemned men rode in on their way to execution. Lancelot loses all social status by stooping to this level. Second, Lancelot remains courteous to a fault, enduring all of Guinevere's cruelty and testing, including purposely losing a tournament (at Guinevere's command) and being disgraced in front of his fellow knights. Third, his love is adulterous as Guinevere is married to King Arthur. And finally, he makes a religion out of his love for his lady. He does not merely love Guinevere; he worships her. As Lewis comments, "When he comes before the bed where she lies he kneels and adores her."[144] Lancelot, in effect, turns the bed into an altar. If the *chansons de geste* turned chivalry into the eighth sacrament, the same must be said of courtly romances and their sacrament of "the lady." Of course, scholars still debate how sincere this cult was and how much it was an ironic game of bored nobility.[145]

The movement from Germanic barbarism to Christian chivalry to courtly love marks a civilizing process, particularly in regards to the status of women. It is in this move toward the equality of the sexes (if at first through the exaggerated role reversal of knight and lady) that the medieval transition toward modernity can be seen as early as the twelfth century. The literary form of this movement in the verse and prose romances marks the very early stages of the modern novel. The French word for "novel" is *roman*. Where moderns are taught to see only discontinuity between medieval barbarism and modern enlightenment, a closer look at the medieval tradition reveals a continuity in technological progress (as Lynn White, Jr. shows) and in cultural progress (as C. S. Lewis shows). An examination of this continuity is another important lesson in overcoming the chronological snobbery that so blinds moderns to the insights the medieval mind has to offer.

Remember, following each list are bibliographic references to the relevant primary sources (A) that are listed in chronological order by the author's lifetime and secondary sources (B) that are listed in alphabetical order by the author's name.

---

143. Lewis, *Allegory*, p. 23.
144. Lewis, *Allegory*, p. 29.
145. See once again, Roger Boase, *The Origin and Meaning of Courtly Love*.

OUTLINE OF CLASSIFICATION SYSTEMS

Plato's Classification of the Arts

1. useful arts (using artifacts, e.g. flutist using a flute)

2. productive arts (producing "real" artifacts, e.g. artisan/carpenter making a flute)

3. imitative arts (producing only images, e.g. poetry and painting)

> A. Plato, *Republic*, 601d
> B. Tatarkiewicz, Wladyslaw, "Classification of Arts in Antiquity"

Aristotle's Classification of the Arts (most well know in Latin terminology)

1. liberal arts (*artes liberales*) entailed the free exercise of the mind (by medieval times these were synonymous with the seven liberal arts)
   a. the trivium (grammar, rhetoric, logic)
   b. the quadrivium (arithmetic, music, geometry, astronomy)

2. vulgar arts (*artes vulgares*) required physical exertion (e.g. anything mechanical like playing a musical instrument or carpentry)
   a. cooperative arts (arts helping nature produce things it would produce by itself, e.g. agriculture, medicine, teaching)
   b. productive arts (arts producing things that nature would not produce by itself, e.g. carpentry, architecture)

NOTE: Note the classical contempt for manual labor.

> A. Aristotle, *Politics*, 1337b-1338a
> B. Adler, Mortimer, *Aristotle for Everybody: Difficult Thought Made Easy*, pp. 61-62

Quintilian's Classification of the Arts

1. theoretical arts (consist only in studying things, e.g. astronomy)

2. practical arts (consist in action that does not leave a product, e.g. dancing)

3. productive arts (produce objects that endure after the artist's action, e.g. painting)

> A. Quintilian, *The Orator's Education*, II.xviii
> B. Tatarkiewicz, Wladyslaw, "Classification of Arts in Antiquity"

Cicero's Classification of the Arts

1. Major arts (*artes maximae*): political and military arts

2. Median arts (*artes mediocres*): intellectual arts (seven liberal arts)

3. Minor arts (*artes minores*): painting, sculpture, music, acting, athletics

NOTE: In this first appearance of the "fine arts," they are given last place.

A. Cicero, compare *De Oratore*, 1.2.7 (*artes maximae and artes mediocres*) and 2.42 (*artes minores*)

B. Tatarkiewicz, Wladyslaw, "Classification of Arts in Antiquity"

Plotinus' Classification of the Arts

1. Purely intellectual arts (e.g. geometry, music)

2. Arts improving human action (e.g. rhetoric, politics, military arts)

3. Arts imitating nature (e.g. painting, sculpture, dancing)

4. Arts helping nature (e.g. medicine, farming)

5. Arts producing physical objects (e.g. building, carpentry)

NOTE: The highest arts are the most spiritual, and the lowest arts are the most material.

A. Plotinus, *Enneads*, V.ix.11

B. Tatarkiewicz, Wladyslaw, "Classification of Arts in Antiquity"

OUTLINE OF CLASSIFICATION SYSTEMS (CONTINUED)

Seven Mechanical Arts (Hugh of St. Victor)

1. weaving (*lanificium*)
2. armament (*armatura*)
3. navigation/commerce (*navigatio*)
4. agriculture (*agricultura*)
5. hunting (*venatio*)
6. medicine (*medicina*)
7. acting (*theatrica*)

NOTE: Non-liberal arts are no longer depreciated by being labeled vulgar. Now they are termed mechanical. Hugh of St. Victor reflects Christian appreciation of the physical world based on the doctrine of the Incarnation of Christ.

> A. Hugh of St. Victor, *The Didascalicon of Hugh of St. Victor*, II.xx
> B. "Hugh of St. Victor," *New Catholic Encyclopedia*, 2nd edition, vol. 7_
> Outline of Classification Systems

Classification of the Liberal and Mechanical Arts (Hugh of St. Victor)

	external to nature	internal to nature
Liberal Arts	**trivium:** grammar, rhetoric, logic	**quadrivium:** arithmetic, music, geometry, astronomy
Mechanical Arts	**weaving, armament, navigation** (external cover for nature to protect herself from harm)	**agriculture, hunting, medicine, acting** (internal by which nature feeds and nourishes herself)

NOTE: For Hugh's entire classification of the arts see the list "Classification of Philosophy in Hugh of St. Victor" on page 148 in chapter seven on Philosophy.

> A. Hugh of St. Victor, *The Didascalicon of Hugh of St. Victor*, II.xx
> B. "Hugh of St. Victor," *New Catholic Encyclopedia*, 2nd edition, vol. 7

Seven Wonders of the Ancient World

1. Great Pyramid of Giza

2. Hanging Gardens of Babylon

3. Statue of Zeus at Olympia

4. Temple of Artemis at Ephesus

5. Mausoleum of Maussollos at Halicarnassus

6. Colossus of Rhodes

7. Pharos (Lighthouse) at Alexandria

NOTE: Lists of architectural wonders arose following Alexander the Great's conquests in the fourth century BCE. These sites featured prominently in travel guides for Hellenic tourists. Antipater of Sidon (first century BCE) identified seven works located around the Mediterranean rim that closely approximates the list above. In turn, his list inspired innumerable versions throughout late antiquity and the Middle Ages. Gregory of Tours compiled a list of seven wonders in the sixth century, a list which included the Temple of Solomon and Noah's Ark. Other compilers of lists of architectural wonders (both before and after Antipater) include Herodotus, Strabo, Cassiodorus, and Bede.

"I have set eyes on the wall of lofty Babylon on which is a road for chariots, and the statue of Zeus by the Alpheus, and the hanging gardens, and the Colossus of the Sun, and the huge labor of the high pyramids, and the vast tomb of Mausolus; but when I saw the house of Artemis that mounted to the clouds, those other marvels lost their brilliancy, and I said, 'Lo, apart from Olympus, the Sun never looked on aught so grand'" (Antipater, *Greek Anthology*, IX.58; see also VIII.177).

    A. *Greek Anthology*, IX.58 (see also VIII.177)
    B. Clayton, Peter A. and Martin J. Price, *The Seven Wonders of the Ancient World*

Poetry in Aristotle (modes of imitation)

Means of Expression

1. Rhythm (e.g. dance)

2. Language (e.g. prose)

3. Melody

Combinations: Rhythm + Melody = instrumental music (use of flute or lyre)
Rhythm + Language = epic poetry
Rhythm + Language + Melody = tragedy, comedy, lyric poetry

Objects of Expression

1. Imitation of characters better than us (e.g. epic poetry, tragedy)

2. Imitation of characters like us

3. Imitation of characters worse than us (e.g. comedy)

Manner of Expression

1. Narrative mode (e.g. epic poetry)

2. Mixed mode (e.g. Homer's quasi dramatic style)

3. Dramatic mode (e.g. tragedy, comedy)

   A. Aristotle, *Poetics*, 1447a-b
   B. Ross, W. D., *Aristotle*, pp. 286 ff.

Six Elements of Greek Drama

1. plot

2. character

3. thought (the content of the characters' speech)

4. diction (the style of the characters' speech)

5. music/melody

6. spectacle (costumes and scenery)

NOTE: During the Early Middle Ages drama literally disappeared and only gradually developed again beginning with the passion plays and Nativity plays around the twelfth century. One reason for this eclipse of drama may have been Augustine's harsh criticism of the theater in his books.

> A. Aristotle, *Poetics*, 1450 a-b
> B. Joseph, Miriam, *The Trivium*, p. 228

Five Sources of the Sublime in Literature

1. Command of significant and full-blooded ideas

2. Inspiration of vehement emotions

3. Proper use of powerful figures of thought and speech

4. Excellent choice of words and imagery

5. Effective organization and arrangement of words (general effect of dignity and grandeur)

> A. Longinus, *On the Sublime*, viii.1
> B. Feder, Lillian, *Crowell's Handbook of Classical Literature*, p. 232

Medieval Literature: Three Popular Medieval Books

1. *The Romance of Reynard the Fox [Le Roman de Renart]*

Composed toward the end of the twelfth century, Reynard is the hero of medieval beast epics, satirizing medieval society and institutions from the nobility and clergy to the peasantry. Loosely connected tales revolve around Reynard's summons by King Noble the lion to answer accusations by Isengrim the Wolf.

2. *The Golden Legend* by Jacobus de Voragine

Composed around 1260, this anthology depicts the lives of 180 saints in an array of factual and fictional stories ranging from well known saints to gory descriptions of the death of St. James the Dismembered. Written by the Archbishop of Genoa and arranged according to the saints' feast days throughout the liturgical year.

3. *Romance of the Rose* by Guillaume de Lorris and Jean de Meun

The first part was composed by Guillaume between 1230 and 1235. Jean de Meun finished the work around 1275. This work is an allegorical account of a young man's dream in which he joins forces with the God of Love in pursuit of his beloved Rose against the antagonists of Reason, Rebuff, Wealth, Jealousy, and others. Love triumphs at the end of this most popular of all medieval romances. C. S. Lewis preferred the first part. Northup Frye belittled the second part as an "encyclopedic satire."

NOTE: In addition to these popular works, every self-respecting library in the Middle Ages contained a copy of Ovid's and Virgil's works.

> A. *The Romance of Reynard the Fox*
>   Jacobus de Voragine, *The Golden Legend*
>   Guillaume de Lorris and Jean de Meun, *Romance of the Rose*
> B. Walsh, James, *A Golden Treasury of Medieval Literature*, pp. 181-197

Medieval Literature: Three Major Genres
(following the Old French tradition)

I. The Heroic Epic (*chanson de geste*)

These long narrative poems of warlike deeds merge the Romantic code of chivalry with the Germanic warrior code (the distinction between epic and romance is not absolute).

1. Matter of Rome (Troy): heroic deeds of Alexander the Great & other ancient warriors

E.G. *The Romances of Alexander* (Armenian version = fifth c.)

This collection of pseudo histories of Alexander the Great was compiled over several centuries. Much of the collection is pure fantasy.

2. Matter of France: heroic deeds of Charlemagne and his time

E.G. *The Song of Roland* (c.1095)

This famous Old French epic recalls the betrayal and slaughter by the Saracens of the rearguard of Charlemagne's army in 778 and of Charlemagne's bitter revenge.

E.G. The Poem of the Cid (c.1140)

This poem recalls the legendary exploits of a famous figure in the long struggle of Christian Spain against the Moslems. Two particular themes include the adventures of the historical, exiled Cid and the mythical marriages of his daughters. This poem is not technically a Matter of France, but is deeply influenced by that tradition.

3. Matter of Britain: heroic deeds of King Arthur and his knights

E.G. *The History of the Kings of Britain* (c.1131)

Geoffrey of Monmouth's loose rendering of early British royalty generously mixes fact with legend.

E.G. *Le Morte d'Arthur* (1485)

This is a later compilation of Arthurian legends by the fifteenth century rogue adventurer, Sir Thomas Malory.

NOTE: See "Chivalric Romance" on pages 260-261 below for more Arthurian romances (Matters of Britain).

A. Bodel, Jean, *Chanson de Saisnes*
B. Artz, Frederick, *The Mind of the Middle Ages*, pp. 322 ff.

Medieval Literature: Three Major Genres (continued)

II. The Troubadour Lyric

Short songs of chivalry and courtly love sung by troubadours, minstrels, jongleurs, and Minnesingers. The tradition began in ninth century France and flourished in southern France in the twelfth century.

1. Lyrics in praise of love

E.G. 'The Pangs of Love' by Guillaume IX (1071-1127), the "first troubadour"

I shall make a new song
before the wind blows and it freezes and rains.
My lady is trying me, putting me to the test
to find out how I love her.
Well now, no matter what quarrel she moves for that reason,
She shall not loose me from her bond.

Instead, I become her man, deliver myself up to her,
and she can write my name down in her charter.
Now don't go thinking I must be drunk
if I love my virtuous lady,
for without her I have no life,
I have caught such hunger for her love.

For you are whiter than ivory,
I worship no other woman.
If I do not get help soon
and my lady does not give me love,
by Saint Gregory's holy head I'll die
if she doesn't kiss me in a chamber or under a tree.

What shall it profit you, my comely lady,
if your love keeps me far away?
I swear, you want to become a nun.
And you better know, I love you so much
I'm afraid the pain will prick me to death,
if you don't do right by me for the wrongs I cry against You.

What shall it profit you if I become a monk shut in
and you do not keep me for your man?
All the joy of the world belongs to us,
Lady, if we both love each other,
Now to my friend down there, Daurostre [the *jongleur*],
I say, I command: sing this nicely, do not bray it out.

For this one I shiver and tremble,
I love her with such good love;
I do not think the like of her was ever born
in the long line of Lord Adam.

Medieval Literature: Three Major Genres (continued)

II. The Troubadour Lyric (continued)

2. Lyrics in praise of war and valor

E.G. 'The Joys of War' by Bertrand de Born (c.1140 – c.1214)

My heart is filled with gladness when I see
Strong castles besieged, stockades broken and overwhelmed,
Many vassals struck down,
Horses of the dead and wounded roving at random.
And when battle is joined, let all men of good lineage
Think of naught but the breaking of heads and arms,
For it is better to die than be vanquished and live. . . .
I tell you I have no such joy as when I hear the shout
"On! On!" from both sides and the neighing of riderless steeds,
And groans of "Help me! Help me!"
And when I see both great and small
Fall in the ditches and on the grass
And see the dead transfixed by spear shafts!
Lords, mortgage your domains, castles, cities,
But never give up war!

3. Lyrics in praise of God

E. G. "Canticle of Brother Sun" by St. Francis of Assisi (c.1182 – 1226)

Most high, all powerful, all good Lord! All praise is yours, all glory, all honor, and all blessing. To you, alone, Most High, do they belong. No mortal lips are worthy to pronounce your name.

Be praised, my Lord, through all your creatures, especially through my lord Brother Sun, who brings the day; and you give light through him. And he is beautiful and radiant in all his splendor! Of you, Most High, he bears the likeness.

Be praised, my Lord, through Sister Moon and the stars; in the heavens you have made them, precious and beautiful.

Be praised, my Lord, through Brothers Wind and Air, and clouds and storms, and all the weather, through which you give your creatures sustenance.

Be praised, My Lord, through Sister Water; she is very useful, and humble, and precious, and pure.

Be praised, my Lord, through Brother Fire, through whom you brighten the night. He is beautiful and cheerful, and powerful and strong.

Be praised, my Lord, through our sister Mother Earth, who feeds us and rules us, and produces various fruits with colored flowers and herbs.

Be praised, my Lord, through those who forgive for love of you; through those who endure sickness and trial. Happy those who endure in peace, for by you, Most High, they will be crowned.

Medieval Literature: Three Major Genres (continued)

II. The Troubadour Lyric (continued)

Be praised, my Lord, through our Sister Bodily Death, from whose embrace no living person can escape. Woe to those who die in mortal sin! Happy those she finds doing your most holy will. The second death can do no harm to them.

Praise and bless my Lord, and give thanks, and serve him with great humility.

NOTE: This poem by St. Francis is the earliest surviving piece of Italian literature.

      A. For the poem of Guillaume IX see Frederick Goldin, ed., *Lyrics of the Troubadours and Trouveres: An Anthology and a History*, p. 41.

         For the poem of Bertrand de Born see Barbara Tuchman, *A Distant Mirror: The Calamitous 14th Century*, p. 16.

         For the poem of St. Francis of Assisi see William R. Cook and Ronald B. Herzman, *The Medieval World View: An Introduction*, pp. 250-251.

      B. Artz, Frederick, *The Mind of the Middle Ages*, pp. 330 ff.

Medieval Literature: Three Major Genres (continued)

III. The Chivalric Romance (*roman d'aventure*)

These longer narratives idealize noble knights and their ladies, particularly the knights and ladies associated with King Arthur and his Round Table. These romances slowly gave birth to narratives satirizing courtly love (in the tradition of Ovid's *Art of Love*).

1. Arthurian Romances

E.G. Chrétien de Troyes (c.1140-c.1200)

Erec and Enide, the first Arthurian romance (c.1160)

Erec neglects his honor (*armes*) due to a happy marriage to Enide, his bride and true love (*amors*). Criticism from the court causes him to go questing with his bride, and after many conquests he recovers his glory.

Cliges (c.1162)

Cliges loves and is loved by Fenice, but Fenice is forced to marry the uncle of Cliges who is the emperor of Constantinople. Unlike the Tristan story, she refuses to play Isolde and cheat on her husband. She is united with Cliges in the end after breaking the love triangle by a potion that feigns her death.

Lancelot [*Knight of the Cart*] (c.1170)

This work commissioned by Marie of Champagne portrays the ideal relationship of courtly love (*fin'amors*) in the adulterous affair of Sir Lancelot and King Arthur's wife, Guinevere. The courtly love theme of the knight undergoing many trials and humiliating himself for his lady is prominent in this story.

Yvain [*Knight with the Lion*] (c.1170)

This story is in some ways the reverse of the *Erec* plot. Yvain neglects his bride (*amors*) in stubborn pursuit of his glory (*armes*). However, like *Erec*, and unlike *Lancelot*, *Yvain* is a tribute to marital fidelity.

Perceval [*Story of the Grail*] (c.1180)

This romance cuts back and forth between the adventures of country bumpkin turned knight, Perceval, and King Arthur's noble nephew, Sir Gawain. While this work was never finished by Chrétien and breaks off mid-sentence, it focuses on the spiritual side of knightly quests and contains the first mention of the Grail mysteries in medieval literature.

E. G. Gottfried von Strassburg (fl. 1210)

Tristan (1210)

This classic medieval romance relates the life of Tristan and his adulterous love affair with Queen Isolde of Ireland whom he won for King Mark of Cornwall and then fell in love with himself due to a love potion.

Medieval Literature: Three Major Genres (continued)

III. The Chivalric Romance (*roman d'aventure*) (continued)

E. G. Wolfram von Eschenbach (fl. c.1195-1225)

Parzival (1205-1215)

This work retells and completes Chrétien de Troyes's story of the Holy Grail.

2. *Other Romantic Works*

E.G. Andreas Capellanus (fl. twelfth c.)

Art of Courtly Love (1184-1186)

This work commissioned by Marie of Champagne contains contrived dialogues between men and women of various social classes in twelfth century France, interspersed with advice and rules on winning the affections of the opposite sex. This was considered the primary handbook of courtly love in its day.

E.G. Guillaume de Lorris (fl. 1230) and Jean de Meun (c.1250-c.1305)

Romance of the Rose (first part, c.1230-1235, second part, c.1275)

In this allegorical account of a young man's dream, he joins the God of Love in pursuit of his beloved Rose against the antagonists of Reason, Rebuff, Wealth, Jealousy and others. This was the most popular of all medieval romances. See the more detailed explanation of the plot on page 255 above.

A. See works as listed.
B. Artz, Frederick, *The Mind of the Middle Ages*, pp. 343 ff.
  Loomis, Roger Sherman, *The Development of Arthurian Romance*, pp. 44-66

Medieval Literature: Other Genres

1. Fabliaux (little fables often included in sermons by Dominican friars)

Short bawdy verse tales (with loose roots in Aesop's fables) composed between the twelfth and fourteenth centuries, satirizing the corruption of rulers, clergy, lawyers, and doctors in medieval society. These clever fables created an abundance of anecdotes that influenced later and larger works like Boccaccio's *Decameron*, and Chaucer's *Canterbury Tales*.

2. Bestiaries

In medieval times the natural world or "book of nature" was believed to be a source of instruction like the books of the Bible. Animal behavior served as examples for proper human conduct. "But ask the animals and they will teach you" (Job 12:7). Numerous Latin bestiaries (books of beasts) grew from the popular third century Greek text, the *Physiologus*, into a Christian animal lore that is part science, part fantasy.

3. Debate Poems

Verse compositions where two persons (objects) debate topics (morality, politics, courtly love, etc.) following the general rules of disputation in public debates. Henri d'Andeli's *Battle of the Seven Arts* (1259) personified the fight between logic (championed by Aristotle and Boethius) and grammar (championed by Homer, Virgil, and Ovid).

4. Dream Poems/Visions

Narratives (often allegorical) framed in a dream/vision where the dreamer is often accompanied by a mentor or guide. Cicero's "Dream of Scipio" in his *De Republica,* Macrobius's *Commentary on the Dream of Scipio*, and Guillaume de Lorris and Jean de Meun's *The Romance of the Rose* are all examples of this genre.

5. Lives of the Saints

Hagiography (the writings of the lives of the saints) included both stories of the martyrdom or *passio* of a particular saint (e.g. St. Thomas Becket) and the life or *vita* of a particular saint (e.g. St. Francis of Assisi, "God's troubadour"). One popular anthology was Jacobus de Voragine's *The Golden Legend* (composed c. 1260) depicting the lives of 180 saints in an array of factual and fictional stories.

NOTE: For medieval drama, see p. 273.

> A. For Fabliaux see Robert Hellman and Richard O'Gorman, *Fabliaux: Ribald Tales from the Old French*
> For Bestiaries see *The Book of Beasts: Being a Translation from a Latin Bestiary of the Twelfth Century*
> For Debate Poems see Henri d'Andeli, *Battle of the Seven Arts*
> For Dream Poems/Visions see Guillaume de Lorris and Jean de Meun's *The Romance of the Rose*
> For Lives of the Saints see Jacobus de Voragine, *The Golden Legend*
> B. Walsh, James, *A Golden Treasury of Medieval Literature*

The Ten Commandments of the Code of Chivalry

1. Thou shall believe all that the Church teaches, and shall observe all its directions.
2. Thou shall defend the Church.
3. Thou shall respect all weaknesses, and shalt constitute thyself the defender of them.
4. Thou shall love the country in which thou wast born.
5. Thou shall not recoil before thine enemy.
6. Thou shall make war against the Infidel without cessation, and without mercy.
7. Thou shall perform scrupulously thy feudal duties, if they be not contrary to the laws of God.
8. Thou shall never lie, and shall remain faithful to thy pledged word.
9. Thou shall be generous, and give largesse to everyone.
10. Thou shall be everywhere and always the champion of the Right and the Good against Injustice and Evil.

    A. Geoffroi de Charny, *A Knight's Own Book of Chivalry*
    B. Gautier, Leon, *Chivalry*, p. 26

Woodcut from Spencer's *Fairie Queene,* 1592

The Nine Worthies (models of chivalry)

From Pagan times:

    1. Hector

    2. Alexander the Great

    3. Julius Caesar

From the Hebrew tradition:

    4. Joshua

    5. David

    6. Judas Maccabaeus

From Christian times:

    7. King Arthur

    8. Charlemagne

    9. Godfrey of Bouillon

    A. Jean de Longuyon, *Voeux du Paon*
    B. Gautier, Leon, *Chivalry*, p. 115
       Lewis, C. S., *The Discarded Image*, p. 181

The Chief Rules of Courtly Love

1. Thou shall avoid avarice like the deadly pestilence and shall embrace its opposite.

2. Thou shall keep thyself chaste for the sake of her whom thou loves.

3. Thou shall not knowingly strive to break up a correct love affair that someone else is engaged in.

4. Thou shall not choose for thy love anyone whom a natural sense of shame for bids thee to marry.

5. Be mindful completely to avoid falsehood.

6. Thou shall not have many who know of thy love affair.

7. Being obedient in all things to the commands of ladies, thou shall ever strive to ally thyself to the service of Love.

8. In giving and receiving love's solaces let modesty ever be present.

9. Thou shall speak no evil.

10. Thou shall not be a revealer of love affairs.

11. Thou shall be in all things polite and courteous.

12. In practicing the solaces of love thou shall not exceed the desires of thy lover.

    A. Andreas Capellanus, *The Art of Courtly Love*, I.6
    B. Lewis, C. S., *The Allegory of Love*

Other Rules of Courtly Love (attributed to Arthurian tradition)

1. Marriage is no real excuse for not loving.
2. He who is not jealous cannot love.
3. No one can be bound by a double love.
4. It is well known that love is always increasing or decreasing.
5. That which a lover takes against the will of his beloved has no relish.
6. Boys do not love until they arrive at the age of maturity.
7. When one lover dies, a widowhood of two years is required of the survivor.
8. No one should be deprived of love without the very best of reasons.
9. No one can love unless he is impelled by the persuasion of love.
10. Love is always a stranger in the house of avarice.
11. It is not proper to love any woman whom one should be ashamed to seek to marry.
12. A true lover does not desire to embrace in love anyone except his beloved.
13. When made public love rarely endures.
14. The easy attainment of love makes it of little value; difficulty of attainment makes it prized.
15. Every love regularly turns pale in the presence of his beloved.
16. When a lover suddenly catches sight of his beloved his heart palpitates.
17. A new love puts to flight an old one.
18. Good character alone makes any man worthy of love.
19. If love diminishes, it quickly fails and rarely revives.
20. A man in love is always apprehensive.
21. Real jealousy always increases the feeling of love.
22. Jealousy, and therefore love, are increased when one suspects his beloved.
23. He whom the thought of love vexes, eats and sleeps very little.
24. Every act of a lover ends in the thought of his beloved.
25. A true lover considers nothing good except what he thinks will please his beloved.
26. Love can deny nothing to love.
27. A lover can never have enough of the solaces of his beloved.
28. A slight presumption causes a lover to suspect his beloved
29. A man who is vexed by too much passion usually does not love.
30. A true lover is constantly and without intermission possessed by the thought of his beloved.
31. Nothing forbids one woman being loved by two men or one man by two women.

A. Andreas Capellanus, *The Art of Courtly Love*, II.8
B. Lewis, C. S. *The Allegory of Love*

The Four Stages of Courtly Love

1. The giving of hope

2. The granting of a kiss

3. The enjoyment of an embrace

4. The yielding of the whole person (often delayed indefinitely)

    A. Andreas Capellanus, *The Art of Courtly Love*, I.6
    B. Lewis, C. S., The *Allegory of Love*

Genealogy of King Arthur

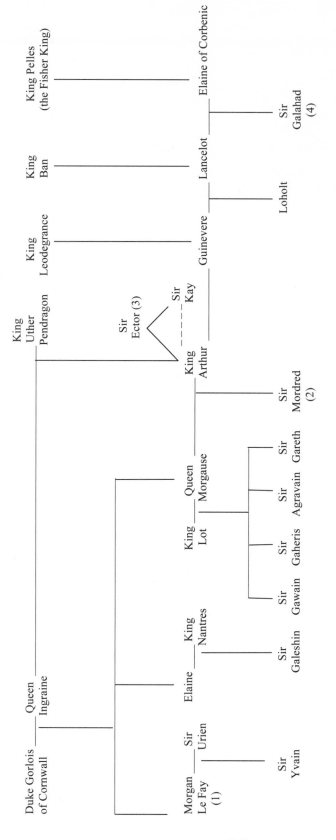

(1) Sorceress and half sister to Arthur. The only enemy of Arthur that he does not kill or whose allegiance he does not win.

(2) Bastard son of Arthur. As foretold by Merlin, Mordred delivers a fatal wound to Arthur in combat and is himself killed in the exchange.

(3) Along with his wife, raises Arthur from infancy to marriage, as arranged by the magician (and mentor to Arthur) Merlin.

(4) Bastard son of Lancelot and the last descendent of Joseph of Arimathea. The only Arthurian knight to complete the quest for the Holy Grail.

A. Sir Thomas Malory, *Le Morte D'Arthur* (other Arthurian sources may have different relationships)

B. Loomis, Roger Sherman, *The Development of Arthurian Romance*
   New Arthurian Encyclopedia

The Legends of the Holy Grail

Grail Source	Grail Story	Grail King	Grail Heroes	Grail Objects
Celtic Branch of Legends				
Anonymous *Peredur* A story found in *Mabinogion* 14th century (Welsh)	Peredur visits his uncle's (mother's brother's) castle and sees two youths bearing a great spear with three streams of blood flowing from its point. He next sees two maidens carrying a large serving dish with a severed head floating in blood. Everyone in the room but his uncle wails and laments upon each occurrence.	Peredur's Uncle	Peredur	Large serving dish with a severed head floating in blood carried by two maidens.
Chretien de Troyes *Perceval: The Story of the Grail* (unfinished) 1180-1190 (French)	Perceval (who has sinned by abandoning his mother) visits the castle of the Fisher King (who is wounded in his thighs) and sees the Grail and the bleeding lance but fails to ask the question, "Who is it that the Grail serves?" Therefore, the Fisher King's wound is not healed.	Fisher King	Perceval (naïve)	First, a boy carrying a bleeding lance. Second, a beautiful girl carrying a grail or serving dish. Third, a girl holding a silver trencher (plate).
Christian Branch of Legends				
Anonymous *1st Continuation of Chretien* 1190-1200 (French)	Gawain visits the castle twice & sees the Grail (moving by itself). Gawain must mend a broken sword to be able to ask THE question. Gawain fails to mend the broken sword. He devotes his search to the bleeding lance.	Fisher King	Gawain (worldly) (amorous)	A serving dish called the Holy Grail miraculously feeds the multitude in the castle. Gawain learns the connection between the Grail, the lance, and the crucifixion of Christ.
Wauchier *2nd Continuation of Chretien* 1200-1210 (French)	Perceval sees the Grail both in the castle and in the forest outside the castle. Perceval fails to mend the broken sword.	Fisher King	Perceval	First, the Holy Grail carried by a girl. Second, a girl carrying a bleeding lance. Third, a boy carrying a broken sword.
Manessier *3rd Continuation of Chretien* 1210-1220 (French)	Perceval learns the broken sword was used to kill the Fisher King's brother, Partinial. Perceval avenges that death and learns that he himself is the Fisher King's nephew. He is crowned Fisher King himself.	Fisher King	Perceval	Perceval learns the lance is the one with which Longinus wounded Christ, that the blood is the blood from that wound, and that the silver trencher was the covering over the Grail. The girl is the Fisher King's virgin daughter.
Gerbert de Montreuil *4th Continuation of Chretien* 1226-1230 (French)	Perceval mends the broken sword but his rewards (the answer to the question and the succession to the Fisher King's throne) are not made clear.	Fisher King	Perceval	
Robert de Boron trilogy (1) *Joseph of Arimathea* (2) *Merlin* (3) Didot-*Perceval* 1200-1210 (French)	(1) Apocryphal gospel telling how Joseph of Arimathea (Jn 19:38-42) buried Christ and sent the Grail and lance to Western Europe via Joseph's brother-in-law, Bron. (2) Connection made between table of the Last Supper (Mk 14:17-25) and Arthur's Round Table. (3) Perceval asks THE question & Fisher King is healed.	Bron = Fisher King	Joesph of Arimathea and Perceval	Pilate gives Joseph the Grail chalice from the Last Supper and gives him the body of Christ and the lance. Joseph fills the Grail with the blood of Christ as he takes Christ from the cross.

The Legends of the Holy Grail (continued)

	Description	Fisher King	Seeker	Grail
Anonymous *Perlesvaus*, also known as *The High Book of the Grail* Before 1210 (French)	Prologue outlines the guardianship of the Grail from Joseph of Arimathea to Arthur's times. Perlesvaus succeeds in Grail task. Gawain and Lancelot fail. Possession of the sword that beheaded John the Baptist is needed in order to enter the Grail castle.	Fisher King	Perlesvaus	Grail clearly identified as a chalice, a "rare sight." Grail scene in the castle chapel includes: First, the Holy Grail. Second, the lance with a bleeding head. Third, the sword that beheaded John the Baptist.
From the Vulgate cycle (possibly composed by Cistercian monks) *Lancelot* 1210-120 (French)	Gawain, Lancelot, and Bors all see the Grail at Pelles's castle at Corbenic, experience its healing powers, but ultimately fail in the quest. Pelles tricks Lancelot into sleeping with his daughter, Elaine, so that she will bear the son (Galahad) who is destined to free his kingdom from the curse that has laid it waste.	Fisher King = Pelles	Gawain Lancelot Bors	The Grail is the most splendid vessel in the semblance of a chalice.
From the Vulgate Cycle *Quest of the Holy Grail* 1220-1230 (French)	The Grail appears (floating in midair) to the knights of the Round Table at Camelot on Pentecost. Later in the story, Perceval presents Partinial's severed head to the Fisher King whereupon the Grail appears carried by two girls. Later still, Galahad anoints the King with blood from the Grail chalice and the King's wounds are healed.	Fisher King = Pelles	Galahad (a virgin)	Galahad, Bors, Perceval, and nine other knights have a vision of Christ and reenact the Last Supper, receiving hosts from the Grail by the hand of Christ. At Galahad's death at the end of the story, the Grail and the lance are assumed into heaven.
From the Vulgate Cycle *History of the Holy Grail* 1230-1240 (French)	Tale of the wandering of Joseph of Arimathea and his descendents from Palestine to Britain. The story parallels the wanderings of the Jews in the desert with the Grail taking the place of the Ark of the Covenenat. The Grail finally reaches its earthly home at the Corbenic castle.	Fisher King = Pelles	Joseph of Arimathea and his descendents	The bowl/Grail and the lance are place by Joseph and his son, Josephus, in an ark as commanded by Christ.
Chymical Branch of Legends				
Wolfram von Eschenbach *Parzival* 1210-1220 (German)	After exotic tales of Parzival's father's travels in Arabia, the remainder of the story follows Chretien's story outline for the most part. Parzival does ask THE Grail question (in this version the question being, "What ails you?") and therefore heals Anfortas's wounds.	Anfortas	Parzival	The Grail is a magic stone called *lapsit exillis* that has fallen from the heavens. The appearance of the Grail is proceeded by an elaborate procession in the castle of Munsalvaesche.
Later Compilation				
Sir Thomas Malory *Morte d'Arthur* 1485 (English)	Malory is a great synthesizer who weaves together many of the strands of the Arthurian legend. However, he mainly follows the *Quest of the Holy Grail* from the Vulgate cycle.	Fisher King = Pelles	Galahad	Follows the *Quest of the Holy Grail* from the Vulgate cycle.

A. Bryant, Nigel, *The Legend of the Grail*
B. Barber, Richard, *The Holy Grail: Imagination and Belief*
Godwin, Malcolm, *The Holy Grail: Its Origins, Secrets and Meaning Revealed*
Williams, Charles, and C. S. Lewis, *Arthurian Torso*

The Three Tables (The Three Great Fellowships)

1. Table of Jesus Christ (Last Supper)	Jesus feeds the 12 apostles
2. Table of the Holy Grail	Joseph of Arimathea feeds 4,000
3. Knights of the Round Table	Established by Merlin; Arthur feeds his knights

   A. *The Quest of the Holy Grail*, chapter 6
   B. Godwin, Malcolm, *The Holy Grail: Its Origins, Secrets, and Meanings Revealed*, p. 123

The Holy Pentangle of Sir Gawain (painted on his shield)

First point = his five senses of sight, hearing, smell, taste, and touch (he remains free from sin)

Second point = his five fingers (that have never failed him)

Third point = Christ's five words on the cross in his hands, his feet, and his side (the source of Gawain's hope)

Fourth point = Mary's five joys* (the source of Gawain's courage)

Fifth point = his knightly virtues: (1) love
    (2) friendship
    (3) freedom from sin
    (4) courtesy
    (5) pity (his greatest virtue)

*NOTE: Mary's five joys included the Annunciation, the Visitation, the Nativity, the Presentation in the Temple, and the Finding in the Temple.

    A. *Sir Gawain and the Green Knight*, section 28
    B. Howard, Donald, *The Three Temptations: Medieval Man in Search of the World*, pp. 226-227

Three Types of Medieval Drama

<u>types</u>	<u>themes</u>	<u>examples</u>
1. mystery plays (or "Cycle" plays)	different biblical stories from the fall of Lucifer to the Last Judgment (the most famous play being the Second Shepherds' Play from the Wakefield Cycle)	*The Wakefield Cycle* (32 plays) (English) *The York Cycle* (48 plays) (English)
2. miracle plays	stories of Christ and the Virgin, and the lives of the saints that focus on spirituality beyond the Bible (the most famous being the Miracle of Theophilus)	Gonzalo de Berceo, *Miracles of Our Lady* (Spanish)
3. morality plays	the struggles between good and evil; heavily allegorical with characters like Everyman, Death, Good Deeds, and Kinsmen	*Everyman* (Dutch)

NOTE: "All of these types of plays were performed by members of the local guilds, and mystery plays were usually produced on *pageants* (roofed wagon-stages) that were rolled into the town square" (Fiero). Note that the fourteenth and fifteenth century medieval mystery plays (performed in the vernacular) are late developments of Latin liturgical plays performed in medieval churches as an integral part of the service of the Mass. For example, the Resurrection of the York cycle finds its origin in the Easter Sepulcher play performed earlier in the Middle Ages. These liturgical plays in turn grew out of tropes or chanted Latin dialogues that were added to the service of the Mass at Easter (e.g., *Quem quaeritis*) or at Christmas as far back as the tenth century.

    A. *Everyman and Medieval Miracle Plays*
       Gonzalo de Berceo, *Miracles of Our Lady*
       The Wakefield Mystery Plays
       The York Mystery Plays: A Selection in Modern Spelling
    B. Fiero, Gloria, *The Humanist Tradition*, 4th edition, vol. 1, pp. 271-272

The York Cycle of Medieval Mystery Plays

guild	play
1. Barkers (tanners)	Fall of Lucifer
2. Plasterers	Creation up to the Fifth Day
3. Cardmakers	Creation of Adam and Eve
4. Fullers (preparers of woolen cloth)	Adam and Eve in Eden
5. Coopers (makers of wooden casks)	Fall of Man
6. Armourers	Expulsion from Eden
7. Glovers	Sacrifice of Cain and Abel
8. Shipwrights	Building of the Ark
9. Fishers and Mariners	Noah and his Wife
10. Parchmenters and Bookbinders	Abraham and Isaac
11. Hosiers	Exodus from Egypt
12. Spicers	Annunciation and Visitation
13. Pewterers and Founders	Joseph's Trouble about Mary
14. Tile-thatchers	Journey to Bethlehem
15. Chandlers (candlemakers)	Shepherds
16. Masons	Coming of the Three Kings to Herod
17. Goldsmiths	Adoration of the Three Kings
18. Marshals (grooms)	Flight into Egypt
19. Girdlers and Nailers	Slaughter of the Innocents
20. Spurriers/Lorimers (spur/bit makers)	Christ with the Doctors
21. Barbers	Baptism of Jesus
22. Smiths	Temptation of Jesus
23. Curriers (men who dress leather)	Transfiguration
24. Capmakers	Woman Taken in Adultery
25. Skinners	Christ's Entry into Jerusalem
26. Cutlers	Conspiracy against Jesus
27. Bakers	Last Supper
28. Cordwainers (shoemakers)	Agony and Betrayal
29. Bowyers and Fletchers	Peter's Denial; Jesus before Caiphas
30. Tapiters (makers of tapestry/carpets)	Dream of Pilate's Wife; Jesus before Pilate
31. Listers (dyers)	Trial before Herod
32. Cooks and Water-leaders	Remorse of Judas
33. Tilemakers	Second Trial before Pilate
34. Shearmen	Christ Led to Calvary
35. Pinners and Painters	Crucifixion
36. Butchers	Mortification of Christ; Burial
37. Saddlers	Harrowing of Hell
38. Carpenters	Resurrection
39. Winedrawers	Christ's Appearance to Mary Magdalene
40. Sledmen	Travellers to Emmaus
41. Hatmakers, Masons, Laborers	Purification of Mary; Simeon and Anna
42. Scriveners	Incredulity of Thomas
43. Tailors	Ascension

The York Cycle of Medieval Mystery Plays (continued)

<u>guild</u>	<u>play</u>
44. Potters	Descent of the Holy Spirit
45. Drapers (dealers in cloth/dry goods)	Death of Mary
46. Weavers	Appearance of Mary to Thomas
47. Ostlers (stablemen)	Assumption and Coronation of the Virgin
48. Mercers (dealers in textiles)	Judgment Day

NOTE: While there is no record of the first performance of the York Mystery Plays, there is a record of the storage of three Corpus Christi pageant-wagons in 1376, showing the plays were already in existence at this time. The plays were organized, financed, and often performed by the York Craft Guilds. The word, "mystery," is a play on words since it represents both a religious truth or rite, and, in its Middle English meaning, a trade or craft. The wagons paraded through the streets of York, stopping at each of 12 playing stations.

A. *The York Mystery Plays: A Selection in Modern Spelling*
B. Cawley, A. C., ed., *Everyman and Medieval Miracle Plays*, pp. 254-256

Annotated Bibliography

ONLINE SOURCES

Arthur Resources: www.clas.ufl.edu/users/jshoaf/Arthurnet.htm
The Arthurnet site provides links to innumerable other sites about the Arthurian tradition.

Medieval Bestiary: http://bestiary.ca
Massive collection of medieval bestiaries (well over 3,000 pages) that can be researched through manuscript families or through the beasts themselves.

Catholic Encyclopedia: www.newadvent.org/cathen
Includes innumerable articles on medieval studies of all types.

Classics Archive: http://classics.mit.edu
Full texts of classics, 441 works, 59 authors (mainly Greco-Roman).

Dartmouth Math Project: www.dartmouth.edu/~matc/math5.geometry
Syllabus devoted to use of geometry in art and architecture through the ages. Discussion of the quadrivium, the Pythagorean tradition, and medieval number symbolism.

Georgetown Site: http://labyrinth.georgetown.edu
Major collection of materials on all aspects of medieval studies.

History of Philosophy: www2.nd.edu/Departments//Maritain/etext/hwp.htm
History of Ancient and Medieval Western Philosophy by Ralph McInerny in conjunction with the Jacques Maritain Center at the University of Notre Dame.

Medieval History Site: www.netserf.org
Best site for finding more specialized sites on medieval history.

Medieval Sourcebook: www.fordham.edu/mvst (click Links)
Full texts of classics and links to other medieval sites.

OMACL: www.omacl.org
The Online Medieval and Classical Library. Numerous literary works.

"Orb" Site: www.the-orb.net
Contains translations of primary materials as well as essays by modern historians. The "encyclopedia" section is especially useful.

Patrologia Latina Database: http://pld.chadwyck.co.uk
Electronic version of Jacques-Paul Migne's massive *Patrologia Latina* (PL).

Princeton Dante Project: www.princeton.edu/~dante
Multimedia edition of the *Divine Comedy* and Dante's minor works (e.g. the *Convivio*) with links to Dante commentaries and other on-line Dante sites including foreign sites.

Sacred Text Archive: www.sacred-texts.com
  Massive collection of Scriptures and other writings from all world religions.

PRIMARY SOURCES

Abelard, Peter [1079-1142]. *Glosses of Peter Abelard on Porphyry* in Richard McKeon's *Selections from Medieval Philosophers*. New York: Charles Scribner's Sons, 1958. An abridged version of Abelard's *Glosses on Porphyry* can be found in Paul Vincent Spade, ed., *Five Texts on the Mediaeval Problem of Universals* (Indianapolis, IN: Hackett Publishing Co., 1994), pp. 26-56. In the argument over the ontological status of universals, Abelard argues for the position that came to be known as moderate realism.

————. *The Letters of Abelard and Heloise*. New York: Penguin Books, 2003. Eight lengthy letters depicting the passionate love affair and tragic marriage between Peter Abelard, the greatest philosopher of his era, and his wife Heloise, who became the abbess of a prominent monastery. Includes letter one, Abelard's *Historia Calamitatum* [The story of my misfortunes].

Adalbero of Laon [d. 1030/1031]. *Carmen ad Robertum Regem* [Song to King Robert]. Jacques-Paul Migne, ed., *Patrologia Latina* (PL). Paris: Garnier, 1853. Vol. 141. The *Patrologia Latina Database* is an electronic version of the first edition of Migne's *Patrologia* and is available (for subscribers) at http://pld.chadwyck.co.uk.

Andreas Capellanus [fl. twelfth c.]. *The Art of Courtly Love*. Translated by John Jay Parry. New York: Columbia University Press, 1969. In the tradition of Ovid's *The Art of Love*, a tongue-in-cheek love manual comprised of contrived dialogues between men and women of various social classes in twelfth century France, interspersed with advice and rules on winning the affections of the opposite sex. Commissioned by Countess Marie of Champagne.

Anselm [1033-1109]. *Proslogion* in *Anselm of Canterbury: The Major Works*. New York: Oxford University Press, 1998. Includes Anselm's famous ontological argument for the existence of God.

Aquinas, Thomas [c.1225-1274]. *Summa Theologica*. 3 vols. New York: Benziger Brothers, 1947-1948. Imitating a structure similar to the public debates or "disputations" of his day in Paris, Thomas's *magnum opus* reviews all of Sacred Doctrine in a series of 611 questions. Each question and answer, including replies and objections, might run for pages.

————. *On Truth*. 3 vols. Chicago: Regnery, 1952-1954. According to James Weisheipl (see his works in Secondary Sources), these questions on truth were disputed in Paris during Thomas's first Parisian regency and distributed over the course of three years.

Aristotle [384-322 BCE]. *The Basic Works of Aristotle*. Edited by Richard McKeon. New York: Random House, 1941. Some of Aristotle's works in this edition are abridged, particularly certain logical works. Complete books of the *Organon* can be found in the Loeb Classical Library series.

———. *Categories. On Interpretation. Prior Analytics*. Loeb Classical Library. Cambridge, MA: Harvard University Press, 2002. Three works in one volume describing Aristotle's theory of terms, of propositions, and of syllogisms, respectively.

———. *Posterior Analytics. Topics*. Loeb Classical Library. Cambridge, MA: Harvard University Press, 2004. Two works in one volume describing Aristotle's theory of demonstrative syllogisms (whose premises are true) and dialectical syllogisms (whose premises are only probable).

———. *On Sophistical Refutations*. Loeb Classical Library. Cambridge, MA: Harvard University Press, 1978. Included in one volume with *On Generation and Corruption* and *On the Cosmos*.

Augustine [354-430]. *The City of God*. 7 vols. Loeb Classical Library. Cambridge, MA: Harvard University Press, 1968. Also in the First Series, vol. 2, of the *Nicene and Post-Nicene Fathers*. Augustine's masterpiece of both political theory and the philosophy of history. A vindication of Christianity against the pagans who blamed the fall of Rome on Christianity.

———. *Confessions*. 2 vols. Loeb Classical Library. Cambridge, MA: Harvard University Press, 1968. Also in the First Series, vol. 1, of the *Nicene and Post-Nicene Fathers*. The story of Augustine's resistance to and final conversion to Christianity. Arguably the first autobiographical work in the Western world.

———. *On Rebuke and Grace*. In the First Series, vol. 5 of the *Nicene and Post-Nicene Fathers*. Grand Rapids, MI: William B. Eerdmans, 1956. A polemical work against the Pelagian heresy in which Augustine defends the doctrine of justification (or salvation) by grace alone.

———. *On the Trinity*. In the First Series, vol. 3 of the *Nicene and Post-Nicene Fathers*. Grand Rapids, MI: William B. Eerdmans, 1956. Perhaps Augustine's most complex theological work.

Averroes [1126-1198]. *On the Harmony of Religion and Philosophy*. Translated by George Hourani. London: Messrs. Luzac & Co., 1967. Averroes argues that religious truth and philosophical truth do not ultimately conflict and that Islamic law commands those that are capable to undertake the study of philosophy.

———. *On Plato's Republic*. Translated by Ralph Lerner. Ithaca, NY: Cornell University Press, 1974. Averroes, known for his commentaries on the works of Aristotle, undertook this paraphrase of the *Republic* because "Aristotle's *Politics* has not yet fallen into our hands" (p. xiii).

Avicenna [980-1037]. *The Canon of Medicine*. Chicago, IL: Kazi Publications, 1999. The *Canon* is a 14-volume medical encyclopedia completed in 1025 that remained an authoritative work up until the early nineteenth century.

Benedict, St. [c.480-547]. *The Rule of St. Benedict*. Translated and edited by Justin McCann. New York: Sheed and Ward, 1999. Classic translation of St. Benedict's timeless rule for monks.

Bernard of Clairvaux [1090-1153]. *Bernard of Clairvaux; Selected Works*. The Classics of Western Spirituality. New York: Paulist Press, 1987. Includes Bernard's classics like *On the Steps of Humility and Pride* as well as *Sermons on the Song of Songs*. Extensive introduction by the famed Bernard scholar Jean Leclercq.

The HarperCollins Study Bible. New Revised Standard Version. New York: HarperCollins, 1993.

Bodel, Jean [c.1167-1210]. *La Chanson des Saisnes* [Song of the Saxons]. Paris: H. Champion, 1992. Bodel, an Old French poet, was the first person to classify epic legends (the *chanson de geste*) into the Matter of Rome (epics of classical antiquity), the Matter of France (epics of Charlemagne), and the Matter of Britain (epics of Arthur).

Boethius [c.480-c.525]. *The Consolation of Philosophy*. New York: Penguin, 1999. Written in prison while awaiting execution, *The Consolation* is a dialogue of alternating prose and poetry between the ailing Boethius and his nurse, Philosophy, who consoles him and enlightens him on the true nature of good and evil, fortune, and happiness.

―――. *Second Commentary on Porphyry's Isagoge*. An abridged version of this text can be found in Paul Vincent Spade, ed., *Five Texts on the Mediaeval Problem of Universals* (Indianapolis, IN: Hackett Publishing Co., 1994), pp. 20-25. Boethius is one of the earliest commentators on the famous *Isagoge*, Porphyry's Introduction to the Categories of Aristotle.

Bryant, Nigel. *The Legend of the Grail*. Cambridge, UK: D. S. Brewer, 2004. "This volume is designed to interweave the principal motifs and narrative strands of the original Grail romances in order to construct a single, consistent and completely accessible version of the Grail story." This compilation includes narratives from: Chrétien de Troyes' *Perceval* in Chrétien de Troyes' *Arthurian Romances* (New York: Penguin, 1991; also see Chrétien de Troyes below), Wolfram von Eschenbach's *Parzival* (see Wolfram von Eschenbach below), *The Quest of the Holy Grail* (New York: Penguin, 1969), *The High Book of the Grail* (Cambridge, UK: D. S. Brewer, 1996), and Robert de Boron's entire trilogy in *Merlin and the Grail* (Cambridge, UK: D. S. Brewer, 2003). The four continuations of Chrétien's *Perceval* can be found in Chrétien de Troyes' *Perceval: The Story of the Grail* (Cambridge, UK: D. S. Brewer, 1986).

Cassiodorus [c.490-c.583]. *An Introduction to Divine and Human Readings*. Translated by Leslie Webber Jones. New York: Columbia University Press, 1969. After holding public offices under four Ostrogothic rulers, Cassiodorus retired to a monastic setting where he strove to transform the monastery into a theological school and scriptorium. Book One of this work discusses the Bible and establishes precise rules for copying and preserving manuscripts. Book Two is a treatise on the seven liberal arts.

Cassian, John [c.365-c.435]. *Conferences*. Mahwah, NJ: Paulist Press, 1985. Drawing on his experience as a monk in Bethlehem and Egypt, Cassian traveled west to found monasteries in Marseilles and the region of Provence. The *Conferences* comprise a study of the Egyptian ideal of the monk.

Chrétien de Troyes [c.1140-c.1200]. *The Complete Romances of Chrétien de Troyes*. Translated by David Staines. Bloomington, IN: Indiana University Press, 1993. The five romances of the French purveyor of the Arthur legends including Eric and Enide, Cliges, The Knight of the Cart (Lancelot), The Knight with the Lion (Yvain), and The Story of the Grail (Perceval). The original verse romances are in prose form here.

Cicero [106-43 BCE]. *De Inventione*. Loeb Classical Library. Cambridge, MA: Harvard University Press, 1976. Included in one volume with *De Optima Genere Oratorum* and *Topica*. Cicero's youthful work on rhetoric which he later criticized in his mature work, *De Oratore*.

———. *De Natura Deorum*. Loeb Classical Library. Cambridge, MA: Harvard University Press, 1979. Study of the theological views of the three schools of philosophy in Cicero's time – the Epicurean, the Stoic, and the Skeptic.

———. *De Oratore*. 2 vols. Loeb Classical Library. Cambridge, MA: Harvard University Press, 2001. Discussion of oratory composed in the form of a conversation between two great Roman orators, Crassus and Antonius, and two of their younger followers.

Dante [1265-1321]. *Dante's Il Convivio/The Banquet*. New York: Garland Press, 1990. Dante's philosophical essay composed after the years of his exile.

———. *Inferno*. Translated by Robert and Jean Hollander. New York: Doubleday, 2000. Dante's journey through the nine circles of Hell based on the Aristotelian classification of sin. Italian and English on facing pages. Verse translation with copious notes.

———. *Purgatorio*. Translated by Robert and Jean Hollander. New York: Doubleday, 2003. Dante's journey up the Mount of Purgatory based on the seven deadly sins. Italian and English on facing pages. Verse translation with copious notes.

———. *Paradiso*. Translated by Robert and Jean Hollander. New York: Doubleday, 2007. Dante's journey through the heavens based on the Ptolemaic system of the celestial spheres. Italian and English on facing pages. Verse translation with copious notes.

Diogenes Laertius [fl. 3rd c.]. *Lives and Opinions of Eminent Philosophers*. 2 vols. Loeb Classical Library. Cambridge: Harvard University Press, 2006. Contains biographies of ancient Greek philosophers by a biographer limited in his philosophical abilities.

Euclid [fl. c.300 BCE]. *The Thirteen Books of Euclid's Elements*. Translated by Sir Thomas Heath. Santa Fe, NM: Green Lion Press, 2002. The basic text on geometry in the Western world for over 2,000 years.

Everyman and Medieval Miracle Plays. Edited by A. C. Cawley. North Clarendon, VT: Tuttle Publishing, 2004. An allegorical morality play, *Everyman* discovers what you cannot take with you when you die and hence falls back on moral and religious values.

Freeman, Kathleen. *Ancilla to the Pre-Socratic Philosophers: A Complete Translation of the Fragments in Diels*. Cambridge, MA: Harvard University Press, 1948. Republished by Forgotten Books in 2008 and available on-line at www.forgottenbooks. org.

Al-Ghazālī [1058-1111]. *The Incoherence of the Philosophers*. Translated by Michael E. Marmura. Provo, Utah: Brigham Young University Press, 2000. The famous attack on philosophy that put Islamic philosophers forever on the defensive. Arabic and English on facing pages.

Geoffrey of Monmouth [c.100-c.155]. *History of the Kings of Britain.* New York: Penguin, 1977. History, mixed with legend, from the founding of Britain by Brutus to the invasion of the Saxons. The legends of Arthur were first recorded here.

Geoffroi de Charny [c.1304-1356]. *A Knight's Own Book of Chivalry.* Philadelphia: University of Pennsylvania Press, 2005. Charny's book offers an exploration and explanation of the values and proper manner of life for Christian knights and men at arms by someone who was a knight himself during the height of the Hundred Years War in the fourteenth century.

Gonzalo de Berceo [c.1190 – c.1264]. *Miracles of Our Lady.* Translated by Richard Terry Mount and Annette Grant Cash. Lexington, KY: University of Kentucky Press, 1997. A collection of miracle tales (often performed as miracle plays) in which people are rewarded for piety and punished for sin through the intervention of the Virgin Mary.

Gottfried von Strassburg [fl. 1210]. *Tristan.* New York: Penguin Books, 1967. The legendary romance relating the life of Tristan and his adulterous love affair with Queen Isolde because of the influence of a magic potion.

The Greek Anthology. 5 vols. Loeb Classical Library. Cambridge, MA: Harvard University Press, 1953. Collection of Greek epigrams from pagan and Christian poets before and after the Christian era.

Gregory the Great [c.540-604]. *Moralia in Job* [Morals on the Book of Job]. Three complete volumes in Latin (volumes 143, 143A, 143B) in *Corpus Christianorum* (Series Latina). The closest English translation is Joseph Gildea's abbreviated version, *Source Book of Self-Discipline: A Synthesis of Moralia in Job by Gregory the Great : A Translation of Peter of Waltham's Remediarium Conversorum* (New York: Peter Lang Publishing, 1991). Gregory's original commentary on the Book of Job comprised over one-half million words.

Guillaume de Lorris [fl. 1230] and Jean de Meun [c.1250-c.1305]. *The Romance of the Rose.* New York: Oxford University Press, 1994. Allegorical account of a young man's dream in which he joins the God of Love in pursuit of his beloved Rose against the antagonists of Reason, Rebuff, Wealth, Jealousy, and others. The most popular of all medieval romances.

Henri d'Andeli [fl. 1259]. *Battle of the Seven Arts.* Berkeley, CA: University of California Press, 1914. Allegory personifying the medieval battle between logic (championed by Aristotle and Boethius) and grammar (championed by Donatus, Homer, Virgil, and Ovid).

Hesiod [eighth c. BCE?]. *Theogony.* Loeb Classical Library edition of *The Homeric Hymns and Homerica.* Cambridge, MA: Harvard University Press, 1977. Hesiod's genealogy of the gods.

———. *Works and Days.* Loeb Classical Library edition of *The Homeric Hymns and Homerica.* Cambridge, MA: Harvard University Press, 1977. An interesting text, given the negative attitude of the ancient Greeks towards work and labor.

Homer [eighth c. BCE?]. *The Iliad*. Translated by Robert Fagles. New York: Penguin Classics, 1998. Tells the story of the wrath of Achilles and his quest for eternal glory during the Trojan War.

―――. *The Odyssey*. Translated by Robert Fagles. New York: Penguin Classics, 1998. Tells the story of the adventures and ultimate homecoming of the cunning Odysseus after the Trojan War.

Hugh of St. Victor [1096-1141]. *The Didascalicon of Hugh of St. Victor: A Medieval Guide to the Arts*. Translated by Jerome Taylor. New York: Columbia University, 1991. "The *Didascalicon* of Hugh of St. Victor aims to select and define all the areas of knowledge important to man and to demonstrate not only that these areas are essentially integrated amongst themselves, but that in their integrity they are necessary to man for the attainment of his human perfection and his divine destiny." Includes discussion of the Hugh's seven mechanical arts along with the traditional encyclopedist's discussion of the Bible and the seven liberal arts.

―――. *On the Sacraments of the Christian Faith*. Cambridge, MA: Mediaeval Academy of America, 1951. Hugh's masterpiece, a dogmatic synthesis of theology and biblical studies.

Iamblichus [fl. mid-fourth c. ?]. *The Theology of Arithmetic*. Translated by Robin Waterfield. Grand Rapids, MI: Phanes Press, 1988. Attributed to Iamblichus, this is the longest work on number symbolism to survive from the ancient world. The work is about the mystical, mathematical, and cosmological symbolism of the first ten numbers.

Isidore of Seville [c.560-636]. *The Etymologies of Isidore of Seville*. New York: Cambridge University Press, 2006. This "encyclopedia" by the seventh century bishop of Seville gathers together all the elements of secular learning at the time and adds a great deal of ecclesiastical information. Its wide use in medieval education is confirmed by the more than one thousand extant manuscripts, second only to the number of manuscripts of the Bible. The Vatican has declared Isidore of Seville the patron saint of the Internet.

Jacobus de Voragine [c.1230-c.1298]. *The Golden Legend*. 2 vols. Princeton, NJ: Princeton University Press, 1993. Anthology depicting the lives of 180 saints in an array of factual and fictional stories ranging from well known saints to gory descriptions of the death of St. James the Dismembered. Written by the Archbishop of Genoa and arranged according to the saints' feast days throughout the liturgical year.

Jean de Longuyon [fl. 1312]. *Voeux du Paon* [Vows of the peacock]. Published as *The Parlement of the Three Ages: An Alliterative Poem on the Nine Worthies and the Heroes of Romance*. London: Oxford University Press, 1915. Book of the nine worthies or champions of chivalry, three in pagan times, three in Old Testament times, and three in Christian times. Professor Gollanez's English edition contains an appendix of early texts that illustrate the Nine Worthies theme.

Joachim of Fiore [c.1132-1202]. *The Book of Concordance*, II.1.2-12 is translated and published in Bernard McGinn, *Apocalyptic Spirituality* (New York: Paulist Press, 1979), pp. 120-148. The remainder of the book has not been translated into English. Joachim of Fiore was the most important apocalyptic author of the Middle Ages.

John of Salisbury [c.1115-1180]. *The Metalogicon of John of Salisbury*. Gloucester, MA: Peter Smith, 1971. A spirited defense of the trivium and of Aristotelian logic by the learned secretary and witness to the death of the famous chancellor Thomas Beckett. John of Salisbury became the revered Bishop of Chartres later in life.

Longinus [first c.?]. *On the Sublime*. Loeb Classical Library. Cambridge, MA: Harvard University Press, 1982. Included in one volume with Aristotle's *Poetics* and Demetrius' *On Style*. Ancient treatise on aesthetics in the tradition of Aristotle's *Poetics*. Longinus might have been a Hellenized Jew.

The Mabinogion. New York: Penguin, 1976. Twelve Welsh prose tales that influenced the Arthurian legends. Composed in the golden age of Celtic storytelling in the thirteenth century or earlier.

Macrobius [fl. late 4th c.]. *Commentary on the Dream of Scipio*. Translated by William Harris Stahl. New York: Columbia University Press, 1990. A commentary on Cicero's *Dream of Scipio*, the concluding section of his *De Re Publica* (which is itself a commentary on the Myth of Er at the end of Plato's *Republic*), Macrobius' work provides the most accessible primary source for understanding the medieval worldview. It includes discussion of the neo-Platonic Trinity, Pythagorean number theory and Plato's lambda, neo-Platonic psychology, the origin and descent of souls from the heavens, the heavenly spheres, and the ten celestial circles. It's all here and Macrobius makes a clearer presentation than encyclopedists like Martianus, Cassiodorus, and Isidore of Seville.

Maimonides, Moses [1135-1204]. *Guide of the Perplexed*. Translated by Shlomo Pines. 2 vols. Chicago: University of Chicago Press, 1974. Monumental translation of Maimonides' *magnum opus* that aims to remain as faithful to Maimonides' original Arabic as possible. "Every Arabic technical term has been rendered by one and the same English term." This edition includes two extensive introductions by Shlomo Pines and by Leo Strauss.

————. *A Maimonides Reader*. Edited by Isadore Twersky. New York: Behrman House, 1972. The thirteen principles of Judaism which were originally set down by Maimonides in his *Introduction to Perek Helek* within his *Commentary on the Mishnah* can be found on pp. 417-423 of Twersky's *Reader*.

Malory, Sir Thomas [c.1405–c.1471]. *Le Morte d'Arthur*. New York: Modern Library, 1994. Considered by many as the classic rendition of the legends of King Arthur and the Knights of the Round Table. First published in 1485 by Willliam Caxton.

Manilius, Marcus [fl. first c.]. *Astronomica*. Loeb Classical Library. Cambridge, MA: Harvard University Press, 1977. Didactic poem on astrology. The first appearance of the astrological system of houses linking human affairs with the path of the Zodiac.

Martianus Capella [fl. fifth c.]. *Martianus Capella and the Seven Liberal Arts.* 2 vols. Translated and edited by William Harris Stahl. New York: Columbia University Press, 1971 and 1977. Volume One is an introduction and commentary on Martianus. Volume Two is a translation of Martianus' *The Marriage of Philology and Mercury*, which is an allegorical tale of a wedding that includes an elaborate presentation of the seven liberal arts.

Nicholas of Lyra [c.1270-1349]. *The Postilla of Nicholas of Lyra on the Song of Songs.* Introduced, translated, and edited by James George Kiecker. Milwaukee: Marquette University Press, 1998. A Franciscan on the theology faculty of the University of Paris from 1309 to 1330, Lyra is something of a transitional figure in biblical exegesis whose work influenced Martin Luther. His work shows both the pre-thirteenth century Platonic spiritual interpretation of Scripture and the post-thirteenth century Aristotelian literal interpretation of Scripture.

Nicomachus [c.60-c.120]. *Introduction to Arithmetic.* Volume 11 in *Great Books of the Western World* edited by Robert Maynard Hutchins. Chicago: Encyclopaedia Britannica, Inc., 1952. Included in this volume are also works by Euclid, Archimedes, and Apollonius of Perga.

Origen [c.185-254]. *Origen On First Principles.* Being Koetschau's Text of the *De Principiis* translated into English, together with an Introduction and Notes by G. W. Butterworth. New edition. Gloucester, MA: Peter Smith Publisher, 1973. The first principles are treated in four books: (1) God and the Trinity, (2) the world and its relation to God, (3) man and free will, and (4) Scripture, its inspiration and interpretation.

Ovid [43BCE-10]. *The Metamorphoses of Ovid.* Translated by Allen Mandelbaum. New York: Harcourt, Inc., 1993. Verse translation of Ovid's treasury of over 250 classical myths woven together by miraculous metamorphoses.

Plato [c.428/427-c.348/347 BCE]. *The Collected Dialogues of Plato.* Edited by Edith Hamilton and Huntington Cairns. Princeton, NJ: Princeton University Press, 2005. The classic collection of Plato's works in one volume.

————. *The Republic of Plato.* Translated by Allan Bloom. New York: Basic Books, 1991. Bloom's translation is known for its literal translation of the original Greek in order to not burden the text with modern philosophical assumptions and language.

Plotinus [c.204-270]. *Enneads.* 6 vols. Loeb Classical Library. Cambridge, MA: Harvard University Press, 1978-1984. Much of Plato's thought passed down to Christian and medieval thinkers through the spiritual genius of Plotinus. His work is also the source of the medieval stages of enlightenment – the purgative, the illuminative, and the unitive.

The Poem of the Cid. New York: Penguin Books, 1985. Bilingual edition. Story of the central figure in the long struggle of Christian Spain against the Moslems. Narrates the Cid's banishment from Castile, victorious campaigns in Valencia, and crowning of his daughters as queens in Aragon and Navarre.

Porphyry [233-c.303]. *Isagoge.* The entire text can be found in Paul Vincent Spade, ed..

Five Texts on the Mediaeval Problem of Universals. Indianapolis, IN: Hackett Publishing Co., 1994. The five texts include work from Porphyry, Boethius, Abelard, Duns Scotus, and Occam. Porphyry sets the stage for but does not engage in the ferocious medieval debate about the ontological status of universal concepts.

Prudentius [348–c.405]. *Psychomachia.* In *Prudentius*, 2 vols. Edited and translated by H. J. Thomson. Loeb Classical Library. Cambridge, MA: Harvard University Press, 1969. The *Psychomachia*, an allegorical account of a great battle between the virtues and the vices, is in volume one.

Pseudo-Dionysius [fifth or sixth c.]. *Pseudo-Dionysius: The Complete Works.* Mahwah, NJ: Paulist Press, 1987. Classic example of triadic, hierarchic neo-Platonic theology. Includes *The Divine Names* (on the divine attributes), *The Celestial Hierarchy* (on the three triads of angelic beings), and *The Ecclesiastical Hierarchy* (on the rites and offices of the Church).

Ptolemy [c.100–c.175]. *Ptolemy's Almagest.* Princeton, NJ: Princeton University Press, 1998. Astronomy textbook from the famous Alexandrian scholar that dominated the astronomy of the Middle Ages.

———. *Tetrabiblos.* Loeb Classical Library. Cambridge, MA: Harvard University Press, 1940. Astrological speculations of the famous Alexandrian scholar.

The Quest of the Holy Grail. New York: Penguin, 1969. The legend of the Holy Grail from the Vulgate Cycle, a legend in which Sir Galahad first figures prominently.

Quintilian [35-c.100]. *The Orator's Education.* 5 vols. Loeb Classical Library. Cambridge, MA: Harvard University Press, 2001. Quintilian's comprehensive training program for orators in the early Roman empire. He gives guidelines for proper schooling of the young; analyzes the structure of speeches; recommends devices that will engage listeners; and counsels on memory, delivery, and gestures.

Al-Qur'ān. Translated by Ahmed Ali. Princeton, NJ: Princeton University Press, 2001.

The Romances of Alexander. Translated by Dennis M. Kratz. New York: Garland Publishing Inc., 1991. Part of the Garland Library of Medieval Literature. Collection of legends concerning the mythical exploits of Alexander the Great. The unknown author is still sometimes called Pseudo-Callisthenes.

The Romance of Reynard the Fox. Translated and edited by Roy Owen. New York: Oxford University Press, 1994. Reynard is the hero of medieval beast epics satirizing medieval society and institutions ranging from the nobility to the clergy to the peasantry.

Sacrobosco [c.1195-1256]. *On the Sphere.* Available in Lynn Thorndike's *The Sphere of Sacrobosco and its Commentators.* Chicago: University of Chicago Press, 1949. Sacrobosco's highly popular medieval textbook provided an introduction to Ptolemaic astronomy. Required reading for the B.A. at Paris and Oxford in medieval times.

Sir Gawain and the Green Knight, Pearl, and Sir Orfeo [fourteenth c.]. Translated by J.R.R. Tolkien. New York: Ballantine Books, 1975. Dark tale of the adventures of King Arthur's most noble knight by an unknown medieval poet. Tolkien's translation emphasizes the alliterative style of the medieval West Midlands where the poem originated.

The Song of Roland [c.1090?]. Translated by Dorothy Sayers. New York: Penguin Books, 1957. The earliest, most famous, and greatest of the Old French epics. Recalls the betrayal and slaughter by Saracens of the rearguard of Charlemagne's army in 778 and of Charlemagne's bitter revenge.

Virgil [70-19 BCE]. *Aeneid.* Translated by Robert Fitzgerald. New York: Random House, 1990. The adventures of Aeneas from the end of the Trojan War through his many wanderings to his conquests in Italy and founding of Rome.

The Wakefield Mystery Plays. Edited by Martial Rose. New York: W.W. Norton, 1969. The complete cycle of thirty-two plays from the Creation of the world to the Last Judgment, given by the town of Wakefield, England in the fourteenth and fifteenth centuries.

William of Sherwood [1190-1249]. *Introduction to Logic.* Translated by Norman Kretzmann. Westport, CT: Greenwood Press, 1966. A classic medieval logic manual.

William of Tudela [fl. 1199-1214]. *The Song of the Cathar Wars: A History of the Albigensian Crusade.* Translated by Janet Shirley. London: Ashgate Publishing, Ltd., 2000. English translation of an early thirteenth c. Provencal poem which narrates key events before, during and after the Albigensian Crusade, which was launched in 1209.

Wolfram von Eschenbach [fl. c.1195-1225]. *Parzival.* New York: Penguin Books, 1980. The retelling and completion of Chrétien de Troyes' story of the Holy Grail. Perhaps the most mystical of the Grail legends.

Wyclif, John [c.1330-1384]. *The English Works of Wyclif Hitherto Unprinted.* Boston: Adamant Media Corporation, 2005. Twenty-eight polemical works by one of the pioneers of the Reformation.

The York Mystery Plays: A Selection in Modern Spelling. Edited by Richard Beadle and Pamela King. New York: Oxford University Press, 1999. This volume offers twenty-two of the forty-eight plays that make up York's famous Corpus Christi cycle, the oldest and best known of the English mystery cycles on biblical themes.

SECONDARY SOURCES

Adler, Mortimer. *Aristotle for Everybody: Difficult Thought Made Easy.* New York: Macmillan, 1978. No one makes Aristotle easier than Adler, the founder of the modern Great Books tradition.

Aeschliman, M. D. *The Restitution of Man: C. S. Lewis and the Case Against Scientism.* Grand Rapids, MI: Eerdmans, 1998. Balanced view of Lewis' critique of science arguing Lewis avoided the two opposed temptations of "science deified" and "science defied."

Artz, Frederick B. *The Mind of the Middle Ages: An Historical Survey.* Third edition, revised. Chicago: University of Chicago Press, 1984. Clear and succinct overview of every aspect of the intellectual history of the medieval mind including philosophy, theology, literature, art, music, and education.

Barber, Richard. *The Holy Grail: Imagination and Belief.* Cambridge, MA: Harvard University Press, 2004. Scholarly yet entertaining analysis of both the original Grail traditions (including Chrétien, Robert de Boron, the Vulgate Cycle, *Perlesvaus*, and Wolfram von Eschenbach's *Parzival*) and the modern interpretations (ranging from Wagner to Charles Williams to the *DaVinci* Code phenomenon).

Barry, Peter. *Beginning Theory: An Introduction to Literary and Cultural Theory.* Manchester, UK: Manchester University Press, 2009. As far from medieval theory as is humanly possible, but an excellent summary nonetheless.

Batteux, Charles [1713-1780]. *Les Beaux Arts réduits à un même principe* [The fine arts reduced to a single principle]. New York: Johanson Reprint Company, 1988. Batteux is generally credited with being the founder of aesthetics in France and the first scholar to set forth a clear cut classification of the fine arts.

Bettelheim, Bruno. *The Uses of Enchantment: The Meaning and Importance of Fairy Tales.* New York: Vintage Books, 2010. Classic work by the famous psychoanalyst on how fairly tales educate children.

Bloomfield, Morton. *The Seven Deadly Sins: An Introduction to the History of a Religious Concept with Special Reference to Medieval English Literature.* East Lansing, MI: State College Press, 1952. Just like the title says.

Boase, Roger. *The Origin and Meaning of Courtly Love: A Critical Study of European Scholarship.* Manchester, UK: Manchester University Press, 1977. Comprehensive analysis of the different theories of origin (e.g. Hispano-Arabic, Crypto-Cathar, Neoplantonic, etc.) and the different theories of meaning (e.g. collective fantasy, play phenomenon, courtly experience) of courtly love.

The Book of Beasts: Being a Translation from a Latin Bestiary of the Twelfth Century. Translated and edited by T. H. White. Mineola, NY: Dover, 1984. Catalog of real and fanciful beasts giving equal precedence to lions, dogs, unicorns, and dragons. Extensive appendix detailing the history of this manuscript and bestiaries as a genre.

Burckhardt, Titus. *Alchemy: Science of the Cosmos, Science of the Soul.* Louisville, KY: Fons Vitae, 1997. A study of spiritual alchemy or the premodern understanding of the relationship between form and matter. Beautifully illustrated summary of medieval cosmology and the spiritual insights of that cosmology.

———. *The Essential Titus Burckhardt.* Edited by William Stoddart. Bloomington, IN: World Wisdom, 2003. Reflections on sacred art, faiths, and civilizations by a student of Frithjof Schuon and Ananda Coomaraswamy.

Burnet, John. *Early Greek Philosophy.* London: Adams and Charles Black, 1975. A classic work on the pre-Socratics.

Cahill, Thomas. *Mysteries of the Middle Ages: The Rise of Feminism, Science, and Art from the Cults of Catholic Europe.* New York: Doubleday, 2006. Shows how religious phenomena like the belief in the Eucharist and the cult of the Virgin Mary sparked new ideas in medieval science and society. Part of Cahill's "Hinges of History" series.

Calter, Paul. *Squaring the Circle: Geometry in Art & Architecture*. Hoboken, NJ: John Wiley & Sons, 2008. A masterpiece of interdisciplinary study and part of the Mathematics Across the Curriculum (MATC) project at Dartmouth College. Calter blends mathematics with a historical overview of art, architecture, and philosophy in Western civilization.

Cantor, Norman F. *Inventing the Middle Ages*. New York: William Morrow and Company, 1991. Critical but not altogether unfavorable analysis of Lewis as a medievalist in the chapter on "The Oxford Fantasists."

Chamberlain, David. "Philosophy of Music in the *Consolatio* of Boethius," *Speculum* 45.1 (1970):80-97. "The [*Consolatio*] may be said to have a main theme that is musical and to embody a more complete philosophy of music than [Boethius's] *De Musica* itself."

Chapman, Ed. "Toward a Sacramental Ecology: Technology, Nature and Transcendence in C. S. Lewis' Ransom Trilogy," *Mythlore* 3.4 (1976):11-17. Argues that Lewis' science fiction embodies ecological themes, in particular a sacramental ecology "wherein man's relationship with nature would be a means by which man could experience a relationship with the sacred, with the numinous world of transcendence."

Chenu, M. D. *Toward Understanding St. Thomas*. Chicago: Henry Regnery Company, 1964. A detailed examination of the works of Thomas Aquinas as well as the milieu in which these works emerged.

Chesterton, G. K. *Orthodoxy*. Wheaton, IL: Harold Shaw, 1994. Combative, witty, insightful and charming, Chesterton's *Orthodoxy* holds a place of preeminence in Roman Catholic apologetics.

Chiarenza, Marguerite Mills. *The Divine Comedy: Tracing God's Art*. Boston: MA, Twayne Publishers, 1989. Following the work of Dante scholars Charles Singleton and John Freccero Chiarenza reads Dante as the medievals read Dante, with no attempt to demythologize him. She assumes that the poem is coherent and that Dante knew exactly what he was doing.

Chittister, Joan. *The Rule of St. Benedict: Insights for the Ages*. New York: Crossroads, 1992. Translation and commentary of St. Benedict's rule for monks.

Clayton, Peter and Martin Price, eds. *The Seven Wonders of the Ancient World*. New York: Routledge, 1996. The authors combine ancient sources with modern scholarship and archeology to recreate a picture of the Seven Wonders.

Como, James T., ed. *C. S. Lewis at the Breakfast Table and Other Reminiscences*. New York: Macmillan, 1979. Reminiscences of twenty-two of Lewis' friends provide portraits of Lewis the tutor, the orator, the atheist, the Christian gentleman, and the breakfast companion among others.

Cook, William R. and Ronald B. Herzman. *The Medieval World View: An Introduction*. 2nd edition. New York: Oxford University Press, 2004. Engaging history of the Middle Ages with a clear emphasis on its intellectual history. A third edition appeared in 2011.

Copleston, Frederick C. *Aquinas*. New York: Penguin, 1991. Lucid but challenging study of Aquinas' philosophical achievement.

————. *A History of Philosophy*. 9 vols. New York: Image Books, 1993-1994. Monumental history of philosophy by the famed Catholic priest and scholar.

Daileader, Philip. *The High Middle Ages*, CD-ROM, Lecture Three (Chantilly, VA: The Teaching Company, 2001). The middle part of Daileader's three part lecture series on the Middle Ages, *The Early Middle Ages*, *The High Middle Ages*, and *The Late Middle Ages*. Daileader devotes a substantial amount of time to intellectual as well as political and social history.

The Dante Encyclopedia. Edited by Richard Lansing. New York: Garland Publishing, 2000. The entry by Ronald Martinez on "Allegory" is particularly useful.

De Lubac, Henri. *Medieval Exegesis: The Four Senses of Scripture*. 3 vols. published; 1 vol. in process. Grand Rapids, MI: William B. Eerdmans, 1998 (vol. 1), 2000 (vol 2), 2009 (vol. 3). "Given the growing discontent and dissatisfaction with historical-critical exegesis among many biblical interpreters of our own generation, de Lubac's prescient essay offers a timely stimulant for those who wish to reconnect historical exegesis with the proclamation of the gospel." Henri de Lubac is one of the leading figures of 20th century Roman Catholicism.

Dictionary of the Middle Ages. 13 vols. Edited by Joseph R. Strayer. New York: Scribner's, 1982-1989.

Dodds, E. R. *Pagan and Christian in an Age of Anxiety: Some Aspects of Religious Experience From Marcus Aurelius to Constantine*. New York: W. W. Norton, 1970. Clear description of the late antique tripartite world – the material world, the daemonic world, and the divine world.

Duby, Georges. *The Three Orders: Feudal Society Imagined*. Chicago: University of Chicago Press, 1980. In depth historical analysis of the medieval tripartite schema of those who pray, those who fight, and those who work.

Durant, Will. *The Story of Civilization*, vol. 2, The Life of Greece. New York: Simon and Schuster, 1939. An early text from Durant's famous multivolume history of civilization.

Eco, Umberto. *The Name of the Rose*. New York: Harcourt Brace, 1983. This murder mystery within a medieval monastery has become a modern classic in the genre of historical fiction. The book is littered with the lists found in *Medieval Literacy*.

Eliade, Mircea. *The Myth of the Eternal Return*. Princeton, NJ: Princeton University Press, 1991. Contrasts the mythical consciousness of traditional cultures with the historical consciousness of modern culture. Archaic men and women did not see themselves as making events in history, but as living out and repeating divinely established patterns *in illo tempore*. In the book's final chapter Eliade argues that modernity has been unable to give an adequate response to the "terrors of history."

Encyclopedia of Philosophy. 8 vols. New York: Macmillan, 1972.

Encyclopedia of Religion. 15 vols. 2nd edition. New York: Thompson Gale, 2005.

Fakhry, Majid. *Al-Fārābi, Founder of Islamic Neoplatonism: His Life, Works and Influence.* Oxford, England: Oneworld, 2002. Introduction to the thought of the first great system builder of Islamic philosophy.

———. *Averroes: His Life, Works and Influence.* Oxford, England: Oneworld, 2001. Covers all the key areas of Averroes' life from his transmission of Aristotelian thought to Western Europe to his conflict with the Ash'arite theologians.

———. *A History of Islamic Philosophy.* Third edition. New York: Columbia University Press, 2004. The first comprehensive survey of Islamic philosophy from the seventh century until today.

———. *Islamic Philosophy, Theology and Mysticism: A Short Introduction.* Oxford, England: Oneworld, 2003. Overview ranging from the philosophy of Al-Kindi to Sufi mysticism to modern Islamic fundamentalism.

Feder, Lillian. *Crowell's Handbook of Classical Literature.* New York: Lippincott & Crowell, 1964. Useful companion to the study of classical literature.

Feuerstein, Georg. *Spirituality by the Numbers.* New York: Putnam, 1994. A real gem for list lovers and history buffs. Arranges the teachings of the world religions into their numeric groups (e.g. five pillars of Islam, five Buddhist precepts, seven Christian sacraments, seven chakras of Hatha Yoga, etc.).

Fiero, Gloria. *The Humanist Tradition*, 4th edition, vol. 1. Prehistory to the Early Modern World. New York: McGraw Hill, 2002. The preeminent illustrated textbook for a study of the Humanities throughout the ages. Particular attention is paid to literature, art history, and the history of music (CDs included). Broad in scope, Fiero's text includes a historical account of Islam as well as the Eastern cultural traditions in China and India.

Gautier, Leon. *Chivalry.* Avenel, NJ: Crescent Books, 1989. Portrays the everyday life of the medieval knight. Includes the Ten Commandments of Chivalry and a defense of the chivalry of the *chansons de geste* against the decadent chivalry of the Arthurian legends. Written by a hopeless romantic in the late 1800s.

Gilson, Etienne. *Reason and Revelation in the Middle Ages.* New York: Charles Scribner's Sons, 1966. A classic work by a leading modern Thomist on the three spiritual families of thought in the Middle Ages – the Augustinian emphasizing the primacy of faith, the Latin Averroist emphasizing the primacy of reason, and the Thomist emphasizing the harmony of reason and revelation.

Godwin, Malcolm. *The Holy Grail: Its Origins, Secrets and Meaning Revealed.* New York: Barnes & Noble, 1998. Popular yet all inclusive account of the various Grail traditions. Includes useful maps and charts as well as beautiful illustrations.

Goldin, Frederick, ed. *Lyrics of the Troubadours and Trouveres: An Anthology and a History*. Gloucester, MA: Peter Smith, 1983. Selections of troubadour love songs with the Old French and English on facing pages.

Goleman, Daniel. *Emotional Intelligence*. New York: Bantam Books, 1995. Intelligence is a much broader concept than I.Q. The qualities that mark people who excel in real life include self-discipline, social deftness, persistence, empathy, altruism, and compassion.

Goody, Jack. *The Domestication of the Savage Mind*. New York: Cambridge University Press, 1977. Regarding theories of the "mind" of human societies, Goody challenges the modern dichotomy between advanced and primitive, open and closed, or domesticated and savage (and all such "we-they" distinctions). Particular attention is paid to the function of classification and list-making in the premodern mentality.

Grant, Edward. *The Foundations of Modern Science in the Middle Ages: Their Religious, Institutional, and Intellectual Contexts*. New York: Cambridge University Press, 1996. Argues for the continuity of Western thought by showing how the roots of modern science were planted in the ancient and medieval worlds, specifically through the translation of Greek and Arabic scientific treaties into Latin in the twelfth and thirteenth centuries, through the flourishing of the medieval university, and through the medieval transformation of Aristotle's natural philosophy.

———. *God and Reason in the Middle Ages*. New York: Cambridge University Press, 2001. Through an in-depth study of the medieval university curriculum, Grant shows the "spirit of inquiry" at the heart of medieval scholasticism which ultimately paved the way for the rationalism of the Enlightenment.

———. *Physical Science in the Middle Ages*. New York: Cambridge University Press, 1977. Concise introduction to the history of physical science (particularly Aristotelian science) in the Middle Ages, from its feeble state in the Early Middle Ages to its revitalization in the High Middle Ages.

Grube, G. M. A. *Plato's Thought*. Boston: Beacon Press, 1958. Essays on Plato ranging from his theory of ideas and theory of art to his analysis of the soul, the gods, education, and statecraft.

Guardini, Romano. *The End of the Modern World*. Wilmington, DE: ISI Books, 1998. Apocalyptic vision of the degradation of nature, human personality, and culture in the postmodern world after nature is reduced to "raw material" in the service of political "power."

Hamilton, Edith. *Mythology*. New York: Little, Brown & Co., 1998. Comprehensive and popular exposition of Greek, Roman, and Norse mythology.

Harmon, Michele. "A Contemplation of Cultural Literacy," *Bulletin of the New York C. S. Lewis Society* 21.3 (1990):1-5. Argues that Lewis' *Discarded Image* provides a needed "transcendent cultural literacy" grounded in the Middle Ages that goes beyond the cultural literacy recommended by E. D. Hirsch.

Haskins, Charles Homer. *The Renaissance of the Twelfth Century*. Cambridge, MA:

Harvard University Press, 1955. Haskins, a Harvard professor in the early part of the 20th century, popularized the idea of a twelfth century Renaissance.

Heidegger, Martin. *The Question Concerning Technology and Other Essays*. New York: Harper and Row, 1977. Several essays by Heidegger including the title essay which describes the essence of technology as *Gestell* – the enframing, setting-upon, and ordering of nature which reveals nature as *Bestand* (stock, inventory, raw material, resource).

Heilbron, J. L. *The Sun in the Church: Cathedrals as Solar Observatories*. Cambridge, MA: Harvard University Press, 1999. With dry wit, Heilbron describes the diplomatic discretion on all sides of the debate that allowed Italian clerics to teach and advance sun-centered astronomy despite the medieval Church's prohibition on the subject. Incredible charts on medieval astronomy are part of the text.

Hellman, Robert and Richard O'Gorman. *Fabliaux: Ribald Tales from the Old French*. Westport, CT: Greenwood Press, 1976. Satiric anecdotes of husbands, lovers, rulers, and clergy including "The Man Who Had a Quarrelsome Wife," and "The Priest's Breeches."

Hirsch, E. D., Jr., Joseph F. Kett, and James Trefil. *Dictionary of Cultural Literacy: What Every American Needs to Know*. 2nd edition. Boston: Houghton Mifflin, 1993. A dictionary of the common stock of knowledge necessary for America to be a literate society and functioning democracy.

Hopper, Vincent Foster. *Medieval Number Symbolism*. Mineola, NY: Dover, 2000. Hopper shows "how deeply rooted in medieval thought was the consciousness of numbers, not as mathematical tools, nor yet as the counters in the game, but as fundamental realities alive with memories and elegant with meaning."

Hourihane, Colum, ed. *Virtue and Vice: The Personifications in the Index of Christian Art*. Princeton, NJ: Princeton University Press, 2000. The concept of opposing forces of good and evil is one of the most dominant themes in the history of Christian art. The complex interrelationship of these moral traits received considerable study in the medieval period. Rich resources for this study are made available by this volume, which publishes the complete holdings of the more than 230 personifications of Virtues and Vices in the Index of Christian Art's text files.

Howard, Donald. *The Three Temptations: Medieval Man in Search of the World*. Princeton, NJ: Princeton University Press, 1966. A study of medieval texts that equated the three temptations of Adam and Eve with the three temptations of Christ and identified them all with the three lusts in I John 2:16: the lust of the flesh (*Troilus and Criseyde*), the lust of the eyes (*Piers Plowman*), and the pride of life (*Sir Gawain and the Green Knight*).

Jones, W. T. *A History of Western Philosophy*, vol. 1, The Classical Mind. Second edition. New York: Harcourt Brace, 1969. History of philosophy from the pre-Socratics, through Plato and Aristotle up to the late classical period of the Stoics, the Epicureans, and the Skeptics.

———. *A History of Western Philosophy*, vol. 2, The Medieval Mind. Second edition. New York: Harcourt Brace, 1969. History of philosophy from Plotinus through Augustine and Aquinas up to Roger Bacon, Duns Scotus, and William of Occam.

Joseph, Miriam. *The Trivium: The Liberal Arts of Logic, Grammar and Rhetoric*. Philadelphia: Paul Dry Books, 2002. An understanding of the nature and function of language that links all three parts of the trivium within a seamless Aristotelian framework. Sister Joseph was professor of English at Saint Mary's College from 1931 to 1960.

Kass, Leon. *The Beginning of Wisdom: Reading Genesis*. New York: Free Press, 2003. Extensive commentary on all fifty chapter of Genesis by the famous bioethics scholar. Kass reads Genesis philosophically, in search of a wisdom that neither presupposes the extremes of scientific biblical criticism nor of religious fundamentalism.

Kelly, Amy. *Eleanor of Aquitaine*. Cambridge, MA: Harvard University Press, 1950. Captivating history of Queen Eleanor whose own life almost provides the "plot" for the last three quarters of the twelfth century.

Kenny, Anthony. *The Five Ways: St. Thomas Aquinas' Proofs of God's Existence*. Notre Dame, IN: University of Notre Dame Press, 1980. Critical evaluation of each of the five proofs. Warning: Kenny includes a fair amount of logical symbolism in the text that may intimidate the "lay" reader.

Kneale, William, and Martha Kneale. *The Development of Logic*. Oxford: Clarendon, 2008. No stone is left unturned in this monumental history of logic from Plato and Aristotle to Frege and Goedel.

Knowles, David. *The Evolution of Medieval Thought*, 2nd edition. London and New York: Longman, 1996. A uniquely readable introduction to the thought of Western thinkers from Plato to Occam by the great monastic historian. A classic that cannot be recommended highly enough.

Kreeft, Peter. *A Shorter Summa*. San Francisco: Ignatius Press, 1993. Ultra-condensed readings (with commentary and footnotes) from the *Summa Theologica*. By a prominent C. S. Lewis scholar.

———. *Socratic Logic*. Third edition. South Bend, IN: St. Augustine's Press, 2008. Introduction to and unabashed defense of traditional Aristotelian logic including more commentary on the philosophy of logic than is traditionally found in logic texts. The structure of the book follows the "three acts of the intellect."

Lambert, Malcolm. *Medieval Heresy*. Third edition. Oxford, UK: Blackwell Publishing, 2002. Comprehensive history of the origin and nature of the great heretical movements of the Middle Ages as well as the response and inquisitional process of the medieval churches of Rome and Byzantium.

Lawrence, C. H. *Medieval Monasticism*. Third edition. New York: Longman, 2001. History of the Western monastic tradition from its fourth-century origins in the deserts of Egypt and Syria through its varied forms (Benedictine, Cluniac, Cistercian, etc.) in the Middle Ages.

Lewis, C. S. *The Abolition of Man.* New York: Touchstone, 1996. Perhaps the clearest and most concise defense of natural law in the twentieth century.

————. *The Allegory of Love: A Study in Medieval Tradition.* New York: Oxford University Press, 1985. Lewis' first great work of medieval scholarship originally published in 1936. A study of the courtly love tradition that first appeared in eleventh-century Provencal France, Lewis argues that this notion of romantic love is one of the few truly original ideas in Western civilization. "Compared with this revolution the Renaissance is a mere ripple on the surface of literature" (p. 4).

————. *Christian Reflections.* Grand Rapids: William B. Eerdmans, 1978. Edited by Walter Hooper. Fourteen essays that defend orthodox Christianity against various modern criticism like psychoanalysis, utilitarianism, subjectivism, historicism, and biblical criticism (e.g. Rudolf Bultmann).

————. *The Collected Letters of C. S. Lewis*, edited by Walter Hooper, vol. 1, Family Letters 1905-1931. San Francisco: HarperSanFrancisco, 2004.

————. *The Collected Letters of C. S. Lewis*, edited by Walter Hooper, vol. 2, Books, Broadcasts, and the War 1931-1949. San Francisco: HarperSanFrancisco, 2004.

————. *The Collected Letters of C. S. Lewis*, edited by Walter Hooper, vol. 3, Narnia, Cambridge, and Joy 1950-1963. San Francisco: HarperSanFrancisco, 2007.

————. *"De Descriptione Temporum."* Pp. 9-25 in *They Asked For a Paper: Papers and Addresses.* London: Geoffrey Bles, 1962. Lewis' inaugural address (1954) upon becoming the Professor of Medieval and Renaissance English Literature at the University of Cambridge. Famous lecture where Lewis claims to read medieval texts as a native, not as a foreigner. Also available in Lyle W. Dorset, ed., *The Essential C. S. Lewis* (New York: Touchstone, 1996), pp. 471-481.

————. *The Discarded Image: An Introduction to Medieval and Renaissance Literature.* London: Cambridge University Press, 1964. Lewis' last great work of medieval scholarship that sketches a map of his beloved Medieval Model. This book is based on his two most popular lecture series to undergraduates at Oxford, the Prolegomena to Medieval Literature and the Prolegomena to Renaissance Literature.

————. *English Literature in the Sixteenth Century: Excluding Drama.* New York: Oxford University Press, 1975. Part of the Oxford History of English Literature series. The introduction, "New Learning and New Ignorance," discusses Lewis' ambivalence towards the loss of the medieval worldview.

————. *God in the Dock: Essays on Theology and Ethics.* Edited by Walter Hooper. Grand Rapids, MI: William B. Eerdmans, 1970. Forty-eight essays of Christian apologetics. Most striking in this collection is Lewis' robust sense of humor and thinly veiled sarcasm. *God in the Dock* is perhaps the most readable of Lewis' more academic works.

————. *Mere Christianity.* New York: Touchstone, 1996. Originally given as a series of radio broadcasts and then published as three separate books during World War II: *The Case for Christianity* (1943), *Christian Behaviour* (1943), and *Beyond Person-*

ality (1945). Rejecting the boundaries that divide Christian denominations, Lewis explains and defends the common ground on which all those of Christian faith can stand together vis-à-vis modernity.

————. *Of Other Worlds: Essays and Stories.* Edited by Walter Hooper. New York: Harcourt, Brace & World, Inc., 1967. A somewhat odd collection of essays gathered together by Walter Hooper. Most of the essays revolve around the topics of storytelling, science fiction, and writing for children.

————. *Studies in Medieval and Renaissance Literature.* London: Cambridge University Press, 1998. Along with essays on Dante and Spenser, includes Lewis' "Imagination and Thought in the Middle Ages," his most concise overview of the Medieval Model.

————. *Surprised by Joy: The Shape of My Early Life.* New York: Harcourt, Brace & World, 1955. Lewis' highly readable autobiography and story of his conversion from atheism to Christianity. Includes fascinating accounts of his early love of mythology as well as medieval and Renaissance literature.

————. *That Hideous Strength.* New York: Scribner Classics, 1996. The third book of Lewis' Space Trilogy (which includes *Out of the Silent Planet* and *Perelandra*), this work is his fictional version of the critique of modern technology found in the *Abolition of Man.* A frightening tale that stands alongside such classics as George Orwell's *1984* and Aldous Huxley's *Brave New World.*

The C. S. Lewis Readers' Encyclopedia. Edited by Jeffrey D. Schultz and John G. West, Jr. Grand Rapids, MI: Zondervan, 1998. A complete guide to Lewis' 52 published books, 153 essays, and numerous miscellaneous writings, including prefaces, letters, book reviews, and poems.

Liddell and Scott's Greek-English Lexicon. Oxford: Clarendon Press, 1974.

Lings, Martin. "Reminiscences of C. S. Lewis in the 1930s," audiotape from an address to the C. S. Lewis Society in Oxford, England in the early 1990s.

————. *Symbol & Archetype: A Study of the Meaning of Existence.* Louisville, KY: Fons Vitae, 2006. Traces the spiritual journey of all religions from their symbols to their Archetypes.

Locke, John. *The Second Treatise of Government: An Essay Concerning the True Original, Extent, and End of Civil Government.* Indianapolis, IN: Bobbs-Merrill, 1952. A classic work, following Hobbes, in the intellectual tradition of social contract theory.

Loomis, Roger Sherman. *The Development of Arthurian Romance.* New York: Norton, 1970. A critical study of Arthurian literature in the Middle Ages stressing the sources and origins of that literature.

Lovejoy, Arthur O. *The Great Chain of Being: A Study of the History of an Idea.* New York: Harper Torchbooks, 1960. Studies the paradox between otherworldliness and worldliness in the medieval Platonic tradition. Includes an insightful summary of Plato's *Timaeus.*

Machiavelli, Niccolo. *The Prince*. Translated by Harvey C. Mansfield, Jr. Chicago: University of Chicago Press, 1985. Considered the first expression of political realism, Machiavelli counsels princes how to acquire and maintain political power through a judicious use of ruthlessness, deception, and cruelty.

Marrou, H. I. *A History of Education in Antiquity*. New York: Sheed & Ward, 1956. An encyclopedic history of education from the ancient Greeks to the fall of the Roman Empire.

Martin, Thomas L., ed. *Reading the Classics with C. S. Lewis*. Grand Rapids, MI: Baker Academic, 2000. Includes a chapter on Classical Literature and a chapter on Medieval Literature. Praises Lewis as an interpreter of the Latin texts of late antiquity and the Early Middle Ages (cf. *The Discarded Image*). Criticizes Lewis' enthusiasm for the medieval doctrine of courtly love (cf. *The Allegory of Love*) as a projection of nineteenth century Romanticism.

Menocal, María Rosa. *The Ornament of the World: How Muslims, Jews, and Christians Created a Culture of Tolerance in Medieval Spain*. New York: Little, Brown and Company, 2002. A series of vignettes about medieval Andalusia where literature, science, mathematics, and architecture flourished along with religious tolerance.

Merton, Thomas. *The Wisdom of the Desert: Some Sayings of the Desert Fathers*. New York: New Directions, 1960. Collection of sayings (with introduction) of fourth century Christian hermits in the deserts of Egypt, Palestine, Arabia, and Persia.

Mitcham, Carl. *Thinking Through Technology*. Chicago: University of Chicago Press, 1994. Tracing the changing meaning of technology from ancient times to our own, Mitcham analyzes the engineering approach to technology which assumes the centrality of technology in human life, as well as the humanities approach to technology which is concerned with its moral and cultural boundaries.

Nasr, Seyyed Hossein. *The Need for a Sacred Science*. Albany, NY: SUNY Press, 1993. Scholarly study of the sacred sciences of traditional (premodern) civilizations understood in the light of their cosmological and metaphysical significance and not as crude precursors of modern science or as historical relics of occultism.

New Arthurian Encyclopedia. Edited by Norris J. Lacy. New York: Garland Press, 1996.

New Catholic Encyclopedia. Second edition. 14 vols. Edited by Bernard Marthaler. New York: Thomson Gale, 2003.

New Dictionary of Catholic Spirituality. Edited by Michael Downey. Wilmington, DE: Michael Glazier, 1993.

New Dictionary of Theology. Edited by Joseph Komonchak, Mary Collins, and Dermot Lane. Wilmington, DE: Michael Glazier, 1987.

Otis, Brooks. *Ovid as an Epic Poet*. Second edition. New York: Cambridge University Press, 1971. Far from being a haphazard collection of Greek myths, Otis argues that Ovid's *Metamorphoses* is a carefully constructed work of art with a definite structure and plan.

Otten, Willemien. "Nature and Scripture: Demise of a Medieval Analogy," *Harvard Theological Review* 88.2 (1995):257-284. Study of the medieval doctrine of the two books of God (nature and Scripture), especially in Alan of Lille, Bernard of Chartres, William of Conches, and Thierry of Chartres.

Parens, Joshua and Joseph C. Macfarland, eds. *Medieval Political Philosophy: A Sourcebook*, 2nd edition. Ithaca. NY: Cornell University Press, 2011. A selection of works in medieval political philosophy from the Islamic, Jewish, and Christian traditions.

Park, David. *The Grand Contraption: The World as Myth, Number, and Chance*. Princeton, NJ: Princeton University Press, 2005. Highly readable history of science from ancient mythology, Plato, Aristotle, and the Middle Ages through the early modern period of Copernicus and Newton through the more recent discoveries of evolution, relativity, and the Big Bang.

Patch, Howard. *The Goddess Fortuna in Medieval Literature*. Cambridge, MA: Harvard University Press, 1927. Masterful study, particularly of "Fortune's Wheel" in chapter five.

Pieper, Josef. *The Four Cardinal Virtues*. Notre Dame, IN: University of Notre Dame Press, 1966. Originally published in four separate volumes, Pieper brings together all four virtues and redefines the original significance of these virtues for modern times.

Planck, Max. *A Survey of Physical Theory*. Mineola, NY: Dover Publications, 1994. Exploration of the basic ideas intrinsic to the study of physics by the Nobel laureate and creator of the quantum revolution in modern physics.

Prothero, Stephen. *Religious Literacy: What Every American Needs to Know – and Doesn't*. San Francisco: HarperSanFrancisco, 2007. While claiming to be religious, only one-half of American adults can name even one of the four gospels. Most Americans cannot name the first book of the Bible, the Ten Commandments, one sacred text of Hinduism, the holy book of Islam, or the Four Noble Truths of Buddhism. Prothero tackles the problem with a history of religious literacy in the United States and a dictionary of the most important religious concepts.

Rosemann, Philipp. *Peter Lombard*. New York: Oxford University Press, 2004. Scholarly, yet accessible, introduction to Peter Lombard's life and thought.

Ross, W. D. *Aristotle*. London: Routledge, 1995. The best one-volume commentary on Aristotle for intermediate and advanced students.

Rubenstein, Richard. *Aristotle's Children*. New York: Harcourt, Inc., 2003. Lively and dramatic account of the tension between faith and reason in the Middle Ages sparked by the Latin translations of Aristotle's works.

Russell, Jeffrey Burton. *A History of Heaven: The Singing Silence*. Princeton, NJ: Princeton University Press, 1997. A philosophical history from ancient Greek and Hebrew sources through Dante. While a history, the book is also a remarkable defense of the "metaphorical ontology" of the medieval mind.

————. *Inventing the Flat Earth: Columbus and Modern Historians*. New York: Praeger, 1997. Neither Columbus nor virtually any educated person before his time believed the Earth was flat. Russell sets the record straight and examines how the flat Earth myth was first propagated in the 1820s and 1830s and then grew to the point of historical dogma by the late nineteenth century.

Ruthven, Malise. *Islam: A Very Short Introduction*. New York: Oxford University Press, 2000. Just like the title says.

Shakespeare, William. *As You Like It*. New York: Washington Square Press, 1997. Shakespeare's famous pastoral comedy.

Southern, R. W. *The Making of the Middle Ages*. New Haven, CT: Yale University Press, 1961. According to historian Norman Cantor, *The Making of the Middle Ages* is arguably "the single most widely read and influential book written on the Middle Ages in the twentieth century." Southern legitimated the study of twelfth century romanticism and individualism within modern academia.

————. *Medieval Humanism*. New York: Harper and Row, 1970. "The contents of this book bring together two sides of medieval history which should never be separated: the practical business-like and earthy, and the intellectual, spiritual and aspiring."

————. *Western Views of Islam in the Middle Ages*. Cambridge, MA: Harvard University Press, 1962. Traces the generally hostile and occasionally conciliatory attitudes of Western Christendom to Islam during the Middle Ages.

Steiner, George. *Real Presences*. Chicago: University of Chicago Press, 1991. Argues that any "coherent account of the capacity of human speech to communicate meaning and feeling is, in the final analysis, underwritten by the assumption of God's presence."

Strauss, Leo and Joseph Cropsey. *History of Political Philosophy*. Third edition. Chicago: University of Chicago Press, 1987. Provocative essays on major political philosophers in the Western tradition by Straussian scholars.

Strauss, Leo. *An Introduction to Political Philosophy: Ten Essays by Leo Strauss*. Detroit, MI: Wayne State University Press, 1989. Ten important essays that illustrate Strauss' revival of classical political philosophy. "The Three Waves of Modernity" in particular shows the importance of premodern thought for the defense and support of liberal democracy in the face of communism and fascism.

————. *Xenophon's Socratic Discourse: An Interpretation of the Oeconomicus*. With a literal translation of the *Oeconomicus* by Carnes Lord. South Bend, IN: St. Augustine's Press, 2004. Xenophon's *Oeconomicus* is generally acknowledged to be the oldest surviving work devoted to economics and constitutes the classic statement of economic thought in ancient Greece.

Tatarkiewicz, Wladyslaw. "Classification of the Arts in Antiquity," *Journal of the History of Ideas* 24.2 (1963):231-240. Outlines an ancient classification of the arts according to an eightfold schema that includes classification by the Sophists, Plato, Aristotle, Seneca, Quintilian, Cicero, and Plotinus.

————. *The History of Aesthetics*. 3 vols. Bristol, UK: Thoemmes Continuum, 1999. Comprehensive account of the development of European aesthetics from the time of the ancient Greeks to the 1700s. The book achieved bestseller status in the author's native Poland. Covering ancient, medieval and modern aesthetics, Tatarkiewicz writes substantial essays on the views of beauty and art through the ages and then goes on to demonstrate these with extracts from original texts from each period.

Tuchman, Barbara. *A Distant Mirror: The Calamitous 14th Century*. New York: Alfred Knopf, 1978. A history of the cataclysms suffered by Europe in the fourteenth century (the Black Plague, the Hundred Years' War, the papal schism, and popular revolts) as seen through the eyes of Enguerrand de Coucy VII, "the most skilled and experienced of all the knights of France."

Vattimo, Gianni. *After Christianity*. New York: Columbia University Press, 2002. Relying on Joachim of Fiore's thesis on the "Spiritual Age" of history, Vattimo argues that postmodernity leads towards religion, not away from it.

Veatch, Henry. *Aristotle: A Contemporary Appreciation*. Bloomington: Indiana University Press, 1974. Veatch argues that Aristotelian thought is not irreconcilable with modern science and that Aristotle more adequately addresses certain issues neglected by modern thought. He concludes that not only does Aristotle continue to be a live option in philosophy, but "the only option open to a man of healthy common sense."

Vernant, Jean-Pierre. *The Universe, the Gods and Men; Ancient Greek Myths*. New York: Harper Collins, 2001. Enchanting retelling of the early Greek myths from the myths of creation to the Trojan War to the stories of Dionysus and of Oedipus.

Wagner, David L., ed. *The Seven Liberal Arts in the Middle Ages*. Bloomington, IN: Indiana University Press, 1983. Chapters on each of the seven liberal arts by different scholars with an overview by the editor.

Walsh, James. *A Golden Treasury of Medieval Literature*. Boston: Stratford, 1930. Folcroft Library Editions, 1973. Asserts that *Reynard the Fox*, *The Golden Legend*, and *The Romance of the Rose* were the three most read medieval books outside the Bible.

Ward, Michael. *Planet Narnia: The Seven Heavens in the Imagination of C. S. Lewis*. New York: Oxford University Press, 2008. Argues that the seven medieval planets hold the key to the inner structure of Lewis' *Chronicles of Narnia*. An informative account of each medieval sphere.

Watson, George. "The Art of Disagreement: C. S. Lewis (1898-1963)," *The Hudson Review* 48.2 (1995):229-239. Reflections on Lewis' Socratic and sometimes combative teaching style by a former student.

Weisheipl, James A. "Classification of the Sciences in Medieval Thought," *Mediaeval Studies* 27 (1965):54-90. Scholarly account of the seven liberal arts and the three philosophies which reached their full development in thirteenth century scholasticism.

————. *Friar Thomas D'Aquino: His Life, Thought & Works*. Washington, DC: Catholic University of America Press, 1983. Unsurpassed history of Thomas's life, thought, and works including a fifty-page "brief" annotated catalogue of the authentic works of Thomas.

White, Jr., Lynn. *Medieval Religion and Technology*. Berkeley, CA: University of California Press, 1986. Collection of nineteen essays that trace the roots of modern technology as far back as the Early Middle Ages. Furthermore, White argues that religious more than secular interests sparked the inventiveness visible in medieval engineering. "The classical Renaissance, which in some areas of life was an inundating wave, created scarcely a ripple in technology" (p. 91).

————. *Medieval Technology and Social Change*. New York: Oxford University Press, 1988. Classic description of technological innovations like the stirrup and the horse-drawn heavy plow which created medieval institutions like feudalism and the manorial system.

Wieruszowski, Helene. *The Medieval University*. New York: Van Nostrand, 1966. Erudite discussion of early monastic and cathedral schools and the subsequent rise of the universities and the standard medieval curriculum. Each chapter is supplemented by relevant readings from papal and royal decrees, city statutes, medieval letters and manuals, and university documents.

Wild, John. *Introduction to Realistic Philosophy*. New York: Harper and Brothers, 1948. Sympathetic introduction to the basic concepts and principles of classical realistic philosophy as gleaned from the texts of Aristotle and Thomas Aquinas.

Williams, Charles, and C. S. Lewis. *Arthurian Torso*. New York: Oxford University Press, 1952. A rather odd compendium of Williams' prose history of the Grail/Arthur legend and Lewis' commentary on Williams' Arthurian poetry.

Wright, Ronald. *An Illustrated Short History of Progress*. Toronto: House of Anansi Press, 2006. Wright argues that the current runaway growth in human population, consumption, and technology can only be addressed by examining the patterns of progress and disaster that humanity has repeated around the world since the Stone Age.

Yandell, Stephen, "The Allegory of Love and The Discarded Image: C. S. Lewis as Medievalist," in Bruce Edwards, ed., *C. S. Lewis: Life, Works, and Legacy*, vol. 4, Scholar, Teacher, and Public Intellectual (Westport, CT: Praeger Publishers, 2007), pp. 117-141. Impressive study of Lewis' "taxonomic impulse" and work as a medievalist, including his academic training, his scholarly publications, and his sheer "love of the labyrinthine." For a related work discussing both Tolkien and Lewis' love of the labyrinthine symbolism of the number four, see Yandell's "'A Pattern Which Our Nature Cries Out For': The Medieval Tradition of the Ordered Four in the Fiction of J.R.R. Tolkien," *Proceedings of the J.R.R. Tolkien Contemporary Conference*, edited by Patricia Reynolds and Glen H. GoodKnight (Napoleon, MI: Mythopoeic Press, 1995):375-392.

Select Index

APPENDIX:
LISTS ON EASTERN
TRADITIONS

APPENDIX:
Lists on Eastern Traditions

Despite Lewis' portrayal in some academic circles as a Christian fundamentalist, he was not opposed to what now goes by the name of multiculturalism (although he would no doubt be critical of its current manifestations). In fact he implicitly approves a multicultural approach to Truth in his criticism of modern technology entitled *The Abolition of Man*. The Appendix of *Medieval Literacy* mirrors the appendix to Lewis' book where he cites multiple cultural sources revealing a universal natural law that he refers to simply as the Tao. His sources include Ancient Egyptian, Anglo-Saxon, Australian Aborigine, Babylonian, Christian, Confucian, Greek, Hindu, Jewish, Native American Indian, Old Norse, and Roman. However, in that same book he recommends immersion in Old Western Culture as the readiest path to an appreciation of other traditional cultures.

For Lewis, the natural law written into the heart of every human being does not discriminate according to color, creed, or gender. It is Lewis' assessment that natural law is ultimately one doctrine, whether it derives from an Eastern religion like Taoism or a Western one like Christianity. He asks, almost rhetorically, "If we lump together, as I have done, the traditional moralities of East and West, the Christian, the Pagan, and the Jew, shall we not find many contradictions and some absurdities?"[1] His answer is basically – not as many as one might think. If natural law is truly natural, then it would stand to reason that it is also universal (cf. St. Thomas, *Summa Theologica*, I-II, q. 91, a. 2 that approves the following quote from St. Paul).

As St. Paul says: "When Gentiles, who do not possess the law, do instinctively [*physei* = by nature] what the law requires, these, though not having the law, are a law to themselves. They show that what the law requires is written on their hearts" (Romans 2:14-15). While Lewis was not a philosophical or moral relativist; neither was he parochial about philosophy and religion. He refused to engage in "denominational disputes" within Christianity and, while not a Perennialist (see page 16 in this book's Introduction), Lewis was open to the truth found in religions other than Christianity.

In all religious traditions there are moral warnings similar to the Ten Commandments (not to murder, lie, steal, etc.) as well as the same moral imperatives to care for the poor, the sick, the aged, and small children. In defending natural law Lewis kept his eye on the big picture, refusing to be led astray into moral minutiae. He declined to fiddle while Rome burned. Perhaps Lewis felt some affinity to Pascal's observation that human beings know too little to be dogmatists and too much to be skeptics. Perhaps not.

In compiling these lists I have found Georg Feuerstein's *Spirituality by the Numbers* particularly useful in sketching a broad premodern worldview that encompasses both East and West. Feuerstein, an internationally known yoga scholar, discusses an array of spiritual lists from Hinduism, Jainism, Confucianism, Judaism, Buddhism, Islam, and Christianity, not to mention Native American Indian traditions.

The following lists detailing Eastern traditions make no claim to completeness. In-

---

1. Lewis, *Abolition*, p. 56.

deed, in order to avoid a second volume exceeding the length of *Medieval Literacy*, I have limited this Appendix to major themes from the traditions of Hinduism and Buddhism. Hinduism is emphasized because of its antiquity – certainly one of the oldest surviving religions, so ancient it is called the eternal religion. And Buddhism is emphasized because of its universality. Buddhism is pan-Asian insofar as the Theravāda tradition spread from its origins in northern India to southern India (now relegated to the island of Sri Lanka) and to Southeast Asia. The Mahāyāna tradition moved north and east from India to Tibet and from China (via India) to Korea, Japan, and Vietnam.

The classical literature of the East exceeds the wildest aspirations of the written word in the West. For example, the *Mahābhārata* the Indian counterpart to Homer's *Iliad* is the longest epic in world literature. At 75,000 verses it dwarfs the *Iliad* (15,693 of hexameter verse in the original Greek), not to mention Dante's *Divine Comedy* (14,230 verses). In addition, the number and length of the Sacred Scriptures of the Hindu and Buddhist traditions far exceed those of Judaism, Christianity, and Islam. Hindu and Buddhist sacred texts easily run into the hundreds of volumes (see pages 344 and 357 below).

THE FOUR AGES AND MYTH OF THE ETERNAL RETURN

The length of Eastern texts mimics the expansive Eastern view of time. In the Hindu tradition one total cycle of time (*mahāyuga*) within an endless series of similar cycles is equivalent to 4,320,000 years. This one cycle is comprised of four different ages to be discussed momentarily. The early British colonizers of India viewed these monstrous numbers of Eastern cosmology as blasphemous. In his famous address to Parliament on February 2, 1835, the "Minute on Indian Education," Thomas Macaulay repeatedly refers to the "absurd history" of the Hindoos.[2] And the British Alexander Hamilton spends a great deal of space in his *Key to the Chronology of the Hindus: In a Series of Letters* (1820) confronting the "astronomical numbers" of Hindu cosmology and history. Hamilton goes to great lengths to show that, when reduced properly, the astronomical numbers of Hindu time agree with the shorter dates in the Bible.[3]

Unlike the Eastern cyclical view of time, the great monotheistic religions of the West (Judaism, Christianity, and Islam) emphasize the creation of the world and a linear view of time and history. In these three religions history progresses from the creation of the world through unique acts of God (the Exodus of the Jews, the Incarnation of Christ, the flight of Mohammad to Medina) towards a final judgment and end of the world. The entire time frame of this drama according to a literal reading of the Book of Genesis may be as brief as 6,000 years. By comparison, time in the East is neither progressive nor finite.

Ironically, the cosmology of the pagan West (classical Greece and Rome) contradicts the time frame of the biblical West. This bifurcation of worldviews in the West between the classical pagan worldview and the Judeo-Christian worldview was held together during the medieval period. The following chart by C. S. Lewis scholar Peter Kreeft shows how this tension between "Athens and Jerusalem" played out in the West.[4]

---

2. Thomas Macaulay, *Speeches by Lord Macaulay, With His Minute on Indian Education* (New York: AMS Press, Inc., 1935).

3. Alexander Hamilton, *Key to the Chronology of the Hindus* (Whitefish, MT: Kessinger Press, 2008).

4. Peter Kreeft, *Heaven: The Heart's Deepest Longing* (San Francisco: Ignatius Press, 1989), p. 18.

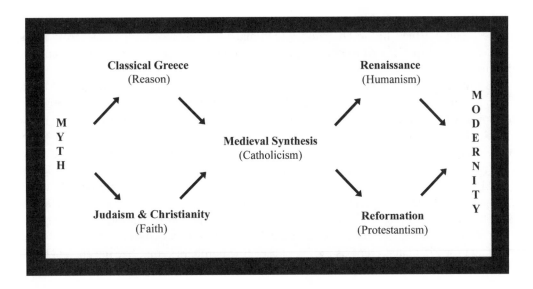

We noted in chapter two on Mythology that both Hesiod and Ovid in the Western classical tradition adhered to a historical doctrine of four declining ages borrowed from the East – gold, silver, bronze, and iron. Plato mimics this doctrine in the *Republic* by describing the natural cycle of political regimes as a decay or devolution from aristocracy to timocracy to oligarchy to democracy to tyranny (545c ff.). These periods of gradual decline are repeated over and over again as part of an eternal pattern; time being merely the "moving image of [an unmoving] eternity" (*Timaeus* 37d). Plato's disciple Aristotle asserted the universe to be eternal without beginning or end. This particular doctrine of Aristotle's cast an aura of heresy around his medieval defenders including St. Thomas.

One of C. S. Lewis' friends/students, Martin Lings, argues that, while this doctrine of the four ages originates in the East, it is neither necessarily heretical nor ultimately antithetical to the three monotheistic religions of the West.

> According to world-wide tradition, the "life" of the macrocosm consists of thousands of years of spiritual prosperity leading gradually down, from Golden Age to Silver Age to Bronze Age, until it reaches a relatively short final period in which the prosperity is increasingly marred by its opposite. This period, the Iron Age or, as the Hindus term it, the Dark Age, is the late autumn and winter of the cycle, and it roughly coincides with what is called "historic" as opposed to "prehistoric."[5]

In the Hindu tradition as mentioned earlier each cycle (*mahāyuga*) of these four ages (a cycle that is repeated over and over again) is 4,320,000 years long. The four *yugas* or ages are named after four dice throws:

1. *Kṛtayuga* (1,728,000 years) = the age of truth (winning age)
2. *Tretāyuga* (1,296,000 years) = "thrice-lucky age" (age of mostly winning)
3. *Dvāparayuga* (864,000 years) = "twice-lucky age" (age of mostly losing)
4. *Kaliyuga* (432,000 years) = the dark age (losing age)

---

5. Martin Lings, *The Eleventh Hour: The Spiritual Crisis of the Modern World in the Light of Tradition and Prophecy* (Cambridge, UK: Archetype, 2002), p. 53.

The four ages successively degenerate. In the *Tretāyuga* humans lose 25% of their goodness and virtue. In the *Dvāparayuga* humans lose 50% of their virtue. And in the *Kaliyuga* they lose 75% of their original virtue. Currently we are only 5,000 years into the current *Kaliyuga*.

Similarly the Buddhist tradition has a vast conception of time. The Buddha is said to have remembered numerous previous lifetimes – 91 *kalpas* of time in all. To impress his disciples with the magnitude of cosmological time, the Buddha described a *kalpa* as the length of time it would take for a man to wear away a great stone mountain seven miles high, seven miles wide, and seven miles long by stroking it once every hundred years with a piece of cloth (*Samyutta Nikāya*, 15.5)!

Martin Lings believes that the linear view of time in the monotheistic West has been exaggerated in modernity. He finds clues to the theory of the four ages in the Hebrew Scriptures, for example in the incredible longevity of human life before Abraham. For example Adam lived for 930 years (Genesis 5:5), Noah for 950 years (Genesis 9:29), and Abraham for 175 years (Genesis 25:7). These large numbers symbolize the ancient belief that the world is winding down or devolving, not evolving. Lings observes:

> The ancient and worldwide tradition of the four ages does not contradict the Book of Genesis, but, like the evidence of science, it does suggest an allegorical rather than a literal interpretation. It suggests, for example, that certain names indicate not merely single individuals but whole eras of prehistory and that the name Adam in particular may be taken as denoting not only the first man but also the whole of primordial humanity, spanning a period of many thousand years.[6]

As the lists on medieval exegesis in chapter eight on Theology show, the medieval mind interpreted Scripture in both literal and allegorical senses. While some medievals literally may have believed the world was created in approximately 4,000 BCE (following the genealogies in the Hebrew Scriptures), others interpreted the Genesis account allegorically, following the biblical injunction that with the Lord, "one day is like a thousand years, and a thousand years are like one day" (2 Peter 3:8).

SACRIFICE AND COSMOLOGY

From the allegorical point of view, the story of the Garden of Eden and the long life spans of the Hebrew patriarchs hint at the perfection of a distant Golden Age. Archaic man looked for perfection in the past, not in the future. In Hinduism, that perfection could be reenacted in the present by precisely executing sacrifices and rituals originally performed by the gods. The ancient sacrifices of the Vedic religion mimicked these archetypal actions to ensure that the world would continue. According to Mircea Eliade the early texts reiterate: "We must do what the gods did in the beginning. . . . Thus the god did; thus men do. . . . This Indian adage summarizes all the theory underlying rituals in all countries."[7]

Ancient men and women performed sacrifices, says Eliade, to restore the primordial unity, innocence, and bliss that existed in the earliest times. "Each Brahmanic sacrifice

---

6. Martin Lings, *Ancient Beliefs and Modern Superstitions* (Cambridge, UK: Archetype, 2001), p. 3.

7. Mircea Eliade, *The Myth of the Eternal Return* (Princeton, NJ: Princeton University Press, 1991), p. 21.

marks a new Creation of the world."[8] Mythic men and women viewed the universe as a clock running down. They lived in terror of a constantly degenerating universe (cf. the modern notion of entropy) that could only be regenerated by religious sacrifice.

Far from being an expression of blood lust, sacrifice repeats the original drama of creation and the unity of all beings. One must remember that while in the Western Judeo-Christian tradition, there is one creation of the world by God and one Incarnation of God in Jesus Christ, in the East particularly in Hinduism there are many creations of the world and many incarnations of the divine. Furthermore, in the Western religious traditions God creates the universe out of nothing (*ex nihilo*).

In the East, at least in Hinduism, the divine being creates the universe out of itself. Everything in the universe is ultimately one with the divine and creation itself is the ultimate sacrifice. The eternal Divine pours itself out into the creation or empties itself out into the universe and into time. (Note that this theory is mentioned in the Christian notion of *kenosis* or divine emptying in Philippians 2:5-7 where "Christ Jesus, who, though he was in the form of God, did not regard equality with God as something to be exploited, but emptied himself, taking the form of a slave, being born in human likeness.")

According to the *Ṛgveda* 10.90 the universe is created out of the primordial sacrifice of the primordial man Puruṣa (alternately identified as the divine being or Lord of Creation Prajāpati). Thomas Hopkins notes, "The primary act of creation is the creation of the sacrifice; that being created, all else is formed from it."[9] More specifically the world is created out of sacrifice, out of the dismemberment of Puruṣa with his mouth becoming the *brāhmans* or priestly caste, his arms becoming the *kṣatriyas* or military caste, his thighs becoming the *vaiśyas* or artisan caste, and his feet becoming the *śūdras* or laborer caste (see *Ṛgveda* 10.90.12 as well as the list on page 331). In a similar Babylonian myth, the god Marduk creates the cosmos from the dismembered body of the sea monster Tiamat.[10]

In the ancient Vedic system, the elaborate sacrificial cult restores and reaffirms the natural and social order of the universe (macrocosm) through the rituals and mantras performed in the microcosm of the sacrificial arena (see the chart on page 327). To quote Eliade again:

> Indeed, the construction of the sacrificial altar is conceived as a "Creation of the world." The water with which the clay is mixed is the primordial water; the clay that forms the base of the altar is the earth; the side walls represent the atmosphere. . . . But if the raising of the altar imitates the cosmogonic act, the sacrifice proper has another end: to restore the primordial unity, that which existed before the Creation.[11]

Sacrifice is ultimately an act of world-affirmation, both a repetition of the original world-construction as well as a means of world-maintenance.

Not only does sacrifice symbolically regenerate the different levels or castes of the social order, it also enables the ecological regeneration of the different levels of the cosmological order. The three different altars utilized in the most elaborate of Vedic sacri-

---

8. Eliade, *Eternal*, p. 78

9. Thomas J. Hopkins, *The Hindu Religious Tradition* (Belmont, CA: Wadsworth Publishing Co., 1971), p. 22.

10. Mircea Eliade, *The Sacred and the Profane: The Nature of Religion* (New York: Harcourt Inc., 1987), p. 77.

11. Eliade, *Eternal*, p. 78.

fices include the round altar of the Gārhapatya or householder's fire which represents the flat disc of the earth, the square altar of the Āhavanīya or offering fire which represents the four-directional sky, and the semi-circular altar of the Dakṣina fire which represents the dome of the atmosphere in-between the heavens and the earth (see list on page 326). The correlation of the three fires corresponds to the three primary forms of the natural world.

Vedic sacrifices were both elaborate and expensive affairs. Usually only wealthy members of the kṣatriya caste could afford to be patrons of a sacrifice. Each sacrifice entailed the participation of at least one member from the three classes of priests corresponding to the three primary Vedic texts (see list on page 325).[12] Often these ritual experts would have numerous assistants. Only married men could perform these sacrifices and they were always accompanied by their wives at the ceremonies.

It should be noted that sacrifices were not only performed to reestablish the forces of nature and society, but also to bring particular worldly blessings – wealth, power, health, prosperity, success, progeny, and ultimately immortality – to the patrons of the sacrifice and to the priests who performed the sacrifice.[13] This promise of success still motivates sacrifice today. On November 24, 2009, the world's biggest animal sacrifice took place in Nepal near the border of India with the killing of more than 250,000 animals as part of a festival in honor of Gadhimai, a Hindu goddess of power. "It is the traditional way," explained a 45-year old Nepali driver, "If we want anything, and we come here with an offering to the goddess, within five years all our dreams will be fulfilled."[14]

KARMA AND NATURAL LAW

Within Hinduism the concept of sacrifice was gradually transformed from the expensive ritualistic system with a view to worldly success (not totally outmoded today) into the notion of karma understood as moral sacrifice. This transition can be seen in both the *Upaniṣads* and in the *Bhagavad-Gītā*. Particularly in the *Upaniṣads* there is a movement from the world-affirmation of the sacrificial system to the world-renunciation of the ascetic movements popular at the time. While Hinduism moved toward a synthesis of world-affirmation and world-renunciation in its emphasis on worldly action coupled with the renunciation of the fruits of that action in the *Bhagavad-Gītā*, the tendency toward world-renunciation remained especially strong in Buddhism.

Buddhism critiques the sacrificial Vedic cults of Hinduism in much the same way that Christianity critiques the sacrificial cults of Judaism. The Buddhist Scriptures delight in pointing out over and over how bloody and expensive were the Brahmanic sacrifices. In Buddhist texts, Brahmin priests are repeatedly pictured in similar fashion to the hypocritical high priests and Pharisees in the Christian New Testament – hardly a flattering portrait (see, e.g. *Dīgha Nikāya* 4.11 ff. and 27.3 ff.).

For example, in the *Kūṭadanta Sutta*, the Buddha talks the Brahmin Kūṭadanta out of sacrificing "seven hundred bulls, seven hundred bullocks, seven hundred heifers, seven hundred he-goats and seven hundred rams" (*Dīgha Nikāya*, 5.1). The Buddha persuades

---

12. Over time a fourth sacred text was added to the traditional Triple Veda. See list on the Triple Veda. While the added Veda was not concerned with sacrifice but primarily with magic, it is a canonical text.

13. Hopkins, *Hindu*, p. 34.

14. http://www.guardian.co.uk/world/2009/nov/24/hindu-sacrifice-gadhimai-festival-nepal

Kūṭadanta into a bloodless sacrifice analogous to the interior sacrifice that Jesus and the prophets before him proclaimed. As the Hebrew psalmist notes: "For you have no delight in sacrifice; if I were to give burnt offering, you would not be pleased. The sacrifice acceptable to God is a broken spirit; a broken, contrite heart, O God, you will not despise" (Psalm 51:16-17).

While the Eastern view of infinite time conflicts with the Western biblical notion of finite time, the Eastern notion of *ṛta* (or *rita*) in general and karma in particular has many similarities to the medieval West's doctrine of natural law. Karma refers to the moral law of cause and effect. For example, in the *Dhammapada*, verses 1-2, we read: "If with an impure mind a person speaks or acts, suffering follows him like the wheel that follows the foot of the ox . . . . If with a pure mind a person speaks or acts, happiness follows him like his never-departing shadow." In verse 5, we read: "Hatred is never appeased by hatred in this world. By non-hatred alone is hatred appeased. This is Law Eternal (*dhammo sanantano*)."

In the Buddhist medieval manual the *Abhidhammattha Sangaha*, Bhikkhu Bodhi says in his Guide to passage V.18: "The law of kamma (*kammaniyāma*) is self-subsistent in its operation, ensuring that willed deeds produce their effects in accordance with their ethical quality just as surely as seeds bear fruit in accordance with their species. The direct products of kamma are the resultant (*vipāka*) states of consciousness and mental factors that arise when kamma finds the right conditions to fructify."[15] Note the metaphors to nature. Nothing could be closer to Jesus' adage from his Sermon on the Mount, "By their fruits you shall know them" (Matthew 7:16). Or to St. Paul's injunction, "God is not mocked, for whatever a man sows, that he will also reap" (Galatians 6:7).

However, the law of karma or the eternal law does not diminish the need for particular laws. The Buddha taught both natural law and positive law. An example of natural law would be the Four Noble Truths the Buddha preached at Deer Park to his five earliest disciples (see the list on page 347 below). Briefly, the four truths are: (1) everything in the cycle of rebirth is suffering, (2) suffering is caused by desire, (3) the cessation of desire leads to the cessation of suffering, and (4) the Noble Eightfold Path teaches the cessation of both desire and suffering.[16] Regarding positive law, Buddhism added a multitude of specific rules (*paññati*) or conventional truths (*sammuti-sacca*), e.g., the 227 rules for monks and 311 rules for nuns in the *Vinaya Piṭaka*.

Similarly, St. Thomas classifies law as descending from universal laws to very specific laws. In the *Summa Theologica* (I-II, q. 91, a.1 ff.) he distinguishes (see page 88 in chapter four on Psychology):

1. eternal law (Divine Providence known through the light of revelation)
2. natural law (universal moral standards discovered through the light of reason)
3. positive law (necessary for specific moral situations)
   a. human positive law (specific laws further deduced from natural law)
   b. divine positive law (necessary on account of uncertainty of human judgment)
      i. Old Law = the Decalogue in the Old Testament

---

15. Ācariya Anuruddha, *Abhidhammattha Sangaha: A Comprehensive Manual of Abhidhamma.* Translated and edited by Bhikkhu Bodhi (Onalaska, WA: Buddhist Publication Society, 1999), p. 200.

16. See Walpola Rahula, *What the Buddha Taught* (New York: Grove Press, 1974), p. 16.

ii. New Law = the law of the Gospel in the New Testament

Like medieval Catholicism, medieval Buddhism relishes both lists of specific laws (cf. the *Vinaya Piṭaka* referred to previously) and lists of moral taints. For example, Buddhism's list of fourteen unwholesome mental factors (*Abhidhammattha Sangaha*, II.4), corresponds to the Seven Deadly Sins of the medieval West, one difference being that the Buddhist unwholesome factors refer more to proclivities than actions.

Although self-subsistent in its operation, the law of karma need not entail the fatalism painted by its Western critics. Both Hinduism and Buddhism teach liberation (*mokṣa* for the Hindu and *nirvāṇa* for the Buddhist) from *saṃsāra* – the endless cycle of birth, death, and rebirth. Both religions adhere to what Steven Collins terms "the *saṃsāra-karma-mokṣa* belief system."[17] In this system human beings trapped in the world of rebirth or *saṃsāra* by their volitional actions or *karma* can find liberation from this cycle through asceticism and meditation.

We might note that there are many paths to liberation in this belief system; some are world-renouncing and some are world-affirming. The famous *Bhagavad-Gītā* (one small chapter in the epic *Mahābhārata* mentioned previously) teaches a form of detachment (karma yoga) that does not entail abandoning the world. "Be intent on action, not on the fruits of action; avoid attraction to the fruits and attachment to inaction!" (*Bhagavad-Gītā*, II.47). To achieve this purity, a man (or woman) must simply perform the duties of the social caste he or she is born into (see list of castes on page 331 below), while at the same time renouncing the fruits or outcomes of these actions.

Natural law is built into the structure of the universe. Speaking specifically of Theravāda Buddhism and medieval Catholicism, both systems assume an objective hierarchy of existence and an objective hierarchy of consciousness. The Western hierarchy at the macrocosmic level is explained in chapter three on Cosmology and at the microcosmic level in chapter four on Psychology. Bhikkhu Bodhi describes the natural hierarchy in the Buddhist cosmos in precise and concise fashion in his Guide to passage V.2:

> The outer world is quite real and possesses objective existence. However, the outer world is also a world apprehended by consciousness, and the type of consciousness determines the nature of the world that appears. Consciousness and the world are mutually dependent and inextricably connected to such an extent that the hierarchical structure of the realms of existence exactly reproduces and corresponds to the hierarchical structure of consciousness.[18]

Here Bhikkhu Bodhi refers to the famous 31 realms of existence where humans, demons, and gods reside based on their karma.

The realms move from Hell (the lowest level in the woeful plane of existence) to the state of "neither perception nor non-perception" (the highest level in the immaterial-sphere plane of existence). Both Buddhist and Catholic systems entail a natural reward and punishment for moral acts in that both systems have a series of heavens and hells that are hierarchically structured. In fact, while Dante only has nine levels of Hell, Buddhism has a total of 168 levels![19]

---

17. Steven Collins, *Selfless Persons* (New York: Cambridge University Press, 1999), p. 64.
18. *Abhidhammattha*, p. 188.
19. *Abhidhammattha* (V.4), p. 190.

Both systems eschew moral nihilism. Bhikkhu Bodhi's Guide to the *Abhidhammattha Sangaha* (V.22) summarizes three types of moral nihilism that would surely find little argument from St. Thomas. The three types include:

1. nihilism (*natthika-diṭṭhi*), which denies the survival of the personality in any form after death, thus negating the moral significance of deeds;

2. the inefficacy of action view (*akiriya-diṭṭhi*), which claims that deeds have no efficacy in producing results and thus invalidates moral distinctions; and

3. the acausality view (*ahetukadiṭṭhi*), which states that there is no cause or condition for the defilement and purification of beings, that beings are defiled and purified by chance, fate, or necessity.[20]

These heretical beliefs (wrong view = *micca-diṭṭhi*) are condemned by the Buddha in *Dīgha Nikāya*, 2.16 ff., in *Majjhima Nikāya*, nos. 60 & 76, and in the *Dhammapada* 21-22 among other places.

Similarly St. Thomas condemns the inefficacy of action view when he declares, "Man has free-will: otherwise counsels, exhortations, commands, prohibitions, rewards, and punishments would be in vain" (*Summa Theologica*, I, q. 83, a. 1). The Buddha also emphasizes moral responsibility. In the *Anguttara Nikāya* 6.63, he declares: "It is volition (*cetana*), monks, that I call kamma, for having willed, one performs an action through body, speech, or mind." While the literal meaning of karma is action, the Buddha further defines it as volitional action, wholesome (*kusala*) or unwholesome (*akusala*). It may be that the East and West come closest to each other in their belief in an objective natural law applicable to all human beings.

THE MEDIEVAL PASSION FOR CLASSIFICATION

While the Theravāda Buddhist tradition holds to a modal rather than to the substance ontology characteristic of the medieval West, it does not adhere to the epistemological relativism characteristic of the modern West. In Theravāda Buddhism, the function of perception or apperception (*sañña*) is a fully conscious process of understanding by which newly observed qualities of an object are related to past experience. One of the five famous Buddhist aggregates listed below on page 349, *sañña*, is a rudimentary process of classification that is a natural function and not a social convention. As discussed earlier, consciousness is an objective fact that reflects the structure of the universe.

This passion for classification is a major characteristic of medieval scholasticism, both East and West. As C. S. Lewis observed, the medieval mind had an overwhelming taxonomic impulse to take a perpetual inventory of the universe:

At his most characteristic, medieval man was not a dreamer or a wanderer. He was an organizer, a codifier, a builder of systems. He wanted "a place for everything and everything in its right place." Distinction, definition, tabulation were his delight . . . .
There was nothing medieval people liked better, or did better, than sorting out and tidying up. Of all our modern inventions I suspect they would most have admired the card index [database]. The perfect examples [of their system] are the *Summa* of Aquinas and Dante's *Divine Comedy*.[21]

---

20. *Abhidhammattha*, p. 208.
21. Lewis, *Discarded*, p. 10.

The scholar Raimundo Panikkar makes a similar observation in his enlightening article, "Common Patterns of Eastern and Western Scholasticism."[22] He notes seven patterns common to the medieval East and West which include: (1) the principle of authority, (2) a hierarchical structure of the world, (3) the intrinsic value of tradition, (4) extensive use of commentaries, (5) precise terminology, (6) dialectical methodology, and (7) doctrinal orthodoxy. Almost all of the lists in *Medieval Literacy* reveal a hierarchical structure dependent on a deep respect for tradition and a meticulous use of commentary and repetition to insure doctrinal orthodoxy. This hierarchy can be seen in lists as diverse as the Hindu levels of social caste and Dionysius' nine choirs of angels. It should be noted, however, that despite his respect for authority, that pinnacle of Western scholasticism, Thomas Aquinas, pronounced the argument from authority the weakest of all arguments (*Summa Theologica*, I, q. 1, a. 8).

Both Eastern and Western scholasticism exalt in dry, hierarchical classification systems. Many scholars have attributed the structure of Thomas' *Summa* to the scholastic adage, "Seldom affirm, never deny, always distinguish." Every answer to every one of Thomas' 611 questions in the *Summa* required a far more complex answer than a simple yes or no. Scholasticism celebrated distinctions and subtle shades of grey. Interestingly, in the East the Sanskrit word for color, *varṇa*, is the same as the word for caste which implies classification. Brian Smith observes in his classic work on the Hindu caste system, "Classification is the basis for all of what we call thought, reason, or logic. 'All thinking is sorting, classifying,' as E. H. Gombrich, among others, has observed. To make sense of things is to bring order to them, to organize and structure them by dividing them into classes [castes] or categories."[23]

While critical of the Hindu social caste system, Buddhism, even more than Hinduism, relishes classification *qua* classification. Almost like art for art's sake, most Buddhist traditions (excluding Zen) carry this art of classification to its most medieval extremes. The Buddha himself delighted in lists. He taught the Four Noble Truths to summarize his doctrine, the Five Aggregates to challenge the notion of "self," the Eightfold Path as a step-by-step road to salvation, and the Twelve Factors of Dependent Origination to explain the cycle of karma and rebirth.

The poetic suttas (sayings of the Buddha) abound in lists. The entire *Anguttara Nikāya* breaks down the Buddha's teaching into lists of ones, twos, threes – all the way up to elevens. Similarly, suttas 33 and 34 in the *Dīgha Nikāya* comprise lists of things in twos, threes, fours, etc. – for example, two kinds of meditation (calm and insight), three kinds of feeling (pleasant, unpleasant and neutral), four kinds of material elements (earth, air, fire, and water). Clearly, the early traditions portray the Buddha using these lists as a useful preaching technique in an oral and "illiterate" culture.

Buddhist scholasticism devoted itself to insuring "the accurate transmission of [these] categorical lists."[24] Eventually these mnemonic missionary devices developed into a full-blown metaphysical system. The Abhidhamma Mātikā or schedule of categories that underpins Theravāda philosophical psychology consists of 22 sets of triple classification

---

22. Raimundo Panikkar, "Common Patterns of Eastern and Western Scholasticism," *Diogenes* 83 (1973):103-113.

23. Brian K. Smith, *Classifying the Universe: The Ancient Indian Varṇa System and the Origins of Caste* (New York: Oxford University Press, 1994), p. 3.

24. Collins, *Selfless*, p. 109.

(*tika*) and 100 sets of double classification (*duka*). According to the *Pali-English Dictionary*, *mātikā* means "tabulation, register, summary, or condensed contents."[25] The root of *mātikā* is *mātar* which means "mother."[26] Note the similarity of *mātikā* to the condensed *summae* of medieval Western theologians.

The Abhidhamma Mātikā makes no distinction between scientific and ethical classification. For example, the first triad in the schedule is that of wholesome, unwholesome, and morally indeterminate (*Dhammasaṅganī* 1 ff.).[27] All types of consciousness are classified according to this triad. In Buddhism the worlds of fact and value are intertwined. Epistemology and ethics, fact and value, are cut from the same cloth of consciousness.

This "scholastic list-making tendency"[28] finds it apotheosis in the *Visuddhimagga*, the mother of all classification systems by the great fifth century commentator, Buddhaghosa. The later twelfth century abbreviated scholastic manual of Abhidhamma philosophy, *Abhidhammattha Sangaha*, encapsulates this passion for classification, including elucidation of 89 types of consciousness, 52 mental factors, 31 realms of existence, 28 material phenomena, 10 fetters, 10 defilements, 7 *jhāna* factors, 7 factors of enlightenment, 5 aggregates, 4 noble truths, 12 parts of dependent arising, and 24 conditions (all mentioned in chronological order as discussed in the text), just to mention a few.

The Theravāda tradition resembles the extreme realism tradition of the medieval West. The *Abhidhammattha Sangaha* (I.1) distinguishes ultimate realities (*paramattha-sacca*) from conventional realities (*sammuti-sacca*). The four ultimate realities are: (1) consciousness, (2) mental factors, (3) matter, and (4) *nibbāna* or nirvana. While ultimate realities have an autonomous self-existence or *sabhāva*, conventional realities do not. Conventional realities are illusory and include individual entities like this particular man named Socrates or that particular horse named Barbaro or this particular marble coffee table.

In Theravāda Buddhism, the ultimate realities can be expanded to encompass 72 kinds of self-existent entities.[29] These *dhammā* include distinct universal entities like consciousness, the 52 mental factors (e.g. perception, volition, faith, mindfulness, envy, compassion), the 18 concretely produced material phenomenon (e.g. earth, air, fire, and water), and *nibbāna*. These 72 universal entities are the only things in the world that truly exist. Everything else to some extent is a mirage.

This position is close to Plato who held that the "Form" of envy is more real than the envious person who "participates" in envy. For Plato, universals have more reality than particulars. The universal – man – is ultimately more real than the particular man, Socrates. Socrates is merely an example, albeit a notable one, of the universal category, man. Plato's belief in the real existence of universal concepts or Forms was categorized as extreme realism by the medieval West in contrast to nominalism.

According to the doctrine of extreme realism universal concepts are spiritual enti-

---

25. T. W. Rhys Davids and William Stede, *Pali-English Dictionary* (Delhi, India: Motilal Banarsidass Publishers, 1993), p. 528.

26. Rhys Davids, *Pali-English*, p. 527.

27. See Caroline A. F. Rhys Davids, *A Buddhist Manual of Psychological Ethics (Buddhist Psychology) of the Fourth Century Bc: Being a Translation, Now Made for the First Time, from the Original ... Abhidhamma-Pitaka Entitled Dhamma-Sangani* (Columbia, MO: South Asia Books, 1996).

28. Collins, *Selfless*, p. 129.

29. *Abhidhammattha* (VII.1), p. 264.

ties that exist independently of all particulars. According to the doctrine of nominalism, universals are simple conventions used to describe particulars which share a "family" resemblance with each other; mere linguistic conveniences with no real existence. The medieval West attempted a compromise between these two extremes in the doctrine of "moderate realism" which held that universals exist within the particulars as a common likeness and exist in the human intellect as a concept formed from the focus of the intellect on that likeness. Universals are neither independent entities nor subjective mental states, but mental abstractions reflecting real similarities among individual particulars. Proponents of moderate realism included Aristotle, Abelard, and Thomas Aquinas (see the list on page 175 in chapter seven on Philosophy).

Theravāda Buddhism's doctrine of "no-self" is an extreme form of Plato's dismissal of particular individual entities. The only ultimate realities for the Buddha are those mentioned above – impersonal universal categories. Buddhist "lists" function like Plato's "ideas" in their transcendent existence. Interestingly, Buddhism includes universal material entities like the element of earth among its ultimate categories while Plato only has universal immaterial concepts in his world of Forms.

Steven Collins relates the utilization of these lists to Theravāda monastic discipline and meditation:

> The ability to classify any experience or concept into a known, non-valued impersonal category was held to be a technique for avoiding desire for the object thus classified. . . . Meditation is the application of the lists of impersonal elements (*dhammā*) by a monk to his own experience – those lists which in Buddhist doctrine replace the idea of a self.[30]

Though not adhered to by all medieval scholastic traditions, this extreme realism that Buddhism and Platonism share illustrates one rationale for the medieval fascination with lists, categories, and classes – indeed, for this book, *Medieval Literacy*.

In the West, however, the moderate realism of Aristotle and Thomas emerged as the dominant tradition. Ultimately, the West exalted the status of the individual and the particular over the universal and the categorical. What Thomas most admired in Aristotle was Aristotle's "worldliness." For Aristotle, what is most real is the combination of form and matter in the individual thing, for example, the individual man Socrates.

Thomas found this worldliness confirmed in the Judeo-Christian tradition, particularly in the doctrine of the Incarnation (John 1:17) where the "Word became flesh and lived among us."[31] Thomas also found this worldliness affirmed in God's answer to Moses when Moses asks God his name. God responds, "I am Who Am" (Exodus 3:13-14). Thomas, arguably the first existentialist in the West, interprets the Divine name to mean that God is the one and only being whose essence is to exist. God is *actus purus*, the pure act of being.[32] Since all created things are made in the image of God, the most exalted quality of any individual or particular creature is simply its existence.

Where the Buddha infers that all existence is suffering and Plato asserts that the Good is "beyond Being" (*Republic*, 509b), Thomas affirms all existence as reflecting the glory of God. According to Josef Pieper, this "theologically founded worldliness" is the

---

30. Collins, *Selfless*, pp. 113, 91.
31. Josef Pieper, *Guide to Thomas Aquinas* (San Francisco: Ignatius Press, 1991), p 131.
32. Pieper, *Guide*, p. 137.

"essence of the Christian West."[33] To conclude, the dominant theological tradition in the medieval West exalts the particular over and against the universal, whereas in the East (and in Plato) universal categories are given more prominent status.

Remember, following each list are bibliographic references to the relevant primary sources (A) that are listed in chronological order by the author's lifetime and secondary sources (B) that are listed in alphabetical order by the author's name. Also note that italicized words in the Hinduism lists are transliterations from Sanskrit and italicized words in the Buddhism lists are transliterations from Pali.

---

33. Pieper, *Guide*, p. 134 and p. 133.

HINDUISM

The "Horizontal" Trinity (*trimūrti* or "three forms" of the Absolute among the gods)

deity	function
1. *Brahmā*	the Creator
2. *Śiva*	the Destroyer
3. *Viṣṇu*	the Preserver

NOTE: There are few places in Indian literature where the *trimūrti* is mentioned. Early western students of Hinduism may have overemphasized the parallel between the Hindu and Christian trinity (cf. Doniger below).

    A. A twenty-foot high sculpture of the *trimūrti* can be found in the Elephanta Caves located on Elephanta Island in the Mumbai harbor.

    B. Doniger, Wendy, *The Hindus: An Alternative History*, p. 384
Smith, Huston, *The World's Religions*, p. 62
Stoddart, William, *Hinduism and Its Spiritual Masters*, p. 19
Zimmer, Heinrich, *Myths and Symbols in Indian Art and Civilization*, pp. 132-136

The "Vertical" Trinity (three internal dimensions of the Absolute)

1. *sat* = infinite being (also referred to as truth or reality)

2. *cit* = infinite consciousness (also referred to as knowledge)

3. *ānanda* = infinite bliss (also referred to as infinity)

NOTE: The translation of the *Upaniṣads* by Juan Mascaró mentions three attributes of Brahman. The translation by Patrick Olivelle mentions three things plus Brahman.

    A. *Taittirīya Upaniṣad*, 2.1

    B. Feuerstein, Georg, *Spirituality by the Numbers*, p. 45
Smith, Huston, *The World's Religions*, p. 60
Stoddart, William, *Hinduism and Its Spiritual Masters*, p. 20.

HINDUISM (CONTINUED)

The Three Regions of the Cosmos

region	type of gods (*devas*)	example of gods
1. sky or heavens	celestial gods	Viṣṇu, Varuṇa
2. atmosphere	atmospheric gods	Indra, Rudra
3. earth	terrestrial gods	Agni, Soma

    A. *Ṛgveda*, 10.121.5
    B. Hopkins, Thomas, *The Hindu Religious Tradition*, pp. 11-13

The Triple Veda

Vedic text	Vedic priest	description of text
1. *Ṛgveda* (Knowledge of Verses)	Hotṛ	hymns to gods to be used during sacrifices
2. *Samaveda* (Knowledge of Songs)	Udgātṛ	adapts hymns to music to be used during sacrifices
3. *Yajurveda* (Knowledge of Sacrifice)	Adhvaryu	mantras for priests to be used during sacrifices
(4.) *Atharvaveda* (Knowledge of the Fire Priest)	Brāhmaṇ	the text is devoted to magic more than sacrifice; the Brāhmaṇ priest eventually became the conductor or overseer of the sacrifice and the activities of the other priests

NOTE: The *Atharvaveda* was added later in the tradition. Each Vedic priest mentioned above is the specialist in the corresponding particular text. The Brāhmaṇ priest was required to have knowledge of all the Vedas.

    A. See above texts.
    B. Doniger, Wendy, *The Hindus: An Alternative History*, pp. 104-105
       Hopkins, Thomas, *The Hindu Religious Tradition*, pp. 29-30

HINDUISM (CONTINUED)

The Three Vedic Sacrificial Fires

fire	altar shape	cosmos
1. Āhavanīya or offering fire (used as the fire of offering to the gods)	square altar	represents the four-directional sky
2. Dakṣina or southern fire (used as the fire of offering to one's ancestors)	semi-circular altar	represents the dome of the atmosphere
3. Gārhapatya or householder's fire (used to prepare the food for the sacrifice)	round altar	represents the flat disk of the earth

A. *Chāndogya Upaniṣad*, 4:11-13
   Laws of Manu, 2.231
B. Doniger, Wendy, *The Hindus: An Alternative History*, p. 130
   Hopkins, Thomas, *The Hindu Religious Tradition*, pp. 18-19
   Knipe, David, *Hinduism*, pp. 33-36

HINDUISM (CONTINUED)

Chart of the Vedic Sacrificial Arena

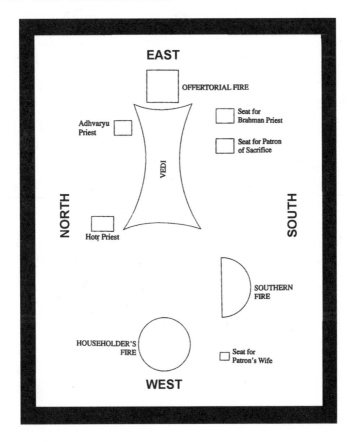

NOTE: The patron of the sacrifice symbolizes Puruṣa, the primordial sacrifice. The dimensions (in terms of ratios) of the altars are based on the personal physical dimensions (in terms of ratios) of the patron.

SOURCE: Figure 3: Sacrificial Area (p. xliii) from *Upaniṣads* (Oxford World Classics) by Patrick Olivelle (2008). By permission of Oxford University Press.

HINDUISM (CONTINUED)

Three Vedic Debts

debt	debtor	payment
1. debt to the sages (*rishis*)	paid by the student	fulfilled by learning the Vedas
2. debt to the ancestors (including parents)	paid by the householder	fulfilled by begetting male heirs
3. debt to the gods	paid by the forest-dweller	fulfilled by performing sacrifices

NOTE: These debts are paid during the first three stages of human life listed below on page 333. A human being only has the right to seek liberation (*mokṣa*) after faithfully fulfilling the above three debts.

A. *Laws of Manu*, 6.35-37
B. "Indian Religions: Mythic Themes," *Encyclopedia of Religion*, 2nd edition, vol. 7

HINDUISM (CONTINUED)

Three Paths to God (yoga = yoke or discipline)

path	technique	temperament
karma yoga *(path of work)*	Work with no attachment to the fruits of one's work.	active temperament (will)
bhakti yoga *(path of devotion)*	Devotion to a personal God distinct from one's self.	emotional temperament (feeling)
jñāna yoga *(path of knowledge)*	Realization of the transpersonal infinite Self beyond the finite self.	Realization of the transpersonal infinite Self beyond the finite self.

NOTE: Note the similarity of the above three yogas to the Platonic tripartite soul on page 78 in chapter four on Psychology. The emphasis in the *Bhagavad-Gītā* is on fulfilling one's duties through a life of action. "Better to do one's own duty imperfectly than to do another man's well" (18.47). However, all spiritual action must renounce the fruits of that action (2.47). Detached action is the ultimate sacrifice.

    A. *Bhagavad-Gītā*
    B. Doniger, Wendy, *The Hindus: An Alternative History*, p. 283.
       Hopkins, Thomas J., *The Hindu Religious Tradition*, pp. 90-95
       Smith, Huston, *The World's Religions*, pp. 29-50

HINDUISM (CONTINUED)

Three *Guṇas*

1. *sattva* = lightness, lucidity, goodness

2. *rajas* = energy, passion, activity

3. *tamas* = darkness, heaviness, inertia

NOTE: The *guṇas* are the cosmic tendencies or qualities of nature of all animate and inanimate objects. They are often contrasted with the *doṣas* or faults of these objects. Note that Buddhism also has three marks of existence that pertain to all phenomena, the Three Marks of Existence on page 346.

    A. *Bhagavad-Gītā*, 14.5-20
       Laws of Manu, 1.15-20 and 12.24-29
    B. Doniger, Wendy, *The Hindus: An Alternative History*, p. 200
       "Guṇas," *Encyclopedia of Religion*, 2nd edition, vol. 6
       Stoddart, William, *Hinduism and Its Spiritual Masters*, p. 41

HINDUISM (CONTINUED)

Four Castes or Stations of Life (*varṇas*)

castes	guṇa	animal	color
1. *brāhmaṇs* = spiritual leaders	*sattva*	cow	white (fair)
2. *kṣatriyas* = political leaders	*rajas*	horse	red (ruddy)
3. *vaiśyas* = artisans and farmers	*tamas*	dog	yellow (sallow)
4. *śūdras* = laborers	*tamas*	dog	black (dark)

NOTE: *Varṇa* means both color and caste. The four stages of life, the four stations in life, and the attendant duties of each (articulated in the most summary fashion in *The Laws of Manu*) are part of the interconnected *varṇāśrama dharma* system that delineates: "(1) the notion that one's particular duty (*dharma*) is calibrated to the class (*varṇa*) into which one was born and the stage of life (*āśrama*) one is presently passing through; and (2) the belief in *karma* and the cycle of rebirth (*saṃsāra*) whereby one's social position in this life is ethically determined by moral actions in past lives" (see Brian Smith below).

According to the *Ṛgveda*, the universe was produced from the primordial sacrifice of a divine creator or cosmic man, Puruṣa, with his mouth becoming the *brāhmans*, his arms becoming the *kṣatriyas*, his thighs becoming the *vaiśyas*, and his feet becoming the *śūdras*. The reader might note the similarity of the caste system to Plato's three classes of philosophers, guardians, and workers as well as to the three orders of feudal society – the clergy who pray, the knights who fight, and the serfs who work.

      A. Puruṣasūkta (Poem of the Primeval Man) in the *Ṛgveda*, 10.90
         Bṛhadāraṇyaka Upaniṣad, 1.4.11-15
         Bhagavad-Gītā, 4.12 and 18.41-44
         The Laws of Manu, 10.1-4
      B. Doniger, Wendy, *The Hindus: An Alternative History*, pp. 40-41 and 116-118 and 286
         Feuerstein, Georg, *Spirituality by the* Numbers, pp. 73-75
         Hopkins, Thomas J., *The Hindu Religious Tradition*, pp. 74-86
         Smith, Brian K., *Classifying the Universe*, p. 10
         Smith, Huston, *The World's Religions*, pp. 55-59

HINDUISM (CONTINUED)

Chart of Four Castes and of Vedic Sacrificial System

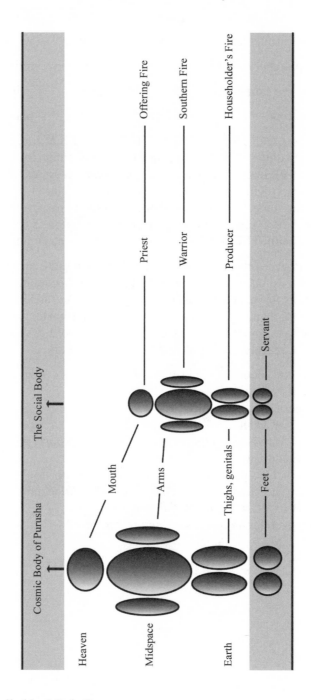

SOURCE: Compiled by Mark Grote.

HINDUISM (CONTINUED)

Four Stages of Life (*āśramas*)

1. Stage of the student (*brahmacārin*) = the period of learning and chastity (ages 1-21)

2. Stage of the householder (*gṛhasthin*) = the period of marriage, children, and earning a living (ages 22-42)

3. Stage of the forest-dweller (*vānaprasthin*) = the period of solitude and renewed studies, living as a hermit with a meager livelihood (ages 43-84)

4. Stage of complete renunciation (*saṃnyāsin*) = the forest-dweller abandons life as a hermit for the life of a wandering mendicant (no home or belongings, live by begging)

    A. *Laws of Manu*, 6.87 (chapter six discusses all four stages at length)
       Vatsyayana, *Kamasutra*, 1.2.1-6
    B. Doniger, Wendy, *The Hindus: An Alternative History*, p. 207
       Feuerstein, Georg, *Spirituality by the Numbers*, p. 68
       Hopkins, Thomas J., *The Hindu Religious Tradition*, pp. 74-86
       Smith, Huston, *The World's Religions*, pp. 50-55

HINDUISM (CONTINUED)

Four Goals of Life (*puruṣārthas*)

goal	description	śāstra text
1. *dharma*	duty (virtue, moral integrity)	*Laws of Manu* (c.100 CE)
2. *artha*	political power (wealth, fame)	*Arthaśāstra* (c.200 CE)
3. *kāma*	pleasure (sensual, aesthetic)	*Kāmasūtra* (c.100-200 CE)
(4.) *mokṣa*	spiritual liberation (similar to Buddhist *nirvana*)	

NOTE: Originally, the goals formed a Trio of the worldly aims of the householder (the first three above), but eventually the goal of the renunciant (*mokṣa*) was added to the list. The goals of the original Trio do not necessarily compete with each other. For example, a couple might have "sex for the sake of offspring (*dharma*), for the sake of gaining political power (*artha*), or for sheer pleasure (*kāma*)" (Doniger, p. 204). Note that the original Trio bears a loose resemblance to the tripartite soul of Plato.

> A. *The Laws of Manu*, 7.151
>   Vatsyayana, *Kāmasūtra*, 1.5.1-12
> B. Doniger, Wendy, *The Hindus: An Alternative History*, pp. 201-211
>   Feuerstein, Georg, *Spirituality by the Numbers*, p. 69
>   Smith, Huston, *The World's Religions*, pp. 13-19

HINDUISM (CONTINUED)

The Four Major Addictions (royal vices)

activity	object
1. gambling	dice
2. drinking	wine (intoxicants)
3. fornicating	women (sex)
4. hunting	animals (meat)

   A. *Laws of Manu*, 7.50
     Kautilya, *Arthaśāstra*, 1.17.35-38 and 8.3.2-61
   B. Doniger, Wendy, *The Hindus: An Alternative* History, pp. 320-325

HINDUISM (CONTINUED)

The Four Cosmic Ages (*yugas*)

1. *Ḳrtayuga* (1,728,000 years) = the age of truth (winning age)

2. *Tretāyuga* (1,296,000 years) = "thrice-lucky age" (age of mostly winning)

3. *Dvāparayuga* (864,000 years) = "twice-lucky age" (age of mostly losing)

4. *Kaliyuga* (432,000 years) = the dark age (losing age)

NOTE: The total cycle (*mahāyuga*) is 4,320,000 human years. The four *yugas* are named after four dice throws. The four ages successively become more degenerated. In the *Tretāyuga* humans lose 25% of their goodness and virtue. In the *Dvāparayuga* humans lose 50% of their virtue. And in the *Kaliyuga* they retain only 25% of their original virtue. Currently we are only 5,000 years into the current Iron Age. These four ages compare closely with the classical Greek notion of the declining four ages from Golden to Silver to Bronze to Iron. While the Hindu concept of time is cyclical and degenerative as is the classical Greek notion, the modern Western notion is limited and progressive.

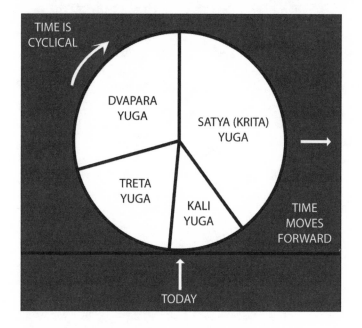

SOURCE: http://hinduism.iskcon.com/concepts/111.htm

A. *The Laws of Manu,* 1.68-74
B. Doniger, Wendy, *The Hindus: An Alternative* History, pp. 57-58
   Feuerstein, Georg, *Spirituality by the Numbers*, pp. 84-85
   Hopkins, Thomas J., *The Hindu Religious Tradition*, pp. 99-102

HINDUISM (CONTINUED)

Five Great Elements (*mahābhūtas*)

1. *ākāśa* = space

2. *vāyu* = air

3. *agni* = fire

4. *āp* = water

5. *pṛthivī* = earth

NOTE: Note the similarities between this list and the five elements in Western thought. Buddhism has four great elements (earth, air, fire, water) as well as five aggregates. Also note that in Sāṃkhya Yoga there is a dualism between nature (*prakṛti*) and spirit (*puruṣa*).

> A. *Taittirīya Upaniṣad*, 2.1
>   Patanjali, *Yoga Sutra*, 3.44
> B. *"Sāṃkhya," Encyclopedia of Religion*, vol. 12

Five Bodies or Sheaths (*kośas*)

1. *annamaya kośa* = the body made of physical matter

2. *prāṇamaya kośa* = the body made of vital breath

3. *manomaya kośa* = the body made of thought energy

4. *vijñānamaya kośa* = the body made of higher intelligence

5. *ānandamaya kośa* = the body made of bliss consciousness

NOTE: Each body is a covering of the Spirit or Self (*atman*).

> A. *Taittirīya Upaniṣad*, 2.8
> B. Feuerstein, Georg, *Spirituality by the Numbers*, pp. 105-106

HINDUISM (CONTINUED)

Five Vital Breaths (*prāṇa*)

1. *prāṇa* = ascending breath including inhalation and exhalation

2. *apāna* = breath associated with the lower half of the trunk

3. *vyāna* = diffuse breath circulating in all the limbs

4. *udāna* = rising breath responsible for speech

5. *samāna* = digestive breath

    A. *Taittirīya Upaniṣad*, 1.7
       Patanjali, *Yoga Sutra*, 3.39-40
    B. "Prāṇa," *Encyclopedia of Religion*, 2nd edition, vol. 11

Five Afflictions (*kleśa*)

1. *avidyā* = ignorance

2. *asmitā* = egoism

3. *rāga* = passion

4. *dveṣa* = hatred

5. *abhiniveśa* = clinging to life

NOTE: See the list on the Three Poisons in Buddhism on page 347.

    A. Patanjali, *Yoga Sutra*, 2.3-9 and 4.28-30
    B. Eliade, Mircea, *Yoga: Immortality and Freedom*, p. 41

HINDUISM (CONTINUED)

Five Restraints (*yamas*)

1. *ahiṃsā* = restraint from violence (nonviolence)

2. *satya* = restraint from falsehood (truthfulness)

3. *asteya* = restraint from stealing

4. *brahmacarya* = restraint from sexual activity

5. *aparigraha* = restraint from avarice

NOTE: Note the similarity with the five Buddhist precepts on page 352.

> A. Patanjali, *Yoga Sutra*, 2.30
> *Laws of Manu*, 10.63
> B. Eliade, Mircea, *A History of Religious Ideas*, vol. 2, p. 62
> "Yoga," *Encyclopedia of Religion*, 2nd edition, vol. 14

Five Disciplines (*niyamas*)

1. *śauca* = cleanliness

2. *santoṣa* = serenity

3. *tapas* = asceticism

4. *svādhyāya* = study of sacred lore

5. *īśvara-praṇidhāna* = dedication to the Lord of Yoga

NOTE: These famous lists of do's (*niyamas*) and don'ts (*yamas*) by Patanjali have often been referred to as Hinduism's Ten Commitments. Compare with the Judeo-Christian list of the Ten Commandments on page 89 in chapter four on Psychology.

> A. Patanjali, *Yoga Sutra*, 2.32
> B. Eliade, Mircea, *A History of Religious Ideas*, vol. 2, p. 62

HINDUISM (CONTINUED)

Six Schools or Viewpoints (*darśanas*) of Hindu Metaphysics
(in traditional ordered pairs)

school	chief characteristic	texts
1. *Nyāya*	Logic	Gautama's *Nyāya Sūtra* (c. 200 BCE - 150 CE)
2. *Vaiśeṣika*	Natural philosophy (atomistic cosmology)	Kaṇāda's *Vaiśeṣika Sūtra* (c. 200 BCE - 100 CE)
3. *Sāṃkhya*	Cosmology (dualistic cosmology)	Īśvara Kṛṣṇa's *Sāṃkhya Sūtra* (350 CE)
4. *Yoga*	Mysticism	Pantanjali's *Yoga Sūtra* (200 BCE or 300-500 CE)
5. *Mīmāṃsā*	Interpretations of Vedic rituals	Jaimini's *Mīmāṃsā Sūtra* (c. 300-100 BCE)
6. *Vedānta*	Spiritual metaphysics	Bādarāyaṇa's *Vedānta Sūtra* (c. 300-100 BCE)

A. See texts as listed.
B. Feuerstein, Georg, *Spirituality by the Numbers*, pp. 114-117
   "Indian Philosophy," *Encyclopedia of Religion*, 2nd edition, vol. 7
   Stoddart, William, *Hinduism and Its Spiritual Masters*, p. 69

HINDUISM (CONTINUED)

Seven Psycho-Spiritual Centers (Chakras) in Haṭha Yoga

chakra	location
1. *mūlādhāra-cakra*	sacrococcygeal nerve plexus at the base of the spine (potential energy)
2. *svādhiṣṭhāna-cakra*	sacral plexus near the genitals (sexual energy)
3. *maṇipūra-cakra*	solar plexus behind the naval (psychic energy)
4. *anāhata-cakra*	cardiac plexus at the heart (love energy)
5. *viśuddha-cakra*	pharyngeal plexus at the throat (speech and bodily energy)
6. *ājñā-cakra*	pineal plexus behind the point between the eyebrows (mental energy or the "third eye")
7. *sahasrāra-cakra*	ventricular plexus at the crown of the head (Divine energy)

A. Svātmārāma, *Haṭhayogapradīpikā*, chapter three

B. Eliade, Mircea, *Yoga: Immortality and Freedom*, p. 234
Feuerstein, Georg, *Spirituality by the Numbers*, pp. 124-126
Hopkins, Thomas J., *The Hindu Religious Tradition*, pp. 127 ff.

HINDUISM (CONTINUED)

Illustration of the Chakras

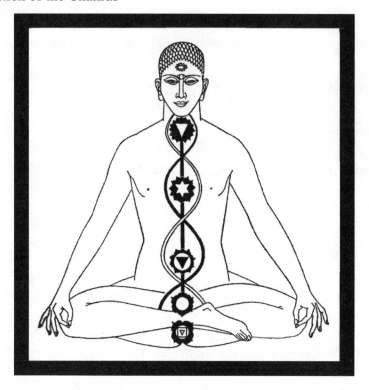

SOURCE: William Stoddart, *The Essential Titus Burckhardt*, p. 215

HINDUISM (CONTINUED)

Eight Limbs of Yogic Practice

1. *yama* = moral principles, e.g., the five restraints cited above

2. *niyama* = disciplines, e.g., the five disciplines cited above

3. *āsana* = posture, e.g., physical and spiritual postures of *haṭha-yoga*

4. *prāṇāyāma* = breath control, e.g., regulation and slowing down of the life force

5. *pratyāhāra* = withdrawal of the senses

6. *dhāraṇā* = concentration

7. *dhyāna* = meditation

8. *samādhi* = contemplation, e.g. coalescing of subject and object (the yogi becomes what he or she meditates on)

NOTE: Note that Buddhism also has an Eightfold Path (see page 350).

A. Patanjali, *Yoga Sutra*, 2.29-55 and 3.1-3
B. Eliade, Mircea, *A History of Religious Ideas*, vol. 2, pp. 62-65
Eliade, Mircea, *Yoga: Immortality and Freedom*, pp. 48-49
Feuerstein, Georg, *Spirituality by the Numbers* , pp. 149-152
"Yoga," *Encyclopedia of Religion*, 2nd edition, vol. 14

HINDUISM (CONTINUED)

Hindu Scriptures

Śruti Texts (texts which are heard [śruti]; Vedic scriptures of divine origin)

• *Saṃhitās* (the Vedas in the strictest sense, used only by the priestly class in sacrificial rites; the first three are also referred to as the the triple, eternal Veda):

1. *Ṛgveda* (Knowledge of Verses): 1028 hymns to various gods during sacrifices

2. *Samaveda* (Knowledge of Songs): adapts Rig Veda hymns to music during sacrifices

3. *Yajurveda* (Knowledge of Sacrifice): instructions, mantras for priests during sacrifices

(4.) *Atharvaveda* (Knowledge of the Fire Priest): magic not related to the sacrifices

• *Brāhamaṇas*: commentaries on the Vedas

• *Āraṇyakas* (Jungle Books): commentaries on Vedic rituals by hermits and forest dwellers

• *Upaniṣads*: meditations on Vedic ritual, on the soul (*ātman*) and the Absolute (*Brahman*)

Smṛti Texts (texts which are remembered [smṛti]; post-Vedic literature of human origin)

• *Vedāṅgas*: also called the "limbs of the Veda" composed to help interpret the Vedas (note the similarity between the Vedāṅgas and the Seven Liberal Arts)

1. *Śksa*: writings on phonetics
2. *Chandas*: writings on metrics and verse
3. *Vyākaraṇa*: writings on grammar
4. *Nirukta*: writings on etymology
5. *Jyotiṣa*: writings on astronomy
6. *Kalpa*: writings on ritual

• *Mahābhārata*: extraordinary epic (75,000 verses!) on a winless civil war (the Hindu *Iliad*); the *Bhagavad-Gītā* forms Book 6, Chapters 23-40 of this work

• *Rāmāyaṇa*: epic about Rama's search for his missing wife (the Hindu *Odyssey*)

• *Śāstras*: scholastic treatises (often in dialogical format) that form the basis for later jurisprudence (e.g., *Laws of Manu, Kāmasūtra, Arthaśāstra*)

• *Puranas*: often called "the fifth Veda," these medieval comendiums of myth and history were available to all four castes of Hindu society (unlike the Vedas that were reserved for the priestly class alone)

A. Many of these Scriptures available at www.sacred-texts.com/hin/index.htm.
B. Basham, A. L., *The Origins and Development of Classical Hinduism*
   Stoddart, William, *Hinduism and Its Spiritual Masters*, pp. 59-60

BUDDHISM

Threefold *Sāsana* (the threefold dispensation of the Buddha)

dispensation	description	simile of the water reservoir
1. *pariyatti*	the religion of the text; the Three Piṭakas; the foundation	the earthen embankments
2. *paṭipatti*	the religion of practice; good works and meditation	the water in the pond
3. *paṭivedha*	the penetration/realization of Buddhist truths; the goal or ornament (Enlightenment)	the lotuses that blossom on the pond

NOTE: "Regarding the recitation of Scripture [performed during the First Synod] it is said: Scripture [which is called] 'Pariyatti' constitutes the foundation of the *Sāsana* established by our Lord, the Blessed One." Scholarship, the religion of the text, ranks higher than good works, meditation, and even Enlightenment. Sacred scholarship is like the embankments of a reservoir. The reservoir will only contain water when the embankments are secure. And there will only be lotuses when there is water.

A. Mehti Sayadaw, *Vaṃsadīpanī* [Treatise on the Lineage of Elders], I.1.11
B. Pranke, Patrick, "The 'Treatise on the Lineage of Elders' (*Vaṃsadīpanī*): Monastic Reform and the Writing of Buddhist History in Eighteenth-Century Burma," pp. 49-50

BUDDHISM (CONTINUED)

Three Refuges or The Triple Gem

1. Buddha = the doctor

2. dhamma (teaching) = the medicine

3. sangha (order of monks) = the nurse administering the medicine

NOTE: There is no initiation ceremony in Buddhism (like the sacrament of Baptism in the Christian tradition). One is a Buddhist if he or she takes refuge in the Buddha, the Dhamma, and the Sangha and observes the basic five moral precepts (listed below on page 352).

> A. *Dīgha Nikāya*, 1.1.5-6
> B. Feuerstein, Georg, *Spirituality by the* Numbers, p. 64
> Rahula, Walpola, *What the Buddha Taught*, p. 80

Three Marks of Existence (*lakkhaṇa*)

1. impermanence (*annica*)

2. suffering or dissatisfaction (*dukkha*)

3. no-self (*anatta*)

NOTE: Like the three *guṇas* in Hinduism, these three marks accompany everything in the phenomenal world.

> A. *Dhammapada*, 277-279
> B. Feuerstein, Georg, *Spirituality by the Numbers*, pp. 54-56
> Smith, Huston, *The World's Religions*, p. 117

BUDDHISM (CONTINUED)

Three Poisons or Fires

1. greed or attraction (*lobha*) = the cock at the center of the Wheel of Life

2. hatred or repulsion (*dosa*) = the snake at the center of the Wheel of Life

3. ignorance or delusion (*moha*) = the pig at the center of the Wheel of Life

NOTE: These three poisons epitomize the factors leading to the cycle of rebirth. See the Hindu list on the Five Afflictions on page 338 above.

> A. *Dīgha Nikāya*, 33.1.10
> B. Stoddart, William, *Outline of Buddhism*, p. 32

The Four Noble Truths

1. The truth of Suffering (*dukkha*)

2. The truth of the Arising (*samudaya*) of suffering due to thirst or desire (*tanha*)

3. The truth of the Cessation (*nirodha*) of suffering

4. The truth of the Path (*magga*) which leads to the cessation of suffering

> A. *Dīgha Nikāya*, 22.17 ff.
> *Majjhima Nikāya*, no. 141
> *Samyutta Nikāya*, 56.11
> *Visuddhimagga*, XVI
> *Abhidhammattha Sangaha*, VII.38
> B. Feuerstein, Georg, *Spirituality by the* Numbers, pp. 67-68
> Smith, Huston, *The World's Religions*, pp. 99-103

BUDDHISM (CONTINUED)

The Four Stages of Enlightenment

1. Stream Entrant
   After conquering the first three fetters or hindrances, one becomes a Stream Entrant, guaranteed of no more than seven re-births before enlightenment. Re-birth will only be in a higher plane.

2. Once-Returner
   For one in whom the fourth and fifth fetters have been greatly weakened, *Nirvana* will be realized at most in one more re-birth.

3. Non-Returner
   One who has completely destroyed the fourth and fifth hindrances will never be reborn as a human or animal or anything lower. This person will be re-born in a heavenly plane and realize enlightenment there.

4. Arahant
   The "enlightened one" or "Arahant" has destroyed all ten fetters and attained enlightenment or Nirvana.

NOTE: For a list of the ten fetters or hindrances to enlightenment, see the list on page 354 below, The Ten Fetters to Enlightenment.

> A. *Abhidhammattha Sangaha*, I.26-28 and IX.38-41
> B. Snyder, David, *The Complete Book of Buddha's Lists – Explained*, p. 237

BUDDHISM (CONTINUED)

The Five Aggregates

1. form/matter (*rūpakkhandha*) = sense objects and sense faculties

2. feeling (*vedanākkhandha*) = bare affective quality of experiencing an object

3. perception (*saññākkhandha*) = awareness of categories; recognizing "this is the same"

4. kamma formations (*sankhārakkandha*) = conditioned and conditioning response

5. consciousness (*viññānakkandha*) = general awareness of objects

NOTE: Aggregate or *rāsi* denotes a group, mass, or heap. The contact of form/matter and consciousness give rise to the three mental (*nāma*) aggregates of feeling, perception, and mental factor/kamma formation. The concurrence of a sense organ, a sense object, and its corresponding consciousness is called contact or *phassa*. See below:

sense faculties (*indriyas*)	sense objects	consciousness (*viññāna*)
(internal bases/*āyatanas*) (aggregate of matter):	(external bases/*āyatanas*) (aggregate of matter):	(aggregate of consciousness):
eye	visible forms	visual consciousness
ear	sounds	auditory consciousness
nose	odors	olfactory consciousness
tongue	tastes	taste consciousness
body	tangible things	physical consciousness
mind-organ	thoughts	mental consciousness

    A. *Dīgha Nikāya*, 22.14
       Majjhima Nikāya, 10.38
       Visuddhimagga, XIV
       Abhidhammattha Sangaha, VII.34
    B. Feuerstein, Georg, *Spirituality by the Numbers*, pp. 93-94
       Rahula, Walpola, *What the Buddha Taught*, pp. 20-25

BUDDHISM (CONTINUED)

The Eightfold Path (sub-divided)

Wisdom (*paññā*)

   1. Right View (*sammā diṭṭhi*)

   2. Right Intention (*sammā sankappa*)

Ethical Conduct (*sīla*)

   3. Right Speech (*sammā vācā*)

   4. Right Action (*sammā kammanta*)

   5. Right Livelihood (*sammā ājīva*)

Meditation (*samādhi*)

   6. Right Effort (*sammā vāyāna*)

   7. Right Mindfulness (*sammā sati*)

   8. Right Concentration (*sammā samādhi*)

   A. *Dīgha Nikāya*, 22.21
     Majjhima Nikāya, no. 117 and no. 141
     Visuddhimagga, XVI
     Abhidhammattha Sangaha, VII.30
   B. Feuerstein, Georg, *Spirituality by the Numbers*, pp. 152-154
     Smith, Huston, *The World's Religions*, pp. 193-112
     Stoddart, William, *Outline of Buddhism*, p. 29

BUDDHISM (CONTINUED)

The Eightfold Path (wisdom)

Right View: The Four Noble Truths

1. suffering – understand it

2. the arising of suffering – eradicate it

3. the cessation of suffering – realize it

4. the path to cessation of suffering – follow it

> A. *Majjhima Nikāya*, 9:13-19
> *Visuddhimagga*, XVI
> *Abhidhammattha Sangaha*, VII.38
> B. Rahula, Walpola, *What the Buddha Taught*, pp. 49-50

Right Intention: The Four Sublime States

1. universal love and good will (*mettā*) for all living beings without distinction

2. compassion (*karuṇā*) for all living beings who are suffering

3. sympathetic joy (*muditā*) for others' success and happiness

4. equanimity (*upekkhā*) amidst all life's vicissitudes

> A. *Majjhima Nikāya*, 7.13-16 and 127.7
> *Visuddhimagga*, IX
> *Abhidhammattha Sangaha*, IX.9
> B. Feuerstein, Georg, *Spirituality by the Numbers* , pp. 78-80
> Rahula, Walpola, *What the Buddha Taught*, p. 75

BUDDHISM (CONTINUED)

The Eightfold Path (ethical conduct)

Right Speech

Deliberate abstinence from:

1. lies
2. slander
3. harsh or rude talk
4. idle gossip

    A. *Majjhima Nikāya*, 117.19
       Abhidhammattha Sangaha, II.6
    B. Rahula, Walpola, *What the Buddha Taught*, p. 47

Right Action: The Five Precepts

Deliberate abstinence from:

1. killing
2. stealing
3. sexual misconduct
4. lying
5. taking intoxicants

    A. *Majjhima Nikāya*, 117.25
       Abhidhammattha Sangaha, II.6
    B. Rahula, Walpola, *What the Buddha Taught*, p. 47

Right Livelihood

Deliberate abstinence from:

1. trade in poison
2. trade in intoxicants
3. trade in weapons
4. trade in slaves
5. trade in animals for slaughter

    A. *Anguttara Nikāya*, 5.177
       Abhidhammattha Sangaha, II.6
    B. Rahula, Walpola, *What the Buddha Taught*, p. 47

APPENDIX: Lists on Eastern Traditions

BUDDHISM (CONTINUED)

The Eightfold Path (meditation)

Right Effort

1. To discard evil states that have arisen

2. To prevent the arising of evil states

3. To develop wholesome states that have not yet arisen

4. To develop wholesome states of mind that have arisen

> A. *Dīgha Nikāya*, 22.21
> *Saṃyutta Nikāya*, no. 49
> *Abhidhammattha Sangaha*, VII.25
> B. Rahula, Walpola, *What the Buddha Taught*, p. 48

Right Mindfulness

1. mindfulness of the activities (e.g. breathing) of the body (*kāya*)

2. mindfulness of sensations or feelings (*vedanā*)

3. mindfulness of the activities of the mind (*citta*)

4. mindfulness of mental and spiritual objects (*dhamma*)

> A. *Dīgha Nikāya*, no. 22
> *Majjhima Nikāya*, no. 10; no. 18; no. 119
> *Abhidhammattha Sangaha*, VII.24
> B. Rahula, Walpola, *What the Buddha Taught*, pp. 69-74

Right Concentration: Four Jhānas

1. First jhāna consciousness together with applied thought, sustained thought, rapture, pleasure, and one-pointedness (unification of mind).

2. Second jhāna consciousness together with rapture, pleasure, and one-pointedness.

3. Third jhāna consciousness together with pleasure and one-pointedness.

4. Fourth jhāna consciousness together with equanimity.

NOTE: Each jhāna factor overcomes a particular fetter or defilement. Applied thought (*vitakka*) overcomes sloth (*thīna*) and sustained thought (*vicāra*) overcomes doubt (*vicikicchā*). Rapture (*pīti*) overcomes ill will (*dosa*). Pleasure (*sukha*) overcomes worry (*kukkucca*). And unification of mind (*ekaggatā*) overcomes sensual desire (*kāma*).

> A. *Dīgha Nikāya*, 22.21
> *Majjhima Nikāya*, no. 111 and 119.18-21
> *Abhidhammattha Sangaha*, I.18
> B. Feuerstein, Georg, *Spirituality by the Numbers*, pp. 76-77

BUDDHISM (CONTINUED)

The Ten Fetters to Enlightenment

Conquered in the Steam Entrant Stage of Enlightenment:

1. wrong view of self (belief in a permanent personality)

2. doubt about the salvific power of the Triple Gem (Buddha, Dhamma, Sangha)

3. clinging to rites and ceremonies (in the belief they will lead to salvation)

Weakened in the Once-Returner Stage of Enlightenment and conquered in the Non-Returner Stage of Enlightenment:

4. sensual desire

5. ill-will or aversion

Conquered in the Arahant Stage of Enlightenment:

6. craving for material existence

7. craving for immaterial existence

8. conceit

9. restlessness or worry

10. ignorance

NOTE: See the earlier list The Four Stages of Enlightenment on page 348. Note that the last five fetters in this list of ten are often referred to as the subtle five fetters. Also, the *Abhidhammattha Sangaha* makes subtle distinctions between the ten fetters according to the Suttanta Method (VII.10), the ten fetters according to the Abhidhamma Method (VII.11), and the ten defilements (VII.12).

A. *Abhidhammattha Sangaha*, I.26-28 and VII.10
B. Snyder, David, *The Complete Book of Buddha's Lists – Explained*, p. 236

BUDDHISM (CONTINUED)

Twelve Factors of Dependent Origination	Tibetan Wheel of Life Illustration
1. ignorance (*avijjā*) = cause	blind man or woman
2. volitional actions (*sankhārā*) = cause	potter making pots
3. consciousness (*viññāṇa*) = result	monkey jumping from tree to tree
4. mind and matter (*nāma rūpa*) = result	boat w/ two passengers
5. sense faculties (*āyatana*) = result	house w/ five windows & a door
6. contact (*phassa*) = result	embracing couple
7. feeling (*vedanā*) = result	arrow piercing an eye
8. craving (*taṇhā*) = cause	man drinking beer
9. clinging (*upādāna*) = cause	woman plucking fruit from tree
10. process of becoming (*bhava*) = cause	pregnant woman
11. birth (*jāti*) = result	woman in childbirth
12. old age/death (*jarā marana*) = result	corpse

Past Causes

1. ignorance (*avijjā*): ignorance that life is impermanence, suffering and no self
2. volitional actions (*sankhāra*): impulses that create kamma

Present Results

3. consciousness (*viññāṇa*): one of six internal bases or sense faculties becoming aware of one of six external bases or sense objects
4. mind and matter (*nāma rūpa*): life-form of mind and matter
5. sense bases (*āyatana*): six sense organs and corresponding objects
6. contact (*phassa*): contact of six sense organs and corresponding objects
7. feeling (*vedanā*): pleasant or painful sensation from above contact (also includes neutral and equanimous feelings)

Present Causes

8. craving (*taṇhā*): craving for pleasant sensations and aversion from painful ones
9. clinging (*upādāna*): clinging to sensual pleasures and to sense of self
10. process of becoming (*bhava*): existence

Future Results

11. birth (*jāti*)
12. old age and death (*jarā marana*)

    A. *Dīgha Nikāya*, no. 15
      Majjhima Nikāya, 38.17 ff.
      Visuddhimagga, XVII
      Abhidhammattha Sangaha, VIII.3-10
    B. Rahula, Walpola, *What the Buddha Taught*, pp. 53-54

BUDDHISM (CONTINUED)

The Tibetan Wheel of Life

SOURCE: www.payer.de/buddhpsych/psych052.htm

BUDDHISM (CONTINUED)

Buddhist Scriptures: The Pali Canon

Tipiṭaka, the three baskets of the Pali Canon includes:

1. *Vinaya Piṭaka* (The Discipline Basket; 227 rules for monks and 311 rules for nuns) = 5 books

   Pārājika (Major Offenses)
   Pācittiya (Minor Offenses)
   Mahāvagga (Greater Section)
   Culavagga (Lesser Section)
   Parivāra (Epitome of the Vinaya)

2. *Sutta Piṭaka* (The Instruction Basket) = 33 vols.

   Dīgha Nikāya (The Long Discourses) = 3 vols. (34 suttas)
   Majjhima Nikāya (The Middle-Length Discourses) = 3 vols. (152 suttas)
   Samyutta Nikāya (The Connected Discourses) = 5 vols. (over 2,800 suttas)
   Anguttara Nikāya (The Numerical Discourses) = 5 vols. (over 2,300 suttas)
   Khuddaka Nikāya (Collection of Little Texts, e.g. *Dhammapada*) = 17 vols.

3. *Abhidhamma Piṭaka* (The Metaphysical Basket) = 7 books

   Dhammasaṅgaṇī (Enumeration of Phenomena)
   Vibhaṅga (Book of Analysis in three sub-section format)
   Dhātukatha (Discourse on Elements in catechism or Q&A format)
   Puggalapaññatti (Description of Personality Types in sutta format)
   Kathāvatthu (Points of Controversy in polemical format)
   Yamaka (Book of Pairs in question and converse format) = no translation
   Paṭṭhāna (Book of Conditional Relations or The Great Treatise)

NOTE: The Pali Canon currently runs to 45 volumes in the Pali Text Society English translation series of the *Tipiṭaka*. There are several volumes still to be translated. While the Pali Canon represents the original Buddhist Scriptures, this Theravāda tradition is only one of three Buddhist traditions, including the Mahayana and Vajrayana traditions. The Sacred Scriptures of all three traditions contains hundreds of volumes.

   A. Many of the volumes mentioned on this page can be ordered from the Pali Text Society website at www.palitext.com. More modern translations can be ordered from Wisdom Publications at www.wisdompubs.org.
   B. For an outline of these texts, see the Introduction to the *Dīgha Nikāya* (The Long Discourses of the Buddha), pp. 51-53

Bibliography on Eastern Traditions

PRIMARY SOURCES

Anguttara Nikāya (Numerical Discourses of the Buddha: An Anthology of Suttas). Translated by Nyanaponika Thera and Bhikkhu Bodhi. Walnut Creek, CA: Alta Mira Press, 1999. A more modern version than the Pali Text Society edition.

Anuruddha, Ācariya. *Abhidhammattha Sangaha: A Comprehensive Manual of Abhidhamma*. Translated and edited by Bhikkhu Bodhi. Onalaska, WA: Buddhist Publication Society, 1999. A highly condensed medieval manual of Abhidhamma philosophy.

Bhagavad-Gītā. Translated by Barbara Stoler Miller. New York: Bantam Books, 2004. Composed in the first century, the *Gītā* presents the dialogue between the warrior-prince Arjuna and the god Krishna on the moral dilemma of war.

Buddhaghosa. *Visuddhimagga* (The Path of Purification). Onalaska, WA: Buddhist Publication Society, 1991. Considered the most important Theravāda text outside of the *Tipiṭaka* canon of scriptures, this work describes the seven stages of purification leading to nirvana.

Davids, Caroline A. F. Rhys. *A Buddhist Manual of Psychological Ethics (Buddhist Psychology) of the Fourth Century BC: Being a Translation, Now Made for the First Time, from the Original . . . Abhidhamma-Piṭaka Entitled Dhamma-Sangani*. Columbia, MO: South Asia Books, 1996. Classic in Theravāda philosophical psychology including the Abhidhamma Mātikā or schedule of categories.

Dhammapada. Taipei, Taiwan: Buddha Educational Foundation, 1986. An anthology of 423 verses spoken by the Buddha, this is the most succinct and beautiful expression of the Buddha's teachings.

Dīgha Nikāya (The Long Discourses of the Buddha). Translated by Maurice Walshe. Boston: Wisdom Publications, 1995. A more modern version than the Pali Text Society edition.

Kautilya. *Arthashastra*. New York: Penguin, 1992. By India's most illustrious political economist of all time. According to Wendy Doniger, Kautilya makes Machiavelli look like Mother Teresa.

Laws of Manu. Translated by Wendy Doniger and Brian K. Smith. New York: Penguin Books, 1991. Drawing on Brahmin jurisprudence, philosophy, and religion, the *Laws of Manu* provide an encyclopedic model of how life (in all the various castes) should be lived, both in public and in private.

Majjhima Nikāya (The Middle Length Discourses of the Buddha). Translated by Bhikkhu Bodhi. Third Edition. Boston: Wisdom Publications, 2005. A more modern version than the Pali Text Society edition.

Patanjali. *Yoga: Discipline of Freedom* (The Yoga Sutra). Translated by Barbara Stoler Miller. New York: Bantam Books, 1998. The earliest known statement of the philosophical and psychological insights that define yoga as the ultimate mind-body discipline. Most scholars agree it was composed well before the eighth century.

Rig Veda. Translated by Wendy Doniger. New York: Penguin, 2005. Doniger selected 108 hymns for this volume. Chosen for their eloquence and wisdom, they focus on the enduring themes of creation, sacrifice, death, women, and the gods.

Samyutta Nikāya (The Connected Discourses of the Buddha). 2 vols. Translated by Bhikkhu Bodhi. Boston: Wisdom Publications, 2000. A more modern version than the Pali Text Society edition.

Mehti Sayadaw. *Vaṃsadīpanī* [Treatise on the Lineage of Elders]. Translated and edited by Patrick Pranke, "The 'Treatise on the Lineage of Elders' (*Vaṃsadīpanī*): Monastic Reform and the Writing of Buddhist History in Eighteenth-Century Burma." Doctoral dissertation at the University of Michigan, 2004. A history of the monastic lineage in Burma; written to justify a monastic reform as part of the state-supported Sangha hierarchy.

Svātmārāma, *Haṭhayogapradīpikā* (Hatha Yoga Pradipika). Woodstock, NY: YogaVidya.com, 2002. Written in the fifteenth century and said to be the oldest surviving text on hatha yoga.

Upaniṣads. A new translation by Patrick Olivelle. New York: Oxford University Press, 1998. The first major English translation of the ancient Upaniṣads in over half a century, Olivelle's work incorporates recent scholarship. Brief selections from the Upaniṣads can be found in Juan Mascaró's translation of *The Upanishads* (New York: Penguin, 1965).

Vatsyayana. *Kamasutra*. Translated by Wendy Doniger and Sudhir Kakar. New York: Oxford University Press, 2009. Includes an entertaining and learned 57-page introduction that puts the *Kamasutra* in historical context.

SECONDARY SOURCES

Basham, A. L. *The Origin and Development of Classical Hinduism*. Boston: Beacon Press, 1989. Succinct, elegant, and engaging synthesis.

Collins, Steven. *Selfless Persons: Imagery and Thought in Theravāda Buddhism*. New York: Cambridge University Press, 1999. Collins shows how the Theravāda Buddhist tradition has constructed a philosophical account of personal identity and continuity on the apparently impossible basis of the doctrine of *anatta* or no-self.

Doniger, Wendy. *The Hindus: An Alternative History*. New York: Penguin Press, 2009. A massive tome that covers the entire history of Hinduism with both wit and wisdom.

Eliade, Mircea. *A History of Religious Ideas*, vol. 2. Chicago: University of Chicago Press, 1984. Part of his monumental work, the religions of ancient China, Hinduism, Buddhism, Roman religion, Celtic and German religions, Judaism, and early Christianity are all encompassed in this volume.

————. *The Myth of the Eternal Return*. Princeton, NJ: Princeton University Press, 1991. Contrasts the mythical consciousness of traditional cultures with the historical consciousness of modern culture. Archaic men and women did not see themselves as making events in history, but as living out and repeating divinely established patterns *in illo tempore*. In the book's final chapter Eliade argues that modernity has been unable to give an adequate response to the "terrors of history."

————. *The Sacred and the Profane: The Nature of Religion*. New York: Harcourt, Inc., 1987. Tracing manifestations of the sacred from primitive to modern times, Eliade shows how even secularized moderns are still unconsciously nourished by the memory of the sacred in camouflaged myths and degenerated rituals.

————. *Yoga: Immortality and Freedom*. Princeton, NJ: Princeton University Press, 1990. Detailed work based on the author's years of study in various ashrams and universities in India.

Encyclopedia of Religion. 2nd edition. 15 vols. New York: Macmillan Reference USA, 2005.

Feuerstein, Georg. *Spirituality by the Numbers*. New York: G. P. Putnam's Sons, 1994. The internationally know yoga scholar presents numerically organized spiritual concepts from all the world's religious traditions beginning with the Void and ending with 144,000 saved souls in Chrisitianity.

Hamilton, Alexander. *Key to the Chronology of the Hindus*. Whitefish, MT: Kessinger Press, 2008. An attempt to reconcile the vast Hindu concept of time with the short, linear Biblical account of time.

Hopkins, Thomas. *The Hindu Religious Tradition*. Belmont, CA: Wadsworth Publishing Company, 1971. This work has become a classic (and succinct) introduction to the Hindu religious tradition. Particularly helpful in making sense of the early Vedic practices and traditions.

Knipe, David. *Hinduism*. San Francisco: Harper SanFrancisco, 1991. Succinct introduction to Hinduism as well as the history, peoples, traditions, and geography of South Asia. Knipe spent years doing fieldwork in South Asia.

Kreeft, Peter. *Heaven: The Heart's Deepest Longing*. San Francisco: Ignatius Press, 1989. Fascinating exploration of the psychological, philosophical, and theological dimensions of the search for total joy. Includes a lengthy look at C. S. Lewis' argument for the existence of God based on the human desire for God.

Lewis, C. S. *The Abolition of Man*. New York: Touchstone, 1996. Perhaps the clearest and most concise defense of natural law in the twentieth century.

————. *The Discarded Image: An Introduction to Medieval and Renaissance Literature*. London: Cambridge University Press, 1964. Lewis' last great work of medieval scholarship that sketches a map of his beloved Medieval Model. This book is based on his two most popular lecture series to undergraduates at Oxford, the Prolegomena to Medieval Literature and the Prolegomena to Renaissance Literature.

Lings, Martin. *Ancient Beliefs and Modern Superstitions*. Cambridge, UK: Archetype, 2001. Shows modern man to be, in his own peculiar 20th century way, the embodiment of superstition in its most dangerous form.

————. *The Eleventh Hour: The Spiritual Crisis of the Modern World in the Light of Tradition and Prophecy*. Cambridge, UK: Archetype, 2002. Analyzes the parable of the laborers in the vineyard in the light of the concept of the Millennium.

Macaulay, Thomas. *Speeches by Lord Macaulay, With His Minute on Indian Education*. New York: AMS Press, Inc., 1935. A classic of British colonialist attitudes.

Panikkar, Raimundo. "Common Patterns of Eastern and Western Scholasticism," *Diogenes*, 83 (1973):103-113. Notes seven patterns common to the medieval East and West: (1) the principle of authority, (2) a hierarchical structure of the world, (3) the intrinsic value of tradition, (4) extensive use of commentaries, (5) precise terminology, (6) dialectical methodology, and (7) doctrinal orthodoxy.

Pieper, Josef. *Guide to Thomas Aquinas*. San Francisco: Ignatius Press, 1991. According to Pieper, the marriage of faith and reason proposed by Aquinas in his great synthesis of a theologically founded worldliness is not merely one solution among many, but the great principle expressing the essence of the Christian West.

Pranke, Patrick. "The 'Treatise on the Lineage of Elders' (*Vaṃsadīpanī*): Monastic Reform and the Writing of Buddhist History in Eighteenth-Century Burma." Doctoral dissertation at the University of Michigan, 2004. Masterful addition to the field of Burmese Buddhist historiography.

Rahula, Walpola. *What the Buddha Taught*. New York: Grove Press, 1974. Perhaps the best introduction to Theravāda Buddhism available.

Rhys Davids, T. W. and William Stede. *Pali-English Dictionary*. Delhi, India: Motilal Banarsidass Publishers, 1993.

Smith, Brian K. *Classifying the Universe: The Ancient Indian* Varṇa *System and the Origins of Caste*. New York: Oxford University Press, 1994. Comprehensive analysis of the historical predecessors to caste as laid out in Vedic literature. Understanding social hierarchy as part of an essentially religious understanding of *varṇa* is the key to comprehending the Vedic world-view in all its complexity and the persistence of its power in the social realm.

Smith, Huston. *The World's Religions*. San Francisco: Harper SanFrancisco, 1991. The best one-volume book on world religions from the author widely regarded as the most eloquent and accessible contemporary authority on the history of religions.

Snyder, David. *The Complete Book of Buddha's Lists – Explained*. Las Vegas, Nevada: Vipassana Foundation, 2006. A total of 90 lists are presented in this book with 29 of the most important ones explained in detail.

Stoddart, William. *Hinduism and Its Spiritual Masters*. Louisville, KY: Fons Vitae, 2006. An outline of Hinduism using an abundance of illustrations, diagrams, lists, and photographs. Beautiful introduction to and summary of Hinduism.

————. *Outline of Buddhism.* Oakton, VA: Foundation for Traditional Studies, 1998. Survey of Buddhist doctrine as well as useful summary of the myriad schools of Buddhism.

Zimmer, Heinrich. *Myths and Symbols in Indian Art and Civilization.* Edited by Joseph Campbell. New York: Pantheon Books, 1946. This book is a reworking by Joseph Campbell of a lecture course delivered by Zimmer at Columbia University in the winter term of 1942 before his untimely death in 1943.

Select Index on Eastern Traditions

W

will 329

Y

yama 343